Close Encounters of the Bird Kind: Wild Birds in San Francisco and Other Places

Val Shushkewich

Published by Val Shushkewich, 2021.

CLOSE ENCOUNTERS OF THE BIRD KIND: WILD BIRDS IN SAN FRANCISCO AND OTHER PLACES

First edition. May 13, 2021.

ISBN: 979-8201056070

Written by Val Shushkewich.

Also by Val Shushkewich

Arctic Changes: Past to Present in the Far North
Close Encounters of the Bird Kind: Wild Birds in San Francisco and Other Places
17 Reasons to Admire Birds
Pioneering Ornithologists

Table of Contents

INTRODUCTION 1

ACKNOWLEDGEMENTS 3

SECTION I – BIRDS IN SAN FRANCISCO.................................5

Chapter One – Crissy Field Marsh 7

Chapter Two –Mrs. Long-billed Curlew and the Willet 15

Chapter Three – Aquatic Park to Golden Gate Bridge 39

Chapter Four –Coastal Trail West of the Golden Gate Bridge 89

Chapter Five – Marshall's Beach 129

SECTION II – BIRDS IN NATURAL WONDERLANDS 139

Chapter Six –Mercer Slough 141

Chapter Seven – Burnaby Lake and Still Creek 175

SECTION III – BIRD RESCUE 205

Chapter Eight– Volunteering at WildCare 207

Chapter Nine –Oil Spill in San Francisco Bay 233

Chapter Ten –Ode to an American Goldfinch 261

Chapter Eleven –A Stranded Loon 271

CONCLUSION 283

REFERENCES 285

APPENDIX I - Migration Maps for Some of the Birds Seen...... 297

ABOUT THE AUTHOR.. 311

PUBLISHED BOOKS 313

To my husband Ken, who has always helped me in everything I do, and to my parents, Irene and George Cuffe, who were kind to all living creatures and who gave me an appreciation for the natural world.

INTRODUCTION

———

THIS BOOK FOLLOWS THE adventures of a bird lover and naturalist in places that are very wild, and yet are within walking distance of highly-populated urban centers. In spite of their proximity to intense human activity, these places attract numerous, varied bird species. The life habits of the birds seen are described, as well as the impact on the author of being able to observe how these birds conduct their lives.

These localities did not happen by chance. They were carefully planned, and continue to be managed and maintained. They are on land which is potentially prime development property for individual use. However, by preserving them for use by the general public, many more people can experience and enjoy naturalist pastimes. Otherwise, these spaces would be divided up among individual owners, and the general public would neither have access to their beauty, nor be able to enjoy their many pleasures. By keeping these large tracts of land intact, they can be managed in a consistent, coordinated, and planned way for the use and enjoyment of the general public, while also making it possible for wildlife to live there.

The author is a naturalist by inclination, even though she was born in and continues to live in major urban centers. The world of nature has always been a source of contemplation, curiosity and respect for her. She wrote this book in order to share with others the glimpses into the natural world experienced in places she considers to be "little bits of heaven on earth". She hopes that in describing these experiences, it will open others' eyes to look for the amazing wild creatures who are able to survive in the natural world, and whom we often do not pay any attention to.

The author's adventures in areas of urban wilderness are described in chapters one to seven. These areas include Crissy Field Marsh and the Golden Gate Promenade along the San Francisco northern waterfront; the area from Aquatic Park to the Golden Gate Bridge in San Francisco; the Coastal Trail on the west side of the Golden Gate Bridge, Marshall's Beach, Mercer Slough east of Seattle, and Burnaby Lake and Still Creek in Burnaby, British Columbia, Canada.

The author became involved in attempts at bird rescue and rehabilitation. Chapter eight relates her experiences at WildCare, a wildlife rescue and rehabilitation center in San Rafael, California. Chapter nine describes volunteering at the worldwide-known International Bird Rescue center in Cordelia, California during the 2007 Cosco Busan oil spill in San Francisco Bay that affected thousands of migrating and overwintering birds. Chapters ten and eleven recount the author's poignant rescues of a juvenile goldfinch, and of a stranded loon.

Unless otherwise noted, the photos in the book were taken by the author.

ACKNOWLEDGEMENTS

I WOULD LIKE TO THANK Claudia Angle, who was a Museum Specialist and Collection Manager for the Curatorial Project of the Biological Survey Unit of the United States Geological Survey, assisting with the curation and management of the North American bird specimen records in the Smithsonian's National Museum of Natural History.

I met Claudia on my first visit to the National Museum of Natural History where I was fascinated by the bird display cases exhibited on the lower floor of the museum. The mounted birds in the cases looked so natural. Some of the specimens were very old, including a Passenger Pigeon, a species now extinct. I spent hours studying the birds in the display cases. Claudia Angle happened to walk by and told me there were many more bird specimens in the back of the museum and asked if I would be interested in seeing some of them. She then took me to the museum's interior, closed to the general public, where there are many cabinets of carefully-prepared bird specimens. She pulled out some of the trays of birds and explained how scientists used them in their research studies.. Claudia showed me one of the bird skins she was in the process of preserving and explained some of the techniques used by taxonomists.

I had already spent many enjoyable hours observing various bird species, reading about their interesting lives, and looking at bird research studies, but I was mostly unaware of the legacy of naturalists who made bird studies their life's work. When Claudia and I walked by a statue of Spencer Fullerton Baird, she seemed surprised I did not know who he was. She explained that Spencer Baird was the primary person responsible for building up the bird and other collections of the Smithsonian's National Museum of Natural History. My meetings with Claudia Angle further spurred my interest in birds and in the lives of naturalists who love and study birds.

At this time, I would also like to acknowledge and thank Dr. Robert Nero, a well-known scientist, author and poet who combines his passions for birds, wildlife, conservation, and archeology with his great talents for writing and poetry. He has completed extensive field studies of the life histories of the Red-winged Blackbird and the Great Gray Owl. His books *The Great Gray Owl: Phantom of the Northern Forest* and *Redwings* were published by the Smithsonian Institution. Natural Heritage Books (now part of Dundurn Press) also published numerous books of his poetry. Dr. Nero is able to blend scientific field study of unsurpassed excellence with the eloquent and poetic expression of what this study means. Behind his scientific work, there is always a realization of the importance of trying to understand a species. His enthusiasm about and respect for nature and wildlife are sources of inspiration to me.

I spent time with Robert Nero in 2012, and we have corresponded since then. In September 2016, when he was 93 years old, I wrote to him about some of the wildlife I had seen on my slow jogs in natural areas. He wrote back: "Val, your 'slow jogs' sound delightful – that could be a new book subject? Well, think about it." These words, coming from such an inspiring writer, encouraged me to continue to write.

SECTION I – BIRDS IN SAN FRANCISCO

ONE CAN NEVER TELL what delightful surprise is in store for him the moment he loses himself in the big out-of-doors....Interest and attention are keys that unlock new worlds to us.

Cordelia Stanwood

Chapter One – Crissy Field Marsh

THE CITY OF SAN FRANCISCO is an urban environment surrounded by natural areas of great beauty. To the west is the Pacific Ocean and to the east is San Francisco Bay.

Fig 1-1 - Map showing the location of the San Francisco Bay area.

The San Francisco Bay and immediately surrounding areas are a winter home and migratory stop for many species of waterfowl, shorebirds, marsh birds, gulls, terns, pelicans, loons, grebes, raptors, and songbirds. Every spring and fall about 11 million birds of more than 100 species migrate along the Pacific Ocean coast going to or passing through the Bay Area. About three-quarters of them rest and feed in the region's tidal marshes, with many of them staying over the entire winter.

The Bay is a key wintering and stopover area along the Pacific Flyway for waterfowl, including scaup, scoter, canvasback and bufflehead ducks. Indeed, according to California Fish and Wildlife surveys, San Francisco Bay held the majority of California's 1999 wintering scaup (85%), scoter (89%), and canvasback (70%) populations. More than 56% of the State of California's 1999 wintering diving ducks were located in the San Francisco Bay proper, which includes the salt ponds and wetlands adjacent to the North and South Bays.

According to the United States Shorebird Conservation Plan, San Francisco Bay is also used by higher proportions of wintering and migrating shorebirds within the U.S. Pacific coast wetland system than any other coastal wetland. On the Point Reyes Bird Observatory surveys, depending on the season, San Francisco Bay accounted for the following percentages of shorebirds in the wetlands of the contiguous United States Pacific Coast: Black-bellied Plover, 55–62%; Semipalmated Plover, 40–52%; Black-necked Stilt, 58–90%; American Avocet, 86–96%; Greater Yellowlegs, 26–41%; Willet, 57–69%; Long-billed Curlew, 45–65%; Marbled Godwit, 46–68%; Red Knot, 39–76%; Western Sandpiper, 54–68%; Least Sandpiper, 39-73%; Dunlin, 24–38%; and Dowitcher, 49–72%.

Because of the great shorebird numbers, the Western Hemisphere Shorebird Reserve Network has classified San Francisco Bay as a site of "Hemispheric Importance" for shorebirds – the highest possible ranking. [Ref 1-1]

The San Francisco Bay Estuary also provides nesting habitat for a variety of marsh birds including Snowy Egret, Great Egret, Black-crowned Night Heron, Great Blue Heron, and California Clapper Rail. Open waters, large lakes, and salt ponds provide habitat for Loons, Pelicans, and Grebes, including the Pied-billed Grebe, Eared Grebe, Horned Grebe, Clark's Grebe, and Western Grebe. Over 50 species of songbirds make use of the remnant riparian zones around the Bay. Among them are flycatchers, sparrows, thrushes, woodpeckers, warblers, vireos, and swallows.

The first special area I enjoyed traversing is part of the Golden Gate National Recreation Area which comprises the north shoreline of the City and County of San Francisco from Pier 39 to the Golden Gate Bridge.

From Pier 39 in San Francisco, one travels west through Fisherman's Wharf, past Aquatic Park, Fort Mason, and the Marina Green to the St. Francis Yacht Club. This is the start of the 3.4-mile round-trip Golden Gate Promenade, a continuous wide pathway to Fort Point at the foot of the Golden Gate Bridge. The Promenade is popular with walkers, joggers and bicyclists. A restored marsh, an excellent place to see birds, is near the start of the Promenade. The trail crosses a bridge over the marsh's outlet stream and continues west towards the Golden Gate. The broad main path continues west past the marsh and stays close to the bay front, with low sand dunes on the right and a huge grass-covered platform to the left. The grassy platform is a re-creation of the historic Crissy airfield. At 1.3 miles, there is a "Warming Hut" which houses a café and a National Parks Service bookstore. The Golden Gate Promenade from the St. Francis Yacht Club to the base of the Golden Gate Bridge and the brick walls of Fort Point ends at 1.7 miles.

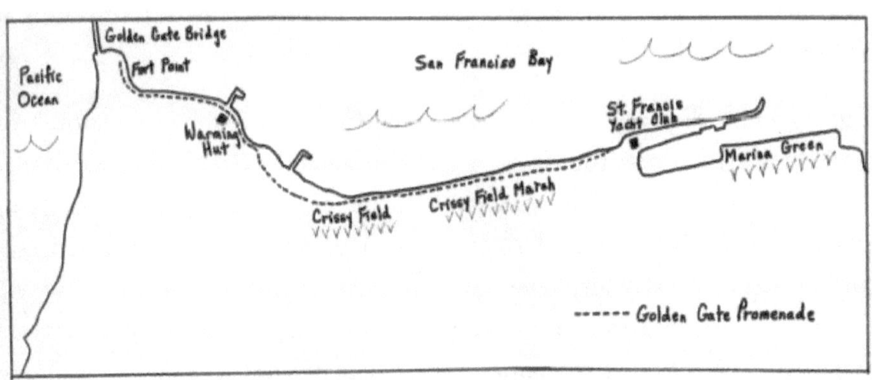

Fig 1-2 - Map showing the location of the Golden Gate Promenade.

Fig 1-3 – View of Crissy Field and the Golden Gate Promenade.

The restoration of Crissy Field is a prime example of the benefits to both humans and wildlife of thoughtful, knowledgeable, well-planned, multi-use habitat restoration. When I first moved to San Francisco in 1988, the Crissy Field marsh and the restored grassy field did not exist. Instead, the site was covered with asphalt.

Crissy Field had served heterogeneous uses. In the 1860's the area contained sand dunes, a large saltwater marsh, and islands. By 1912, the marsh was filled in, and an automobile racetrack was built in preparation for the 1915 Panama-Pacific International Exposition. A grassy meadow was used as a landing strip for early airplanes. In early aviation history this meadow was the only U.S. Army Air Service coastal defense station in the western United States. In 1920, the Army named the airfield in memory of Dana Crissy, a military pilot who died in a plane crash while pioneering a new route across the United States. In 1935, the airfield was paved over. By 1994 when the National Park Service took over Crissy Field from the military, the area consisted of a crumbling-asphalt unused airstrip enclosed by chain-linked fencing. This unaesthetic site was unappealing to both people and wildlife.

DARING PILOTS, YOUTHFUL HEROES

The 91st Observation Squadron

Crissy Field was home to many daring pilots who made their mark on aviation history. Among these famous flyers were Major Dana H. Crissy, who died in a crash attempting to fly to the East Coast from here, and Major Hap Arnold, who later led U. S. Army Air Forces during World War II. In 1924, Lieutenant Russell L. Maughan flew from the East Coast to Crissy Field in one day from "dawn to dusk," and Lieutenant Lowell H. Smith landed here after flying around the world.

The airfield's namesake, Major Dana Crissy, commander of Mather Field in Sacramento, crashed while attempting a transcontinental flight that left here in 1919. The airfield was named in his honor in 1921.

Fig 1-4 – Crissy Field was named for Major Dana H. Crissy.

The restoration of Crissy Field and the creation of the Crissy Field Marsh was a huge project undertaken by the National Park Service when it took over the Presidio from the military in 1994. The $32 million cost was mostly funded through private donations, including an $18 million contribution by the Haas Family, owners of the San Francisco-based Levi Strauss & Company. Today, the area includes a 20-acre tidal marsh, the 1.7-mile Golden Gate Promenade along San Francisco Bay, a 28-acre grass field used for daily recreation and large public events, and 16 acres of dune habitat.

CRISSY FIELD
TRANSFORMED

When the first restoration plans were discussed in 1986,
Evelyn and Walter Haas, Jr. and their family shared the dream
that Crissy Field become a place for people from all walks
of life to enjoy. They made a lead gift to transform 30 acres of
degraded dunes and wasteland into a 100-acre
vibrant waterfront park.

The National Park Service and Golden Gate National Parks Conservancy
honor them here for their vision and generosity.

Fig 1-5 - Plaque commemorating the restoration of Crissy Field.

The process of restoring a tidal marsh to the area took approximately a year to complete, with six months required to excavate fill from the site and another six months to plant about 100,000 native plants raised from seed in the Presidio Native Plant Nursery. Most of the fill removed from the marsh was transferred to the site of the former airfield. The planners of the recreated marsh hoped to restore the wetlands' biodiversity, including fish, birds, and other small aquatic organisms not seen there since the original marsh was filled in. The first native plants were placed in the wetlands in late 1998, with plants continuing to be added on an ongoing basis. In November, 1999, a channel was dug to open the marsh to San Francisco Bay, allowing the tide to flow in and out.

Crissy Field Marsh is a combination freshwater and saltwater marsh, one of the richest environments for the creation of biodiversity. The Tennessee Hollow's spring-fed tributaries provide fresh water, while the twice-daily tide brings in salt water from San Francisco Bay. This coastal wetland system thrives on natural disturbance. Fresh water and storm runoff drain from the land into the marsh, bringing sediment that either settles or is flushed out to the bay. Tides constantly ebb and flow, importing minerals and organic materials. This constant movement and mixing create an opportune environment for a variety of organisms.

The restoration of Crissy Field and the Crissy Field Marsh is a great success. It is a favorite destination for walkers and joggers. Many species of birds not seen there since the marshland was filled in have returned to use the area. Some of the birds are attracted by prey species such as the bay shrimp and Dungeness crab that have also returned.

Fig 1-6 - Crissy Field Marsh.

Fig 1-7 – Where Crissy Field Marsh connects to San Francisco Bay, allowing the tide to flow in and out.

Fig 1-8 - The Warming Hut

Chapter Two – Mrs. Long-billed Curlew and the Willet

FEW PEOPLE SEEM TO notice the birds in Crissy Field Marsh. The Golden Gate Promenade beside the marsh is often crowded with people walking, jogging and bicycling. Only a low wire fence separates the marsh from the Golden Gate Promenade walkway, but people stay on the path and do not look out at the marsh to see the birds. No-one bothers the birds, and the always watchful birds are comfortable going about their lives in the marsh.

I saw a surprising number of different species of birds in Crissy Field Marsh. Since its restoration into a freshwater marsh where the Pacific Ocean tide also flows in and out, it has become an attractive place for a variety of shorebirds and waterfowl who spend time there at various times of the year. I often did not even need my compact binoculars to see the wild birds so close to the path.

Over a period of several years, I regularly saw a Long-billed Curlew with a very long bill in Crissy Field Marsh. Because of her extremely long bill, I knew she was a female. She seemed to own the far eastern side of the marsh and always inhabited this part of the marsh. There were spots of cinnamon among her black/gray/brown/buff body and when she lifted up a wing, she had pure cinnamon-colored wing linings. She was a gorgeous bird, and I loved to watch her. I named her Mrs. Long-billed Curlew.

I was privileged to watch this bird feeding, preening, resting, and interacting with other birds in the marsh, and I grew to admire her. She was almost always at the eastern end of the marsh. She was aware of my standing by the side of the path watching her and taking pictures of her, but she continued going about her business. She seemed as interested in me as I was in her. She often looked straight at me, and sometimes walked towards me.

Fig 2-1 – Mrs. Long-billed Curlew.

Fig 2-2 – Long-billed Curlew walking in Crissy Field Marsh.

There was often a single Western Willet in the same location of the marsh as the Long-billed Curlew and these two birds often fed and rested close to one another in the marsh. They seemed to be friends. Both of these special birds noticed I was watching them, but they did not seem disturbed by my presence. I think they came to know me.

Fig 2-3 – Western Willet in Crissy Field Marsh.

Fig 2-4– Western Willet in breeding plumage at Crissy Field Marsh.

Some of my experiences at the east end of Crissy Field Marsh with this female Long-billed Curlew with the extremely long bill, and this Western Willet who seemed to be her friend, follow. I believe these two birds spent their non-breeding time together at Crissy Field Marsh.

In the late fall and early winter, I saw two large shorebirds feeding in the same area at the restored Crissy Field Marsh. One, a non-breeding Western Willet, was very plain gray. The other, larger one with very different coloring, had a buff and cinnamon underbody with a brown mottled head and back, and a very long downward-curving bill almost as long as its body. It was a Long-billed Curlew.

I watched Mrs. Curlew foraging by walking steadily along the exposed mud bars in the marsh, reaching ahead to pick or probe with the tip of her long bill. She often foraged close to the fence between the Golden Gate Promenade and the marsh and I could see her well, even without binoculars. She looked quite plump. Her bill was very long, curved down and sturdy. Her breast looked buffy/light cinnamon. She had light head stripes. When she turned her back towards me, the mottled black/brown/gray pattern made her appear almost invisible on the muddy surface of the island in the marsh. She probed deeply with her very long bill into dimples in the sandy mud, where she felt for invertebrates. At times, she could twist her head completely around as she felt her way with her long bill down a tunnel in the sand. I watched something she caught move down her long bill.

Fig 2-5 – Long-billed Curlew probing for food in dimples in mud at Crissy Field Marsh.

Fig 2-6 – Long-billed Curlew feeding with her head twisted around. Note the Killdeer at the upper left.

Fig 2-7 – Long-billed Curlew feeding.

On June 21, 2014 there were two Long-billed Curlews on one of the far islands at the marsh. One stood watching and the other had its head tucked under a wing. I heard a faint "curlee" call, and one of the birds flew over my head towards San Francisco Bay. Later as I went by the broad sandbar by the bridge on the eastern side of the marsh, the other Long-billed Curlew was feeling in the holes in the sand with its long bill.

On October 25, 2014 there were many small silver fish leaping out of the water in Crissy Field Marsh. Three Brown Pelicans paraded across the marsh, looking to catch the fish. The Long-billed Curlew and the Willet were wading in the water. The water came up to the curlew's belly. A Common Loon swam by with its head under water to just above its eyes, peering below the surface looking for food. The loon dove and I watched where it went by following the ripples it made on the water's surface. It swam very fast underwater. One time, it quickly surfaced close to where the Willet was standing and startled the Willet.

On December 30, 2014 strong winds blew trees down in San Francisco and the streets were littered with debris from fallen tree branches. That night you could hear the wind howling and the following morning it was still exceptionally windy from the northeast. Going out to Crissy Field Marsh, I noticed the white-capped waves in San Francisco Bay. At the marsh the water level was high. I saw the Long-billed Curlew and Willet sitting together on a rise in the bank close to the bridge on the east side of the marsh. They were together on the south side of this ridge, as much out of the wind as possible. I could just see the Curlew's neck and head looking at me, and part of the Willet's body. They were six inches apart and were resting together out of the wind. What smart birds!

Earlier along the Marina Green, I had seen pigeons sitting below the south side of the curb to get as much out of the wind as possible. On returning from the marsh, I found it tiring trying to run against the strong wind and I mostly walked home.

On June 13, 2015 I went to Crissy Field Marsh about 7:00 am and saw 17 Long-billed Curlews all gathered on a sandspit just by the bridge close to the path. They did not seem afraid of me as I looked at them through binoculars. Some had very long bills and were probably females, and some had shorter bills. They all just stood on the exposed mud bar. It was a foggy day with a very strong westerly wind. In *The Shorebird Guide,* it says about the Long-billed Curlew: "Fall migration takes place between early June and mid-December. Females and failed breeders arrive at wintering sites along the Pacific Coast in mid-June and the Gulf Coast in early July." [Ref 2-1]

On August 16, 2015 a variety of birds were at Crissy Field Marsh. Mrs. Long-billed Curlew was close to the edge of the marsh preening feathers on her side and I saw her run her long bill along the length of a feather— "zipping it up". Three Marbled Godwits landed with a "kerwit" sound and started feeding. The Willet walked along the green grassy bank of the marsh looking for food. I often saw the Curlew and the Willet foraging and resting close to each other. They seemed to watch out for each other and enjoy each other's presence.

On August 30, 2015 eight Marbled Godwits fed on the mudflats at the marsh. Some looked small, while one was much larger than the others with a larger bill. The Marbled Godwits were very close to the path, but did not even look up as people passed. They seemed oblivious to the people going by on the Golden Gate Promenade and to my watching them. This contrasted with the behavior of the Long-billed Curlew and the Western Willet, who were always observant and aware of my presence, and who kept an eye on me as I watched them.

Several times I saw Mrs. Long-billed Curlew and the Western Willet resting side-by-side on the embankment along the edge of Crissy Field Marsh. The Long-billed Curlew had her head turned back under her scapulars, but she had one eye open, observing her surroundings and me. Meanwhile, at times the Willet sat almost back-to-back with her, and as I went by, I could see it also had one eye open, monitoring in the opposite direction. In this way, together the two birds could watch their environment in all directions.

Fig 2-8 - Long-billed Curlew and Western Willet resting together at edge of Crissy Field Marsh.

One day in August the Willet's feathers looked ruffled and its demeanor showed that it felt uncomfortable. I believed it was molting its feathers. The Long-billed Curlew stood a little distance away looking at the Willet. Then they both started preening at the same time.

Fig 2-9 – The Long-billed Curlew and the Western Willet preening together 1.

Fig 2-10 – The Long-billed Curlew and the Western Willet preening together 2.

On May 8, 2018 I went along the San Francisco northern waterfront from 6:00 to 7:30 pm. I had seen neither the Willet nor the Long-billed Curlew for a long time and had presumed they had temporarily flown away to their nesting grounds. However, at Crissy Field Marsh I saw the Curlew. She was walking confidently along the shore beside the path and I could see her clearly. She looked thin, and some of her belly looked more rust-colored than other parts of it. I wondered if she had already gone to her breeding grounds and then returned? This did not seem likely. Was she possibly nesting somewhere close by? Was she not nesting at all that year? I wished I could follow her around to see where she went.

I watched her walking along the shore and poking her long bill into dimples in the mud. Then she inserted her long bill deeper into one of the depressions and pulled up a long, light orange invertebrate. She put this light orange food into the water several times. Was this to clean it before swallowing it; to make it more slippery and easier to swallow; or to drown it? Then she positioned it and swallowed it down her long bill. At several points in this process, she actually stopped to look right at me as I watched her, first through binoculars and then just with my regular glasses on. After she swallowed the light orange dinner, she turned her back towards me and looked out across the marsh.

I walked on, but kept looking back at her, as I admired her so much. She is the "Queen of Crissy Field Marsh". I looked upon her as a friend and she reminded me of the character my Mother had. My Mother was an angel on earth who looked after everybody, and yet was strong in her own convictions and self-worth. This was how I saw the Long-billed Curlew of Crissy Field Marsh.

In the early evening of May 11, 2018 the water level was low in the marsh with much land showing above the water line. Through binoculars, I watched the Curlew walking along the edge of the water quite far away. Suddenly, she stopped walking and froze, looking at something. Then I saw what had attracted her attention. A large dark raptor-type bird had landed on the ground a short distance away from her. It stayed there for some time. She did not move, but just kept looking at this potential predator. Finally, the raptor flew off west over to the far side of the marsh. Both the curlew and I stood and watched as it flew over the edge of the marsh. We saw it swoop down and I heard a small Killdeer cry out. I could not see what had happened. I hoped the Killdeer had been able to escape the raptor.

After a while, the Long-billed Curlew began walking again and I resumed jogging. She was so aware of her surroundings. She immediately noticed the raptor, even though she also had to concentrate on trying to find something to eat.

On July 17, 2018 I went running in the early evening. Fog from the Pacific Ocean poured into the Bay underneath the Golden Gate Bridge. It was overcast and windy. The water level at the marsh was high. I was thrilled to see both the Willet and the Long-billed Curlew together on the only bit of muddy sand close to the edge of the marsh. They were about a foot apart. The Willet was in its breeding plumage and was heavily patterned, unlike the plain gray of its non-breeding plumage. It stood still, while the curlew poked her bill in the mud looking for something to eat. I laughed and called out: "I am so happy to see you!". Whenever I saw them, they made my day. I hadn't really wanted to go running after work, but thought I would feel better if I did, and seeing the two of them, so close together and so close to the path and to me, made me feel happy. Both the Long-billed Curlew and the Willet noticed my watching them and in some of the pictures I took of them, they were looking at me. I think they understood I meant no harm and that I liked them.

October 28, 2018 was an extremely foggy morning out by the Golden Gate Bridge. I left my apartment at 6:30 am and returned about 9:00 am. It was dark until 7:00-7:30 am. There was a somewhat shorter-billed Long-billed Curlew walking along the shore and looking in the mud for breakfast. I believed this was a male curlew who was the spouse of the female Long-billed Curlew. The two of them had separate feeding territories in the marsh. He frequented the more westerly part of the marsh, while she was always closer to the bridge at the marsh's eastern end. That day, I saw her resting, and when a Great Egret came towards her, she moved out of its way.

On November 21, 2018 smoke from the Camp Fire in northeastern California made the air quality very poor in San Francisco. The Camp Fire was the deadliest, most destructive wildfire in California's history. I wore an N-95 air filter mask when I went running. There was finally some relief from the smoke, as it rained. On my way back from Marshall's Beach, it started pouring and I got soaked. I saw the beautiful Long-billed Curlew standing in the water in the pouring rain and putting her head underwater to feel for food.

For some time, the outlet from the marsh to San Francisco Bay had been blocked by a build-up of sand. Water could not flow between the marsh and the Bay as it usually did twice daily when the tide came in. I had noticed the water level in the marsh was always high and none of the islands were above water. I wondered if this affected food availability for the Long-billed Curlew.

On December 8, 2018 the water level was relatively low again and there were islands in the marsh. I was watching the female Long-billed Curlew when I heard another Long-billed Curlew calling and the male curlew flew in to the edge of the marsh a little distance away from her. She opened her very long bill and answered him with her beautiful two-tone cur-lee call, the second note higher than the first. Then she went on looking for food. How lucky I was to witness this exchange between these two beautiful birds!

On the way back from my jog, I noticed four or five crows on the mud bar. They tried to intimidate and distract the Long-billed Curlew so she would drop her food. They flew directly above her, and she had to duck her head. One time she went after one of them with her long bill. This was the only time I saw her do anything that approached being combative. She was always aware of other birds in the marsh, but she did not act aggressively towards them or use her long bill to shoo them away. I never saw her use her long sharp bill to dig at other birds (except to point it at a gull if it harassed her). She walked very close to other birds in her search for food on the mud bars, but she did not try to get them out of her way; rather she went around them. I considered her the "Queen of Crissy Field Marsh" but she did not lord it over other birds or try to intimidate them. I saw her walk near American Coots and other birds, large and small, but she did not bother them.

Mrs. Long-billed Curlew was a very self-assured bird and she did no harm to the other birds. She diligently observed other birds in the marsh and used her extreme intelligence to decide when to make friends with another being, such as the Willet.

The following day on December 9, 2018, hundreds of people, all of them dressed in bright red Santa Claus suits, were participating in a race along the Golden Gate Promenade. The male Long-billed Curlew stood at the edge of the marsh and watched this commotion with some interest. But when I went by Mrs. Curlew, she was completely ignoring all this color and movement of people, and she continued going about her business of foraging for food. I really believed she knew the difference between me and all the people who were oblivious to her presence in the marsh. I didn't really care about what other people thought about me when I stopped to watch her, but I did care about what she thought of me.

For the next several weeks I was away from San Francisco and did not have a chance to go to Crissy Field Marsh until January 1, 2019 from 2:00 pm to 3:30 pm. There were crowds of people walking and bicycling along the Golden Gate Promenade. On the way out, I caught sight of Mrs. Curlew's very long bill and head just visible as she walked along behind a raised edge in the marsh's bank, pushing her bill into soft places in the bank. She looked up several times and she saw me standing there watching her. Then suddenly she took off flying, and made her haunting curlew call. At first I thought she was disturbed by my watching her. But she flew in a wide circle over the eastern part of the marsh and came down on the island. There were many gulls on the island and she shooed one or two of them out of her way with her bill. This was out of character for her. Then she stood for some time and she was looking at me. She made some half-hearted pokes in the mud. Then, a distance away, I heard the male Long-billed Curlew calling and he flew in and landed some distance away. Was he alerted by her calling and was he flying in to protect her, or possibly to challenge a rival for her affections?

When I returned, both birds were just standing together in the marsh.

Fig 2-11 – Mrs. Long-billed Curlew and her mate 1.

Fig 2-12 – Mrs. Long-billed Curlew and her mate 2.

Fig 2-13 – Mrs. Long-billed Curlew and her mate 3.

On January 5, 2019 a major storm system with high winds moved through the area. When I went by the marsh at 7:00 am, it was still dark as the sun rose about 7:30 am. There was just enough light to see the outline of a lone figure at the end of the sandbar. It was Mrs. Curlew. On the way back I saw her standing in the water some distance away while the Willet was at the end of the sandbar. Mrs. Curlew then flew to stand behind the Willet and they stood like this, close together, for a while. The water was rising higher and higher in the marsh, and pretty soon, the mud bar would be covered over. Then the Willet flew off and left the Curlew standing in the rain and the wind. As I went over the bridge, I looked down and saw the water from the Bay pouring into the marsh. I had never seen such a large volume of water flowing in from San Francisco Bay.

January 6, 2019 was even stormier than the day before, and the rain and wind kept up all day. It rained heavily all the way back from Marshall Beach. I saw the outline of the male Curlew on the western sandbar and Mrs. Curlew was feeding on the eastern sandbar quite close to me. I watched her dig down and come up with a pinkish item. Then a Ring-billed Gull flew at her from above, and she crouched down. He came after her again before she had had a chance to get the food down her long bill. She took off in flight and flew high up with the gull in pursuit right behind her. She flew in a half circle and then suddenly made a sharp turn to try to evade the gull. She flew over me and out towards the bay. Finally, the gull turned back. Mrs. Curlew flew around the marsh, coming down lower and landing on the mud bar again. There was nothing in her bill, so I hoped she had been able to swallow the food in flight. Then she resumed feeding. The rain was coming down hard; it was windy as well; and I got soaked through. I wanted to get out of the storm after being outside for only a short time. I hoped Mrs. Curlew would be able to find a sheltered spot to ride out the inclement weather.

Storms kept coming through San Francisco with breaks in between during the first half of January 2019. What I especially noticed about Mrs. Curlew on these days was how she reacted to other birds of other species around her. She seemed to really like the Willet and she often walked close to it. They both went about their business of looking for food, but I believed they liked each other.

On January 19, 2019 I had a chance to go to the marsh three days in a row, as Monday was a Martin Luther King Jr. holiday. On Saturday I ran from 7:00 am to 9:30 am. The tide was at its highest and also there seemed to be a surge from the recent storms. It was just light when I went out past Crissy Field Marsh and I could see only one bird and it wasn't big enough to be the Long-billed Curlew. It was the willet. Then I heard the curlew's cry. Was she calling to me? Sure enough, some distance away, out in the water, there she was. She was getting cleaned up.

On the way back, the water level was even higher in the marsh and no islands were showing. The water was pouring in under the bridge from the Bay. I saw the curlew and the willet resting together on the bank a short distance from the bridge. Mrs. Curlew had her long bill tucked under her scapulars and was standing on one leg. The Willet also had its head turned back. As I approached them from the right, I could see Mrs. Curlew had her eye open watching. The willet was turned the other way. Then as I went past them and was to the left of them, all I could see was the Curlew's back, but the willet had its eye open in this direction. What they were doing was like having eyes all around them so they could see in all directions. They were covering each other's backs. What intelligent birds! No wonder they got along so well together.

On January 27, 2019 Mrs. Curlew was walking along the bank at the edge of the marsh and digging her long bill into the grassy area. She was accustomed to walking on grass, as her breeding area was on grassland of the northwestern plains.

On February 3, 2019 I went from the Marina area to Marshall's Beach from 6:30 to 9:30 am. It was just getting light as I passed the marsh and I saw Mrs. Curlew some distance away. The willet was wading in the water up to its belly. The Curlew made her haunting cry when I approached and I didn't know if it was meant for me or for the willet. On the way back no mud bars showed and the water level was high in the marsh. Both the curlew and the willet were resting close together on the bank. Both of them had their bills tucked back and both had one eye open. It was so nice to see them resting together. They looked out for each other.

The morning of March 2, 2019 was stormy and windy and coming back from my run it started to pour with a strong easterly wind. Mrs. Curlew and the willet were standing close together some distance away in the marsh. Then I saw two gulls attack Mrs. Curlew. She flew off silently in the pouring rain with the gulls in pursuit. I did not see her return to the marsh. The willet stayed in the marsh.

March 10, 2019 was windy and cold in the morning. The sea had large swells that broke into crashing waves at the shoreline. I saw the willet at the marsh. It spread its wings, flashed its white underwing lining and flew from the marsh towards San Francisco Bay, turning west along the shore. Mrs. Curlew was in the marsh preening and then she put her long bill under her feathers and rested, with her eye open watching me.

In the middle of March 2019, the entry to the marsh from the Bay was blocked due to a build-up of sand, and water coming into the marsh from the fresh water spring could not drain into the Bay. Nor could the twice daily tide flow into the marsh from the Bay. The marsh's outlet to the bay had been blocked for some time and the water level in the marsh was the highest I had ever seen it. No islands showed above the waterline and the bank of the marsh was completely under water. The marsh was flooded. On March 16, I saw Mrs. Curlew walking in water in the middle of the marsh. The water was up to her belly and she occasionally put her head far under water to probe in the mud.

March 16, 2019 was the last time I saw Mrs. Long-billed Curlew.

On March 23rd, the marsh was still flooded. Water covered the western end, where there was usually dry ground. The tide in the Bay was out and the water level in the marsh was several feet higher than the water in San Francisco Bay. There was a high sand barrier between the Bay and the water outlet from the marsh. There were no shorebirds in the marsh. I wondered where Mrs. Curlew and the willet were now? Had they migrated somewhere already, or were they at another place close by?

Then, on April 5, 2019 the marsh was suddenly unflooded! The water had exited into the Bay and the water level in the marsh was now extremely low. There was now much unflooded ground in the marsh – as much as I had ever seen. What a shocking change! I wondered what had happened in the last ten days to cause this dramatic change. Was this natural and had the water pressure from the high level in the marsh suddenly forced its way out to the Bay? Had there been human intervention? Most importantly, I wondered if Mrs. Curlew would return to the marsh now, or was she somewhere far away?

Towards the end of April 2019, I saw two Long-billed Curlews, one of whom had a very long bill, at the marsh. However, I knew it was not Mrs. Curlew due to the way this other Long-billed Curlew acted. This other bird walked along similar to the way Mrs. Curlew does, but it was not so observant. It aggressively went after the other Long-billed Curlew, who then flew a distance away and started peacefully feeding. Then the bird with the very long bill purposely rushed over to the other Curlew and chased it off, whereupon the second Curlew flew high up and away from the marsh. I don't believe Mrs. Curlew would act this aggressively.

I believe March 16, 2019 was the last time I could spend time with Mrs. Curlew, this magnificent female Long-billed Curlew, as she would leave Crissy Field Marsh for her breeding ground in the spring of 2019, and I moved away from the San Francisco northern waterfront. When I returned briefly to San Francisco in the first half of July 2019, I saw neither her nor the willet at Crissy Field Marsh

LONG-BILLED CURLEW

The Long-billed Curlew is the largest shorebird in North America, measuring 21 to 26 inches in length. It is an elegant, beautiful bird. Its loud, repeated "curlee" followed by descending sharp whistles, is a joy to hear. The main visible difference between the sexes is that the female has a longer bill, but the female is also larger than the male. Juveniles have much shorter bills.

The Long-billed Curlew is a short-distance migrant. It is one of the earliest breeding shorebirds, returning from wintering grounds from California to Mexico in mid-March. Long-billed Curlews first breed at two to four years old. There is one brood per season. Nest initiation is primarily mid-April to mid-May, with peak hatching mid-May to mid-June. The female abandons her mate and young after two to three weeks. Females and failed breeders first arrive at wintering sites along the Pacific Coast in mid-June. The young can fly after 35-45 days. Males leave the breeding grounds by mid-July, with the young of the year leaving in mid-August.

On its grassland breeding grounds, the Long-billed Curlew feeds primarily on insects such as beetles, grasshoppers and caterpillars. It picks up items on the ground or probes slightly under the surface of soil or mud with its incredibly long bill. In its winter habitat, it eats small crustaceans, mollusks, berries and seeds.

The Long-billed Curlew breeds in short-grass communities, preferring native prairies but also occupying grazed mixed-grass communities and scrub prairie. Its breeding range extends from

south-central Canada, south-central Washington, southeastern Oregon, and southern Idaho to western Nebraska, northeastern New Mexico, northwestern Utah and western Arizona. After the breeding season is over, Long-billed Curlews form flocks and migrate to coastal habitats, mostly from California and Texas into Mexico and Central America. While they are most often encountered on tidal flats and other coastal habitats, wintering curlews also occur on inland grassland and agricultural habitats such as those found in the Central Valley of California, west Texas, and northern Mexico. There used to be many more suitable breeding areas in the Long-billed Curlews' range than there are today. It was found in large numbers on the Great Plains and in the eastern prairies. Suitable areas in its breeding range have shrunk appreciatively and continue to shrink due to agriculture and livestock grazing.

Today, the Long-billed Curlew is considered one of the most threatened shorebird species in America. In the United States Shorebird Conservation Plan, it is categorized as "highly imperiled" due to its already small population size, documented population declines, and significant threats to both its breeding and wintering areas. Based on a total population estimate of 20,000 individuals, the conservation goal calls for increasing population size by 30 percent to 28,500 individuals. (Ref 2-2)

WESTERN WILLET

Willets are grayish overall, but have a bold black-and-white wing pattern easily visible when they fly or unfold their wings. Their breeding and non-breeding plumages are different. Their Basic plumage is largely plain brownish gray, while in alternate plumage, their head, neck and remainder of body are subtly barred and streaked darker. Willets constantly jerk their heads forward and back. Foraging in mudflats, intertidal areas, and shallow marshes, they snatch up food from the surface of the water or probe in the mud with their bills. They eat aquatic insects, marine worms, small crabs, small mollusks and fish. Their diet also includes plant matter such as grass and seeds. Willets breed from central Canada to northeastern California and Nevada, as well as along the Atlantic and Gulf Coast south from Nova Scotia. They winter along the Pacific Coast from Oregon south, as well as along the Atlantic Coast from North Carolina south to northern South America.

Willets form mated pairs that last for many years, even for their whole lives. Although mated pairs are not found together throughout the year, they find each other again at the start of the breeding season. They use displays and calls to re-establish their relationship and begin nesting. Western Willets breed beginning in late April. Along the California coast in San Francisco Bay the mean departure date among tagged wintering birds was April 6.

Two to three weeks after the chicks hatch, the female leaves her mate and young to start her migration. The male remains with the young an additional two weeks until they fledge. Many adults depart the breeding grounds in June and July, with juveniles following soon after.

In a study conducted in 1998 and 1999 on Western Willets breeding at western Great Basin sites in the interior of southern Oregon and northeastern California, and wintering primarily in San Francisco Bay, it was found that Willets arrived synchronously at breeding sites during mid-April and spent less than 12 weeks in the Great Basin. Shortly after chicks fledged, adult willets left the Great Basin for locations primarily at coastal and estuarine sites in the San Francisco Bay area. There was little among-site movement once they arrived at the coast, and birds appeared to be site faithful in subsequent winters. Most of the individual willets tracked stayed in a localized part of San Francisco Bay for seven to nine months of the year, moving from roost sites to feeding areas in response to the tides. Thus, Western

Willets stay briefly at a breeding site and then migrate directly over the mountains to the Pacific Coast, primarily northern California, where they remain in the same area until spring migration. (Ref 2-3).

Climate change and sea level rise are emerging threats for willets, as all the habitats they use are only inches above sea level. It is difficult to know exactly how they will be affected because the response of wetland habitats to changing sea levels is hard to predict.

Fig 2-14 - Long-billed Curlew.

Fig 2-15- Long-billed Curlew 2.

Chapter Three – Aquatic Park to Golden Gate Bridge

DURING THE YEARS 1988 to 2019 on my walks and jogs from Aquatic Park to the Golden Gate Bridge, I saw a wide variety of bird species, depending upon the season and the particular location. The same birds stayed in a certain area for a long time and then suddenly they were gone, having left for other locales. I could predict what type of birds I would probably see, based on their being there for days or weeks at a time. The same species were not necessarily present at the same time every year. One year I might see large numbers of a species and the next year see few or none of this particular species.

In their book, *Union Bay, the Life of a City Marsh*, Harry Higman and Earl Larrison compared a marsh to a wildlife "hotel" where "guests" come and go. (Ref 3-1) Various kinds of birds use the facilities for nesting and raising their families; others over-winter there; and still others pass through on migration to other destinations. This comparison of a marsh to a wildlife hotel applied to my observations of the Crissy Field Marsh, and indeed to the whole area from Aquatic Park to the Golden Gate Bridge along San Francisco Bay. Probably due to the necessarily transient nature of migrant birds, the species and individuals present changed throughout the year.

<u>Western Grebe</u>

One day in February very early in the morning it was still dark and the water in the lagoon by the St. Francis Yacht Club was almost black. As I ran past the lagoon, I noticed a Western Grebe sitting far up on the sand quite a distance from the water. It was fast asleep with its head tucked into its back. I suspected the tide had gone out and stranded it. There was almost no-one around that early, but I was afraid that if the grebe didn't wake up and get into the water soon, a passing dog might see it and go after it. When I returned going the other way and ran back past the grebe, it was still fast asleep. I watched as a Golden Retriever went down onto the sand and along the water. However, the dog didn't seem to notice the grebe sleeping further up on the beach.

The legs of grebes and loons are positioned at the rear of their bodies. This makes it easier for them to propel themselves underwater when they dive. However, it also makes it very difficult for them to walk on land.

I stood at the edge of the sidewalk overlooking the lagoon and loudly cleared my throat trying to wake up the grebe. Still it didn't move. Finally, after my repeatedly loudly clearing my throat, it abruptly lifted its head and looked around. Shortly thereafter, it started to walk towards the water. It was a huge effort for the grebe to walk on land down towards the water. It took several steps holding its body upright over its rear-placed legs and then collapsed on the sand. It covered the distance in five or six phases, some longer than others, and finally made it to the water and the safety of its own environment. I breathed a sigh of relief.

Fig 3-1 – Western Grebe clumsily trying to make it back into the surf. A close look appears that his/her bottom beak is broken off. Courtesy of Kevin Cole from Pacific Coast, USA (en:User:Kevinlcole) / CC BY (https://creativecommons.org/licenses/by/2.0)

Fig 3-2 - Western Grebe in San Francisco Bay.

Western Grebes are large and slender with long necks and long, thin bills. Their plumage is dark gray above and white below, with a clear color division. The top of the face is black, and the bottom white. Western Grebes breed mainly on inland lakes and marshes in the prairie regions of Canada and the United States and spend eight months of the year wintering in the coastal marine waters of western North America, where they form large flocks.

I often observed large flocks of Western Grebes in San Francisco Bay during the day, usually just to the east of the Golden Gate Bridge. They were always resting, never diving, and I wondered why they were not busy diving for food. After reading James Clowater's research study below [Ref 3-2], I understood how they could spend so much time resting during the day and still manage to get enough food to sustain themselves.

RESEARCH STUDY ON WESTERN GREBES

Research has shown that wintering Western Grebes are nocturnal predators. James Clowater studied the foraging behavior of wintering Western Grebes extensively. In the daytime he found they formed large roosting flocks as an anti-predator defense while resting. Early in the day they traveled to these roosting locations. While in the roosting flock they generally did not dive, except for the odd "panic dive" if an eagle or aircraft flew overhead. Birds dispersed from the roosting flocks at dusk and begin foraging after sunset. They were solitary nocturnal foragers feeding on the pelagic-schooling fish, primarily Pacific Herring, that live away from the ocean bottom in the open seas. Pelagic fish commonly school during the day and disperse at night, an anti-predator defense since they lack the advantage of proximity to cover of fish living near the bottom of the sea. The behavior of the predator (the Western Grebe) follows the behavior of the prey (Pacific Herring). As herring disperse at night, it is likely a grebe would encounter only a single or a few herring at a time. Since grebes feed on prey that will quickly flee an approaching predator, there is no advantage to group foraging.

Birds pursuing fish underwater during the day are visually-oriented predators who would be at a disadvantage foraging at night when it is more difficult to see elusive prey. The questions posed by Clowater were: "Why do grebes choose to be nocturnal?" and "How can grebes find their prey in darkness?"

In answer to the first question, Clowater found that grebes foraging at night had their necks angled forward and appeared to be looking into the water, while the odd grebe observed foraging during the day would initiate a dive without appearing to look into the water. Clowater found that birds specializing on agile and elusive fish seldom dive at night. He hypothesized that night-time feeding opportunities were more profitable for Western Grebes because the energetic expense of diving is reduced at night.

In answer to the second question of how grebes can find their prey in the dark, it is believed they use the light from disturbed bioluminescent organisms to show them the location of their prey at night. Bioluminescence is light produced by a chemical reaction which originates in an organism. It can be expected anytime in any region or depth in the sea. Its common occurrence is in the brilliantly luminescent bow wave or wake of a surface ship. In this case, the causal organisms are almost always single-cell algae, often numbering many hundreds per liter. They are mechanically excited to produce light by the ship's passage, or even by the movement of porpoises and smaller fish.

Clowater figured that Western Grebes use bioluminescence to locate their prey in two ways: first of all, if a herring is feeding on the organisms, the algae are disturbed and emit bioluminescent light which attracts the bird to consume the herring; secondly, if herring are feeding near the surface and sense the approach of the grebe, they accelerate to flee and leave a bioluminescent wake which betrays their location to the bird.

Sanderling

At the end of December 1996, heavy tropical rain storms caused severe flooding in the higher country east of San Francisco, from which waters feed out to the Delta, San Francisco Bay, and eventually to the Pacific Ocean. Through the month of January 1997, the Bay was full of tule reeds and logs caused by the runoff from the floods. At Aquatic Park the tide was high, with the water far up on the beach and only one foot from the steps. I watched 20 to 30 Sanderlings up close as they ran along the waterline. They were small (eight inches versus an American Robin's ten inches) with black sticks for beaks, black legs, very white under parts and mottled gray upperparts with black marks. When the Sanderlings flew off if someone approached or a wave threatened to get them wet, they took off and circled as a group. They have a white wing bar which shows when they fly. I sat on the steps and watched them. They knew I was there but didn't move away. They probed in the sand

and among the smaller pieces of wood for food. I saw one who appeared to have only one leg, but who was able to hop about on its one leg and probe in the sand.

On January 25th, 1997 I went for a walk by the beach at Aquatic Park. There were many gulls of several species there and I suspected many of them were migrants. In one area there was enough sand among the rocks for the Sanderlings to comb the beach just below the concrete path. The Sanderlings coexisted with the gulls, moving out of its way if a gull walked by. I saw the Sanderling with one leg hopping around and combing the beach. Then it laid its head back under its wing and rested, with its eye open watching for danger. Several of the Sanderlings were bathing in a water pool among the rocks.

On January 31st the water was still very muddy, and the tide was high. The rocks were completely under water to the edge of the walkway. Debris of logs, plants, and other flotsam floated in the water. I saw the Sanderlings up by the Dolphin Swim and Boat Club where there was still a bit of beach. They did not seem too disturbed by the near presence of the people close by, although the birds must have been keeping very alert as they flew off immediately if anyone got too close. I saw the Sanderling with only one leg in the middle of the others, hopping about and probing in the sand.

Sanderlings nest only in limited areas of the far north, but during migration and winter they are familiar sights on coastal beaches all over the world. They are long-distance migrants, with different populations travelling 3,000 to 10,000 miles between breeding and wintering grounds. Much of the migration is accomplished in long nonstop flights between key stopover points. Because Sanderlings rely heavily on a few staging areas in migration, they are vulnerable to destruction of those sites. Studies show that many individuals return year after year to the same wintering sites. One-year-old birds may remain through the summer on the southern wintering grounds. [Ref 3-3] Some regional populations are in rapid decline, with the apparent causes being habitat degradation and the increasing recreational use of sandy beaches. [Ref 3-4]

Fig 3-3 - Sanderling on rocky coast along San Francisco Bay.

At Aquatic Park, I also saw eight pairs of Red-breasted Mergansers. There were eight males and eight females. The males had long, thin bills and a crest on the back of their dark green heads with distinctive thick white collars around the neck. The smaller females had noticeable orange, long, thin bills, and had distinctive rusk-red-colored heads with crests. All 16 mergansers dove in the water close to the rocks and shore where the pier started.

Red-breasted Mergansers are the most common winter merganser on salt water, especially where rocky coves provide good fishing. They eat fish captured by diving swiftly underwater. The serrated edges on their long-pointed bill allow the birds to more easily grip the fish. To this particular group of mergansers, the cove at Aquatic Park must have seemed like a preferred habitat.

<u>Surf Scoter</u>

From mid-February through mid-April in 1998, I watched 75 Surf Scoters floating in the Bay by the pier at Aquatic Park. They rode the waves on the sheltered side of the Aquatic Park pier. Many of them slept with their heads tucked under their wings, but with their feet still paddling against the current, which was pulling them out towards the Bay. Then, just when I was getting used to seeing so many Surf Scoters at this spot, one day in mid-April they were all gone, having left for their breeding grounds. In the years before and following 1998, I did not see such a large congregation of Surf Scoters in one place on the routes I followed along the San Francisco Bay waterfront. In subsequent winters I only saw one to several in various places near the shoreline.

Male Surf Scoters are velvety-black with a white patch both behind the head on the nape and on the forehead or crown. They have large bills which are swollen on the top and appear orange-colored from a distance, although they are actually multicolored white, red, yellow and black. Female Surf Scoters are various shades of brown. During the summer and fall, the male's bold white nape patch disappears due to heavy wear of the long, white feathers, revealing the short, black feathers beneath, but this nape patch reappears by midwinter. Juvenile males also have white nape patches, though white fore crowns are not evident before their second winter.

Although Surf Scoters are the most common scoter on the Pacific Coast in winter, they were until recently among the least-known of the sea ducks, particularly during the breeding season. They breed on freshwater and shallow lakes in the boreal forests of northern Canada and Alaska. They prefer to nest in sparsely wooded terrain near a pond, bog or stream in the northern boreal forest. They winter in shallow marine coastal waters along coastal North America and south to the northern Gulf of Mexico coast. Rarely diving in water exceeding 30 feet deep, Surf Scoters feed close to the shore where waves break upon the beach. They often dive through foaming wave crests, which is probably the reason for their name. Most Surf Scoters depart for breeding grounds in early spring, but a few, usually young males, may spend their second summer on their wintering grounds

Pair bonds among Surf Scoters are formed on the wintering grounds and pairs migrate together to breeding sites. During the northward passage in the spring, the drakes defend their mates and constantly remain close to them, even if their partners are wounded. Pairs arrive on the breeding grounds from mid-May onwards. Surf Scoters have one of the shortest seasonal pair bonds among waterfowl. In order to undergo their molt migrations on coastal waters, males desert their mates during incubation and within three weeks after arrival on breeding lakes. Pairs may then reunite on the wintering grounds. Therefore, Surf Scoters are single-brooded by females. They have an estimated incubation period of 25-30 days. Surf Scoters have a low annual nest success rate. An indication of possible nest success is the fact that predation caused 76% of nest failures for the Lesser Scaup, another diving duck species breeding in similar areas to the Surf Scoter. Unsuccessful female Surf Scoters depart breeding sites well ahead of successful females, who in turn depart before the young of the year.

Outside of the breeding range, Surf Scoters occur almost exclusively at sea where they spend most of the year. At wintering sites, feeding is mainly during the day and occurs closer to shore than night-time roosting sites.

Population declines of Surf Scoters in most parts of its range have been reported for several decades, especially among birds wintering on the Pacific Coast. The causes for these declines are not clear. They face reduced quality of wintering habitat from increasing contaminants such as selenium, cadmium, and mercury. Declines in Pacific herring may threaten their populations because herring eggs appear to be a critical food during spring migration and throughout the winter on the Pacific Coast. Climate change and sea level rise, resulting in changed water salinity and depth, could alter prey species composition and herring spawning, as well as change the subtidal habitat Surf Scoters depend on for foraging. Climate change is most pronounced at high latitudes and may have its greatest impacts on the most northerly nesting species, such as sea ducks.

Infrequent events may cause mass mortality or affect body condition and fitness of birds. During nonbreeding periods, Surf Scoters aggregate in coastal sites where they are often exposed to a variety of human-caused events, which cause both acute and chronic effects. They are one of the species most frequently caught in oil spills, which have the potential for a catastrophic impact to their populations.

Forty to fifty percent of the Pacific Flyway's Surf Scoter population is believed to overwinter in San Francisco Bay. Over the past 50 years, their populations have declined across their range by 50-60% and a lack of studies focused on the species' breeding, migratory, and wintering ecology make conservation efforts a challenge. Audubon California's Richardson Bay Audubon Center & Sanctuary is addressing local conservation concerns through its new Waterbird Conservation Program. Currently, the Program is focused on nominating new San Francisco Bay Important Bird Areas (IBA) based on the concentration of Surf Scoters and other waterbirds. These new IBAs will help to focus conservation efforts—such as restoration or protections—in these places. Audubon is also hosting an experiment by the United States Geological Survey (USGS) using rafts draped with kelp to attract spawning Pacific Herring. The herring eggs are known to be a significant source of food for Surf Scoters in winter. [Ref 3-5]

Fig 3-4 – Male Surf Scoter in surf in San Francisco Bay.

SURF SCOTER TRACKING STUDIES

Recent studies using satellite transmitters to track movements of individual Surf Scoters have provided very useful information concerning their migrations, and breeding and wintering locales.

A team led by Susan De La Cruz, a biologist with the U.S. Geological Survey, captured and radio marked 90 Surf Scoters to follow them to their nests. One female Surf Scoter was tracked from its coastal wintering grounds in San Francisco Bay to a lake 2,000 miles away that was 80 miles east of Yellowknife in the Northwest Territories. The team was able to locate the satellite-marked hen sitting on six eggs in a downy nest.

Susan De La Cruz commented: "Our preliminary studies showed that most birds marked with satellite transmitters in San Francisco Bay were distributed in a band a few hundred miles wide at the edge of the treeline from Great Slave Lake to Great Bear Lake in Canada's Northwest Territories." (Ref 3-6)

Fig 3-5- Surf Scoters in the winter at San Francisco Bay. Photograph by Dan Gaube, USGS.

Fig 3-6 – Northern boreal forest habitat in interior Canada where scientists located a Surf Scoter from San Francisco Bay and its nest containing six eggs. Courtesy of Matt Wilson, USGS.

Fig 3-7 - Satellite-marked Surf Scoter from San Francisco Bay on a lake near its nest in Canada, showing the six eggs in her nest. Courtesy of Matt Wilson, USGS.

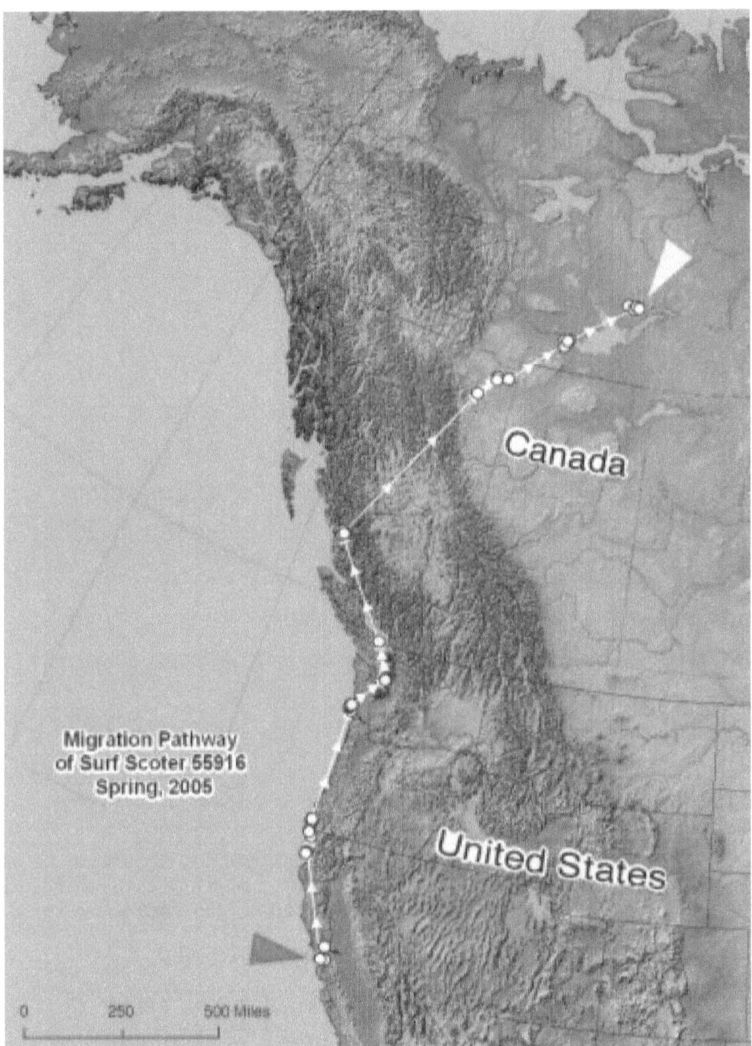

Fig 3-8 – Route of the more than 2,000-mile migration of a satellite-marked female Surf Scoter from her wintering grounds in San Francisco Bay to her breeding grounds in the northern boreal forest of Canada. Modified from a graphic by William Perry, USGS.

Studies have shown that Pacific coast Surf Scoters that wintered in San Francisco Bay had remarkable nesting area fidelity in two consecutive years. For example, eight females marked on the Pacific Coast were tracked to nest locations averaging less than one mile apart in successive years. [Ref 3-7] *This is amazing considering the vastness of the northern boreal forest, and the long stretches of similar terrain they would have had to cross to reach these sites. The "local-knowledge" hypothesis suggests when females return to the same nesting area, they obtain an advantage in terms of food resources, distribution of others of their own species, and predator activity in the area.*

It has been shown that female Surf Scoters using Pacific Flyway wintering sites follow two main routes to their breeding area: a southern inland route involving staging in Puget Sound and the Strait of Georgia and protracted inland migration, or a northern coastal route characterized by short movements along the Pacific coast of British Columbia and southeast Alaska with inland migration initiating from Lynn Canal near Juneau, Alaska. Which route was taken was related to the nesting site latitude in the Canadian northern boreal forest, with the southern inland route chosen by birds nesting further south than those using the northern coastal route. [Ref 3-8]

Each female Surf Scoter kept to the migration route she had used the previous year, but changed the stopover locations between years. Interestingly, the departure dates varied by the wintering sites, but the arrival and settling dates on the breeding grounds were very close to May 30th, suggesting individual birds adjusted their migration timing to meet an optimized reproductive schedule. This is necessary to take advantage of the very short breeding season in the far northern boreal forest, as Surf Scoters have at most only one chance a year to reproduce.

Loon

In May of 1998, I watched two loons in the boat canals by the St. Francis Yacht Club. One was swimming along the boat channel right by the path and I could look down and observe it at very close range. Its rear-positioned legs were strung out behind and it was submerged to just above its eyes, swimming along and looking underwater. Every so often, it dove. It was aware of my presence, and occasionally looked up at me, but showed no fear. From above, it looked like a huge turtle with a large, almost round body and legs splayed out behind. Various types of loons, including Red-throated, Arctic and Common Loons migrate through San Francisco Bay and some overwinter there.

Fig 3-9 – Loon swimming in a boat dock channel by San Francisco Bay.

Whimbrel

In the last half of August 2001, I noticed a Whimbrel walking across the mud bars at Crissy Field Marsh at low tide and foraging by picking up items from the surface rather than by probing in the mud with its bill. It was a large mottled brown shorebird with a long, black, down curved bill; a dark streak through the eye; two pronounced dark stripes on the crown; a pale belly and gray legs. At first, I saw only one bird and then I heard a second bird calling and another Whimbrel flew in and landed. The second bird was missing an entire leg, so it had to hop around.

Whimbrels breed on the high Arctic tundra and are extreme long-distance migrants. I assumed these birds were on migration.

Whimbrels are somewhat similar in appearance and habits to the Eskimo Curlew, although the Eskimo Curlew was smaller and more of a buff color, with no bold head pattern. The Eskimo Curlew is now for all intents and purposes extinct, primarily due to excessive hunting from which it never recovered in the mid to late 1800's. Whimbrels are still numerous perhaps because of their wary behavior and the remoteness of their nesting grounds on the Arctic tundra. There are two distinct North American breeding areas – one along the northern Alaska coast, Yukon and Mackenzie Delta, and another west and south of Hudson Bay. Like many other tundra breeders, Whimbrels in the East fly offshore over the Atlantic during their autumn migration to South America, returning in spring mainly along an interior continental route; while Whimbrels in the West migrate along the West Coast.

Fig 3-10 - Whimbrels.

EXAMPLES OF EXTREME WHIMBREL MIGRATIONS

WINNIE THE WHIMBREL

One group of Whimbrels stage along the lower Delmarva Peninsula in Virginia and feed on fiddler crabs to gain the weight needed to provide the tremendous amount of energy they need for a transcontinental flight. It had previously been assumed all of this group of Whimbrels were from the Hudson Bay breeding population.

However, the Center for Conservation Biology at the College of William and Mary, and The Nature Conservancy in Virginia tracked a female Whimbrel named Winnie by satellite from Virginia all the way to the Mackenzie River area. This documented a previously unknown to science and entirely unexpected migration route between the mid-Atlantic coast and the northwestern Arctic. Winnie completed the nonstop flight of more than 3,200 miles in 146 hours, sustaining an average flight speed of 22 miles per hour for six days.

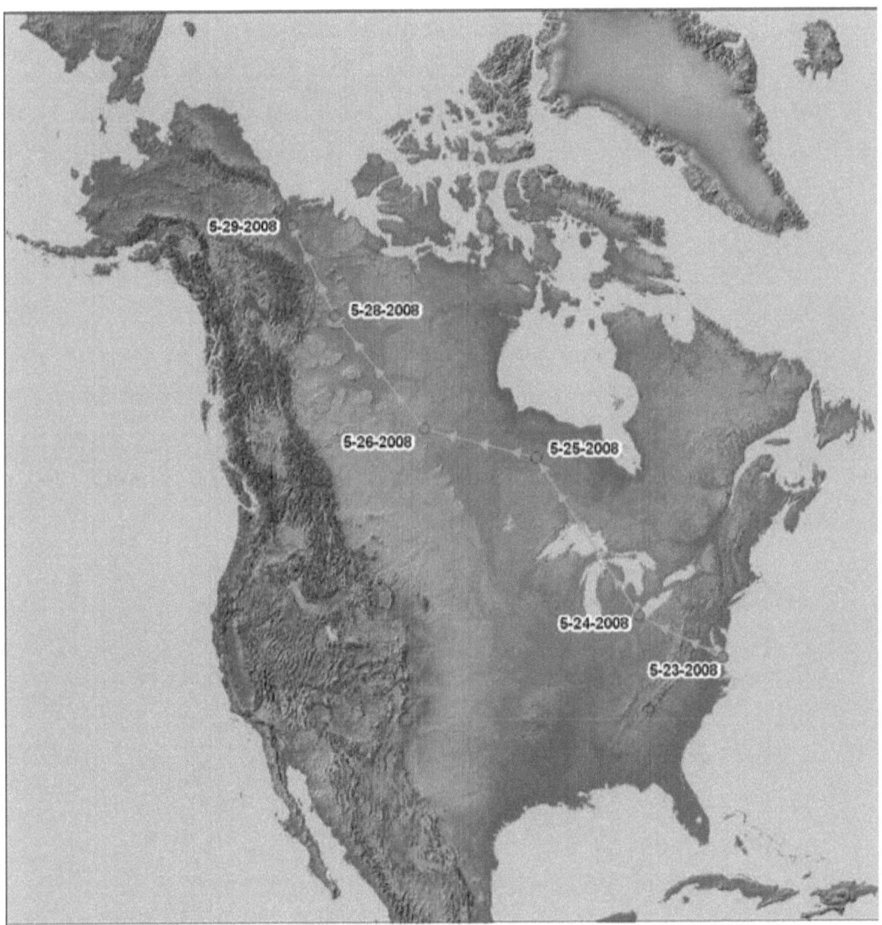

Fig 3-11 - Migration path of Winnie the Whimbrel. Credit: The Center for Conservation Biology.

After Winnie made her record-setting trip to the Mackenzie River, she continued to her breeding grounds in Alaska's Colville River system above the Arctic Circle. She remained on her breeding grounds from June 7 to July 12 when she began moving west along the northern Alaska coast. She staged in the west coast of Alaska until August 2, when she flew south over the north Pacific. Here, she flew into a cyclone and then turned east to Willapa Bay in Washington State, where she stayed for two weeks to rest and refuel.

From here, researchers expected her to fly south down the Pacific Coast, but instead she turned towards the east again, on what would be the last of her great migratory flights. After flying east for another thousand miles and up to seven days, her satellite receiver became stationary in Wisconsin around Lake Superior. Bryan Watts, Director of William and Mary's Center for Conservation Biology believes she encountered stiff headwinds over the high plains, ended up in a poor foraging area, and "just ran out of gas".

Watts said: "How frequently this sort of thing happens, we have no idea. We have evidence of major die-offs over the Atlantic where some birds go out and a storm comes and lots of carcasses wash up. To be lost in a place where you don't have much to feed on, that's a risk the birds take." (Ref 3-9)

THREE OTHER WHIMBRELS

A second example of the extreme migrations undertaken by Whimbrels is documented by three Whimbrels traced by scientists at the Center for Conservation Biology and the Canadian Wildlife Service. The three birds were originally satellite marked on their breeding grounds along the Mackenzie River Delta in far western Canada. In mid-July, the birds flew across the continent to the east coast of Canada and staged for approximately two weeks to build fat reserves. They then flew southeast out over the Atlantic Ocean, reaching the center of the Atlantic Ocean before turning south and making landfall in South America between Guyana and Brazil. At one point their migration route was one thousand miles closer to Africa than to North America. Although this portion of the Atlantic is used by true seabirds that roost on the water, it is so isolated from shore that species such as Whimbrels that cannot land on water were not thought to reach it.

The birds may receive some benefit from venturing this far out to sea in the form of favorable tailwinds. Also, this behavior may have arisen as a successful way to skirt past the hurricane-prone Caribbean.

One of the Whimbrels, named Mackenzie, averaged 30 miles an hour for the six days of the nonstop 4,300-mile flight. (Ref 3-10)

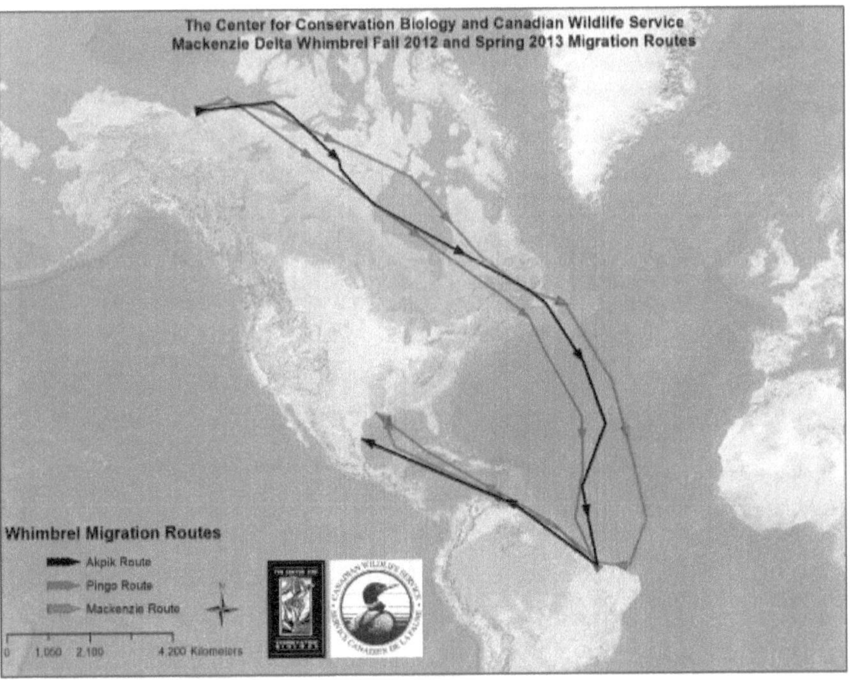

Fig 3-12 - Tracking map – Map of Mackenzie River Whimbrel movements July 2012 through June 2013. Birds have been tracked using solar-powered satellite transmitters. Map by The Center for Conservation Biology (CCB).

Whimbrels are omnivores who use their long downward-curing beaks to hunt for crabs, insects and other small invertebrates living along the shore. During migration, they supplement this diet with berries, which grow naturally in bogs near the coast.

Some migrating Whimbrels were stopping at Miscou Island, New Brunswick before undertaking their marathon flights over the Atlantic Ocean. Here, blueberry growers complained the Whimbrels were eating their crops. But researchers found producers were significantly overestimating the quantity of berries the birds consumed. The challenge of conveying these data and winning over producers fell on Julie Guillemot, a professor of environmental management at the University of Moncton's Shippagan campus. Julie began an outreach program to inform growers of the facts, and about the Whimbrels' migrations.

Lane Stewart, a producer with a 200-acre blueberry farm on Miscou Island said the outreach effort had changed his mind about the Whimbrel, a bird commonly hunted on the island in his grandparents' day. Mr. Stewart was among the producers who allowed biologists onto his property in 2016 to outfit individual birds with GPS transmitters. Lane then took to following the birds' progress on a website showing where they had travelled.

Mr. Stewart commented: "To see such a little bird crossing from one end of the planet to the other – it's kind of impressive. If it's a help for them to eat here, that's okay." (Ref 3-11)

<u>Rafts of Ducks</u>

On January 4, 2008, heavy rain and powerful winds pounded the Bay Area. On the following day, I heard on the news there was a high surf warning with even stronger surges, all along the coast.

When I initially started out the following day about 8:30 am, there was a break in the clouds and no rain. However, I could see the menacing black clouds to the west over the Golden Gate Bridge. Sure enough, it started raining and poured off-and-on along the Golden Gate Promenade. I got soaked, but the temperature wasn't cold, so I didn't mind stopping and standing in the rain to look at birds through my somewhat-waterproofed binoculars. I could tell many of the birds were seeking shelter during the stormy weather.

A large flotilla of Western Grebes, with a few Surf Scoters mixed in, kept inside the more sheltered waters of the Bay to the east of the Golden Gate Bridge.

As I stood in the road leading to Fort Point and looked at this flotilla through my binoculars, an unusually large rogue wave suddenly snuck in from the bay, crashing over the embankment and covering me, soaking me. It had completely caught me off guard as I had been concentrating on the birds. Then I got a small taste of how wild and dangerous this storm could be. After being out for a couple of hours, I began to appreciate what it must be like for a fishing boat, or a bird, to be out in this kind of weather which wasn't even the really stormy weather of the day before.

However, I found it interesting to be out in somewhat stormy weather. They say only mad dogs, fools, and Englishmen go out in a storm. As I am not a mad dog or an Englishman, I must be a fool.

On January 18, 2008, close to shore all along the waterfront of the Marina Green, I saw rafts of several hundred ducks. Most of the ducks were male and female Surf Scoters, while there were also many male and female Greater or Lesser Scaup. I saw one Common Goldeneye couple. The male Goldeneye was quite white with golden eyes and the female had a brown head with gold eyes. All the mixed flock of ducks were just sitting in the water and moving slightly around. One small group among the Surf Scoters dove. The male Scoter dove first and then the others followed him. The flotillas of ducks along the Marina Green waterfront were one of the most amazing sights I had ever seen. In this "mixed flock", they all seemed to be minding their own business while within very close proximity to one another.

On January 25, 2008 there were still rafts of ducks close to the shore along the Marina Green. They seemed to be taking shelter from the series of storms which lasted for many days. I saw large groups of intermingled Surf Scoters and Scaup along with a few Common Goldeneye couples. The Common Goldeneyes seemed more skittish than the other ducks.

Fig 3-13 - Female Common Goldeneye.

<u>Elegant Terns</u>

On September 15, 2012 I went along the Golden Gate Promenade about 8:00 am. For the past several weeks I had heard terns calling noisily as they flew along the waterfront. As I approached the Gulf of the Farallones National Marine Sanctuary Visitor Center at the west end of Crissy Field, I saw hundreds of terns sitting on the pier behind the building.

Fig 3-14 – Pier behind the Gulf of the Farallones National Marine Sanctuary Visitor Center.

A man was just coming out of the white building—which houses a National Oceanic and Atmospheric Administration (NOAA) office—next to the Gulf of the Farallones Visitor Center. He headed towards the elevated walkway pier leading to a little shack. I heard him tell another man that the shack was where some kind of meeting was to take place. I asked the man if he knew what kind of terns were on the pier and told him I had noticed these small terns congregated on this pier about once a year. He answered (with what I believe was a British accent) that they were Elegant Terns. He said: "If you want to get really nerdy and look through binoculars, you can see some smaller ones among them which are Least Terns". I said the terns were very small – half the size of the Herring Gulls. He answered "Yes, aren't they gorgeous!" I felt very happy that someone shared my love of birds, as that is often the word I used to describe a bird – GORGEOUS!

On September 16, and again on September 22, 2012, there were 200 to 300 Elegant Terns along the pier. I saw one or two with the black feathers on their heads sticking up. I walked out on an adjacent parallel pier past the water line to look at them. I was alone and the surf pounded in below the pier. It felt very wild and a little scary, as I can't swim.

On September 29, 2012, there were no Elegant Terns on the pier. However, on October 14, 2012, once again many Elegant Terns were lined up, spaced closely together, on the pier. On some of them I saw the black feathers at the back of their heads sticking out. Several flew around and then landed. When they flew, their white tail feathers fanned out and appeared transparent.

A year later, on October 6, 2013, just before noon, I once again saw 100 to 200 Elegant Terns on the pier. I noticed that these terns liked to sit very close together. Although one end of the pier was vacant, they bunched up at the far end. A tern would fly over and hover, and then gently settle down in a small space between two other birds. Usually, they were very noisy, continuously calling, taking off, and then landing again. However, on this day, they were almost completely silent and seemed to be resting at midday.

Fig 3-15 - Elegant Terns resting on mud bar at Crissy Field Marsh.

Elegant Terns are 17" in length, versus a Herring Gull's length of 25". They breed in colonies and are sometimes associated with other terns, or, in northwestern Mexico, with Heermann's Gulls. In California, they appear to prefer nesting close to the larger Caspian Terns, which are 21" in length. This may help in defense against predators.

In late summer or early fall, after breeding, Elegant Terns move north along the coast, regularly to San Francisco, and rarely to British Columbia. Most move south again in October. Their wintering range extends as far south as Peru and northern Chile.

Elegant Terns are considered vulnerable because their nesting is restricted to only a very few sandy or rocky islands. Their nesting success and extent of dispersal are related to El Niño, a periodic warming over the eastern tropical Pacific Ocean which causes large numbers of fish and marine plants to die.

Elegant Terns forage by flying over the water, hovering and plunge-diving to catch prey below the surface. Feeding flocks of Elegant Terns are very noisy. Their calls are scratchy and grating and are given incessantly by flocks.

Least Terns are 9" in length. The behavior of the Least Tern is very similar to the Elegant Tern, except it sometimes dips down to take prey from the surface of the water or land. Least Terns leave North America and northern Mexico entirely in the winter, moving to tropical waters as far south as Brazil. They breed on coastal beaches and along major inland river systems. They normally depart by late summer for their wintering range in Central and South America.

<u>Pigeon Guillemots</u>

In August of 2012, just inside the entrance to San Francisco Bay on the east side of the Golden Gate Bridge, there were five small, black, pigeonlike birds with large white wing patches sitting together in the water. Through binoculars, I could make out their bright red legs. Two other Pigeon Guillemots were a short distance away.

In June of 2013, I noticed several Pigeon Guillemots in San Francisco Bay to the left of the fishing pier by the Warming Hut. A month later, I had an exciting experience with these Pigeon Guillemots at Fort Point.

Fort Point is a masonry seacoast fortification on the southern end of the Golden Gate Bridge. It was constructed by the United States Army just before the American Civil War to defend San Francisco Bay against hostile warships. When the tide flows in through the narrowed entrance to the Bay, it forms large waves which attract surfers to Fort Point.

Fig 3-16 - Fort Point underneath the south approach of the Golden Gate Bridge.

On July 20, 2013 I was on the road below Fort Point before 7:00 am. From the parking lot outside the Fort, I watched six Pigeon Guillemots swimming in the Bay. Two of the Pigeon Guillemots suddenly took to wing and flew straight towards me. As they flew over me, I saw their bright red legs and dangling feet. They flew directly at the brick walls of Fort Point. Their short wings beat very fast and they were very strong fliers. At the last moment, they swerved and flew back over the Bay. They repeated this four times. I wondered what they were doing. Then one of them flew into an opening in the wall of Fort Point and landed on the wide ledge. The masonry walls of Fort Point are three feet thick and there are wide ledges on its inset windows. The second Pigeon Guillemot also flew into the opening and disappeared from my view. I believed they had made a nest at the back of the ledge.

Fig 3-17 - Pigeon Guillemot on inset window ledge at Fort Point.

Fig 3-18 - Pigeon Guillemots on ledge at Fort Point.

Pigeon Guillemots are members of the Alcidae family that includes the auks, murres and puffins. Like other alcids, they use their wings to "fly" underwater as they search for small fish at the bottom. In flight, their wingbeats are rapid and shallow. Pigeon Guillemots are generally found very close to rocky shores and less often far out over the continental shelf. They are fairly common along the northern Pacific Coast from Alaska to southern California, occurring alone, in pairs, or in small groups.

Pigeon Guillemots first breed at three to five years of age. They are strikingly patterned in breeding season, when their red-orange legs and mouth lining may be important signals in courtship. [Ref 3-12] They nest on hard rock, in deserted holes of puffins and rabbits, or on buildings and wharves, using rock chips, pebbles and debris. Northernmost breeders in Alaska move south in winter to the edge of the pack ice. Birds in the center of the range from British Columbia to Oregon may be permanent residents. Many California birds apparently move north after breeding, as far as British Columbia.

The conservation status of Pigeon Guillemots is declining because of pollution, oil spills and warming climactic trends. As an example of this decline, as of 2010, populations still had not recovered to pre-spill levels following the Exxon Valdez oil spill of 1989. [Ref 3-13]

<u>Common Murre</u>

One Saturday at the end of June 2014, there was a National Park Service pick-up truck parked in the lot at the St. Francis Yacht Club. As I went by, I overheard the ranger speaking to a harmless homeless man who often sits on a bench there. The ranger said to him: "I have a bird in the back of my truck. It is a murre. Would you like to see it?"

I stopped and asked the ranger if I could look too. I thought he had said "BURR" and that a Burrowing Owl was in the crate in the back of his truck. I was expecting to see a small owl. However, when he carefully lifted up a corner of the lid of the crate, and we looked inside, we saw a Common Murre - a fairly large bird with a velvety black back, a large, sturdy black bill and a white belly. The ranger's name was Cody and he said he had found the

Common Murre standing on the ground at the back of the Warming Hut. It was not able to fly, although it had tried flapping its wings. The ranger said no-one was paying any attention to it, but he could not leave it there. Cody said he couldn't understand how it got there or how it had climbed over the high stone seawall by the Warming Hut.

Cody said he had tried calling the International Bird Rescue and Rehabilitation Center in Cordelia, as well as WildCare in San Rafael, but no-one had answered. He had then called a man whom he knew from San Francisco Animal Care and Control (SF ACC), an animal shelter. Cody had to meet the man in the parking lot, as the SF ACC are not supposed to come onto National Park Service property. The man from the SF ACC had inspected the Common Murre and told Cody it was a healthy juvenile that would be able to fly in a few hours, and that it should be left somewhere where it would be safe and close to water. Cody was thinking of leaving the murre at Crissy Field Marsh, and I couldn't think of a better place.

I told Cody I had noticed Pigeon Guillemots that seemed to have a nest in one of the window recesses at Fort Point. Pigeon Guillemots and Common Murres are both of the Alcidae family. Was it possible the Common Murre had walked all the way up the road from Fort Point to the Warming Hut?

When I ran by Crissy Field Marsh the next day, I looked to see if the juvenile Common Murre was still in the marsh, but it was not there.

Fig 3-19 - Several Common Murre on a Rock Ledge. Courtesy of Lisa Hupp, USFWS.

Common Murres are large auks. These "penguins of the north" have set-back legs giving them an upright stance on land. Moving on land is awkward as they shuffle along upright on bent legs. They propel themselves by using their wings to "fly" underwater in pursuit of prey. It is thought that Common Murres ascend through large schools of fish from beneath. (Ref 3-14)

Because they have a very small wing area relative to body weight, they must beat their wings extremely rapidly and maintain high speeds to stay airborne. They can only get airborne by diving off a cliff or by rapidly running over water.

Common Murres typically breed in high-density colonies of up to hundreds of thousands of pairs, where nesting pairs may be in bodily contact with their neighbors. No nest is built, except for a few pebbles brought to the nest site. The single egg is placed on bare rock on an island or on a cliff ledge. They first breed at four to nine years old, with most individuals beginning to breed at age six or seven.

Some 20 days after hatching, the chick leaves its nesting ledge and heads for the sea, unable to fly, but gliding for some distance with fluttering wings. The chick must leap from the cliff ledge with only half-formed wings, or tumble down a grassy slope to reach the water. Once on the ocean, the chick is tended by the male, who feeds it and shows it good foraging areas for a month or two.

In southern populations, Common Murres disperse to find food in the vicinity of the colony and occasionally return to the nest site during the winter.

Common Murres are highly susceptible to being killed in oil spills. The 1989 Exxon Valdez disaster in Alaska resulted in the deaths of nearly 200,000 murres. As tragic as large disastrous events such as the Exxon Valdez spill are, many more birds die from the unregulated dumping of bilge water at sea, which puts thousands of tons of oil into the oceans every year. It takes only a few drops of oil to destroy the insulating qualities of a seabird's plumage, and the result is usually a slow death from hypothermia.

Humans living in northern coastal areas have eaten murres and their eggs for thousands of years. Eggers from San Francisco took almost half a million eggs a year from the Farallon Islands in the mid-19th century to feed the growing city. Today a colony of about 150,000 Common Murres breeds on the Farallon Islands, a group of islands and steep sea pillars in the Gulf of the Farallones. The Farallon Islands lie 30 miles outside the Golden Gate and 20 miles south of Point Reyes, and are visible from the mainland on clear days. The islands are part of the City and County of San Francisco and are a designated wilderness national wildlife refuge. They are closed to the public.

Black Turnstones

October 6, 2013 was a clear day with no fog. Due to the Federal Government shutdown, as the budget had not been approved, the Warming Hut and other buildings on Federal Government property were closed.

The high water level came up to the steps below the path at the northern edge of Marina Green. One black rock stood above the waterline, and when I looked down, I noticed two Black Turnstones sitting on it. Black Turnstones are all black or slate gray above with white bellies. One of the turnstones grew nervous when it saw me looking down on it. When it raised its wings, I saw its conspicuous white stripes. I moved on, as I didn't want the birds to fly away.

Fig 3-20 - Black Turnstones and Sanderlings below walkway at the Marina Green.

On December 1, 2013 at sunrise about 7:00 am, I heard a rattling call along the shoreline beside the Marina Green, and saw several birds flying by. They had distinctive black-and-white markings on their wings. The water was up to the breakwater, with no rocks showing below the path. However, there are concrete steps below the path. I went to the edge of the path and looked down. There was a Black Turnstone on the steps. On a ledge right below the path were four or five more Black Turnstones. I knew they were Black Turnstones as they had made their rattling call.

In December of 2014, I watched a Black Turnstone on the steps below the path at the Marina Green. It flew to the steps, where there were two larger, lighter-colored Surfbirds. The tide was in and the water level was high, so they were waiting to feed on the rocks and steps. Surfbirds are smooth gray above with a white belly with sparse dark spots, and yellow legs. The Black Turnstone is mostly black above with white streaks, and pink legs. The Black Turnstone and Surfbirds stayed together. At one stage a wave washed over the Black Turnstone. Then it started taking a bath in the water, and went out on a rock to clean itself.

Saturday and Sunday, March 5 & 6, 2016, were supposed to be days of heavy rain and storms arriving from the Pacific Ocean. On March 6, 2016, it was pouring at 6:00 am and then at 7:00 am, the sky was completely blue. I went out as far as up the wooden stairs behind the Warming Hut. A cold wind blew from the west. On the way back, I saw four Black Turnstones below the path at the Marina Green. They were sleeping, and were sheltered on the east side of a rock, so they would be out of the wind. Birds are so smart!

Black Turnstones breed only in Alaska, mostly within a little over a mile of the coast. They stage in huge numbers in the protected coves and inlets of Prince William Sound, Alaska, and then winter in small flocks on sea rocks along the West Coast. They are strictly coastal during migration and winter, preferring the tidal zone of rocky shorelines, sand and gravel beaches, intertidal mudflats, and man-made jetties. They winter in coastal areas and nearshore islands from south-central Alaska to Mexico. Southern migration continues into mid-October, with some birds moving later.

The Black Turnstone song is a guttural rattle. Its alarm note has been called a rattling scream.

Least Sandpipers

At the far eastern end of Crissy Field Marsh close to the bridge over the outlet into San Francisco Bay, I often saw flocks of 20 to 30 Least Sandpipers feeding and resting along the edge of the marsh. Sometimes, they flew as a flock from one place and landed together at another place in the marsh.

When they all turned at once, their white undersides blended in with the sky. When they were resting among the rocks and vegetation along the edge of the marsh, they were virtually invisible unless you searched for them.

I first heard the clear "treep" calls of the Least Sandpipers along the shoreline of the marsh. Then several of them went a little higher up and lay down among the small rocks and put their heads under their scapulars. When I ran back past them on my way back from the Coastal Trail, they were all sleeping close together among the small rocks and were excellently camouflaged. None of them seemed to be on guard. They were virtually invisible. If I had not first seen them starting to settle down among the rocks, I would never have known they were there.

On December 12, 2004 much flotsam and jetsam and pieces of wood, brought down from the area draining into the Bay following storms, floated at the edge of the water in Crissy Field Marsh. On the east side of the foot bridge was a space full of pieces of wood and small rocks. Almost perfectly camouflaged against this background were three or four Killdeer and about 20 Least Sandpipers who were puffed up and resting behind pieces of driftwood. Their legs looked yellowish so they were Least Sandpipers and not Sanderlings.

Fig 3-21 - Least Sandpipers resting on northeast side of Crissy Field Marsh.

Fig 3-22 - Least Sandpipers resting on rocks at Crissy Field Marsh.

Least Sandpipers are the smallest American shorebirds. On the coast, they usually avoid sandy beaches and wide-open tidal flats, preferring narrow tidal creeks and the edges of a salt marsh. They prefer grassy areas to the more open flats frequented by most shorebirds.

Least Sandpipers are grayish above in their winter plumage, with yellowish or greenish legs, a short thin bill, and a streaked breast. They are common and relatively tame birds on inland mudflats and wet grassy areas. They feed heavily on insects, but when feeding along the coast their diet is similar to other small shorebirds and includes crustaceans, mollusks, and marine worms. They forage on mudflats, picking up food by sight and sometimes probing.

Least Sandpipers roost near feeding areas, alone or in small groups, among marsh vegetation or on the upper beach in the wrack line where sea vegetation is left up on the shore.

They breed on the northern tundra or in bogs, nesting on the ground near water. The female lays four eggs in a shallow scrape lined with grass and moss. Both parents incubate. The female leaves before the young birds fledge and sometimes even before the eggs hatch. The male typically stays with the young at least until they can fly. The young birds feed themselves and are able to fly within two weeks of birth.

Least Sandpipers are long-distance migrants. They migrate in a broad swath across North America. Eastern populations probably fly 1,800 to 2,500 miles nonstop over the ocean to South America. Western populations migrate through interior North America or down the Pacific Coast.

<u>Marbled Godwits</u>

In early May of 2003, on the shore along the Bay just before the Warming Hut and pier, I watched eight large sandpipers of two different types. Both types had long bills and probed into the sand to the tops of their bills. They were walking carefully up the sand. Several of them had long, down-curved bills and several had long straight bills. I watched them through binoculars. All the birds were about the same size of 18 inches and were speckled gray-brown overall. I believe the birds with the downward-curving bills were Whimbrels. They had dark crown stripes which flowed into their long bills. The other birds had no dark crown stripes and had long straight bills which appeared pinkish at the base. These birds were Marbled Godwits, who

often associate loosely with other shorebirds. These birds were probably on migration together. The Whimbrel summers in Northern Alaska and around Hudson Bay; the Marbled Godwit summers in southern Saskatchewan and southwestern Manitoba. This was an incredible sight, especially when one wondered where these birds had come from and where they were going, and considering the fact this was a short stop on their long migratory journeys.

Numerous large shorebirds were along the shore of the Crissy Field restored marsh in the fall of 2003. I watched one Marbled Godwit taking a bath and preening. It had a long almost straight but slightly upturned bill that was pink at the base and darker towards the end. It began by working its long bill around its lower parts, then lifted water over its back, and vigorously splashed in the water with its wings, wetting itself all over. Then it stepped out of the water and began to preen its belly with its long bill. When it stepped out, I noticed it seemed lame and I could see one of its long, skinny legs was not straight and may have been broken at one time. Later when I watched this particular bird feeding, it went down on one leg, but it could still feed. The Marbled Godwit forages by probing in shallow water and soft mud for aquatic insects and mollusks. I had watched Marbled Godwits feeding at Crissy Field Marsh and submerging their whole head underneath the water as they probed deeply in the soft mud for food.

In early August of 2015, there were six Marbled Godwits feeding all together close to the path at the marsh. Two of them were larger than the others and looked thin. The female Marbled Godwit is larger, longer-billed, and paler underneath than the male.

On August 23, 2015, 15 Marbled Godwits were feeding by the bridge over the marsh. A Black-bellied Plover chased one of them away. On August 29, 2015, I saw eight Marbled Godwits at various places in the marsh. Some were larger and had longer bills than others. There were also two Black-bellied Plovers in non-breeding or juvenile plumage. One of the plovers was about one-half the size of a small Marbled Godwit. I saw it run along the sand, stop to pick something up, and then stand still. This large plover has a dainty appearance.

On September 5, 2015 there were more than 40 Marbled Godwits at Crissy Field Marsh close to the path by the bridge and mudflats. There were occasional squabbles among them as they fed. Their vocalization was soft and quiet, but it carried a long way and sounded like a rapidly repeated "ga-WI da ga-Wi da ga-WI da".

Fig 3-23 - Marbled Godwits. A large shorebird with a long, upturned bill, the Marbled Godwit breeds in the center of the continent and winters along the coasts. Courtesy of Lee Karney, United States Fish and Wildlife Service (USFWS).

ARTHUR CLEVELAND BENT (1866-1954)

Arthur Cleveland Bent was a successful businessman and a dedicated amateur ornithologist. He began submitting papers to "The Auk", the journal of the American Ornithologists' Union, in 1901. In 1910, he approached the Secretary of the Smithsonian Institution with a proposal to complete a series started by Charles E. Bendire, who had issued the first volume of "Life Histories of North American Birds". (Ref 3-18). Bent was 44 years old at the time of his proposal, and he dedicated the remaining 44 years of his life to completing this endeavor.

As a businessperson with a strong work ethic and highly developed organizational skills, Bent was thorough and meticulous in his research. He organized the life history data for each species in a uniform sequence, including Spring Migration, Courtship, Nesting Habits, Eggs, Young, Sequence of Plumages to Maturity, Seasonal Molts, Feeding Habits, Flight, Swimming and Diving Habits, Vocal Powers, Behavior, Enemies, Fall Migration, and Winter Habits.

What Bent originally believed would take six volumes to complete when he began work on his "Life Histories of North American Birds" in 1910, proliferated into 20 volumes by the time of his death in 1954, with a few remaining volumes in the series later completed under the supervision of Harvard-trained ornithologist Oliver L. Austin, Jr. This comprehensive work contains hundreds of avian species biographies.

Bent supplemented his own observations with the published literature and unpublished notes of a network of volunteer contributors and collaborating authors. In order to recruit contributors, he mailed out countless circulars and advertised repeated requests in ornithological publications. (Ref 3-19) *The favorable initial response encouraged him to continue with the project. Over 150 people contributed eggs, notes, and/or photographs for the first volume published in 1919. Bent always acknowledged the names of these collaborators, and by the end of the project, contributions had been received from over 800 author partners.*

The Bent series remains a starting point for serious research on the life history of North American birds. It is also far from dry reading, containing readable descriptions of the lives of birds, written by a large number of enthusiastic nature lovers and observers of birds in the field. It is interesting to note that Bent did not have formal training in ornithology and never received a salary for his monumental work, which none the less won great praise from the ornithological community and has remained a standard reference work to this day.

A. C. Bent wrote about the Marbled Godwit: "Next to the Long-billed Curlew and the Oyster Catchers, the Marbled Godwit is the largest of our shorebirds. For that reason and for other reasons it is rapidly disappearing, and before many years it may join the ranks of those gone but not forgotten. Although shy at times, it is often foolishly tame and is then easily slaughtered. It is large enough to appeal to the sportsman as legitimate game and it makes a plump and toothsome morsel for the table. But, worst of all, its breeding grounds on the prairies and meadows of the central plains are becoming more and more restricted by the encroachments of agriculture." (Ref 3-15)

Fortunately, the Marbled Godwit has not gone the way of the Eskimo Curlew, and can still be seen on the Pacific Coast during the winter.

Bent describes the nesting habitats of the Marbled Godwit as follows: "In southwestern Saskatchewan, in 1905 and 1906, I became better acquainted with the Marbled Godwit on its breeding grounds. Along the lower courses of the streams, near the lakes, but sometimes extending for a mile or more back from the lake, are usually found broad, flat, alluvial plains, low enough to be flooded during periods of high water. These plains are more or less moist at all times, are exceedingly level, and are covered with short, thick grass only a few inches high. Such spots are the chosen breeding grounds of the Marbled Godwit, and so far as our experience goes, the nests of this species are invariably placed on these grassy plains or meadows. The Godwit makes no attempt at concealment, the eggs being deposited in plain sight in a slight hollow in the short grass.

On June 9, 1906, I enjoyed a most interesting experience with an unusually tame individual of this normally shy species. While walking across the flat meadow near the creek, I happened to see a Marbled Godwit crouching on her nest beside a pile of horse droppings. She was conspicuous enough in spite of her protective coloration, for the nest was entirely devoid of concealment in the short grass. Though we stood within 10 feet of her, she showed no signs of flying away, which suggested the possibility of photographing her. My camera was half a mile away in our wagon, but I soon returned with it and began operations at a distance of 15 feet, setting up the camera on a tripod and focusing carefully. I moved up cautiously to within 10 feet and took another picture, repeating the performance again within five feet. She still sat like a rock, and I made bold to move even closer, spreading the legs of the tripod on either side of her and placing the camera within three feet of her. I hardly dared to breathe, moving very slowly as I used the focusing cloth, and changed my plate holders most cautiously, but she never offered to move and showed not the slightest signs of fear, while I exposed all the plates I had with me, photographing her from both sides and placing the lens within two feet of her. She sat there patiently, panting in the hot sun, apparently distressed by the heat, perhaps partially dazed by it, and much annoyed by the ants which were constantly crawling into her eyes and half open bill, causing her to wink or shake her head occasionally. I reached down carefully and stroked her on the back, but still she did not stir, and I was finally obliged to lift her off the nest in order to photograph the eggs." (Ref 3-16)

The Marbled Godwit can still be seen along the estuaries, tidal mudflats, ocean beaches and salt marshes of California, but in nowhere near the same numbers as they were formerly seen. Bradford Torrey writing in 1913 states: "I have seen godwits and willets together lining the grassy edge of the flats for a long distance, and so densely massed I mistook them at first for a border of some kind of herbage. Thousands there must have been; and when they rose at my approach, they made something like a cloud; gray birds and brown birds so contrasted in color as to be discriminated beyond risk of error, even when too far away for the staring white wing patches of the willets to be discernible." (Ref 3-17)

Black-bellied Plover

On September 12, 2015, the fog was in. I saw a seal swimming in the Bay to the east side of the Marina Green. At Crissy Field Marsh, six Marbled Godwits flew in and started cleaning up in the water. A Black-bellied Plover went into the middle of them and started vigorously splashing. The Marbled Godwits then called "too-wit" and all flew off. The Black-bellied Plover proceeded to get out of the water onto the sand, and energetically shook itself off.

Fig 3-24 - Non-breeding Black-bellied Plover. A large shorebird of coastal beaches, the Black-bellied Plover is striking in its black-and-white breeding plumage. It is the largest plover in North America and can be found along the coast in winter northward to Massachusetts and British Columbia. Courtesy of Lee Karney, USFWS.

On November 21 and 22, 2015, the water level at the marsh was high and none of the islands were above the waterline. I saw four winter-plumaged Black-bellied Plovers. They saw me watching them, but it did not bother them. One had his head tucked back. They had very large black eyes, were somewhat fluffed out, and their sides were mottled. They were beautiful!

The Black-bellied Plover is the largest and stockiest of North American plovers. It breeds in the tundra in the northernmost reaches of North America and Eurasia, farther north than other species of its kind.

Fig 3-25 - Non-breeding Black-bellied Plovers at edge of Crissy Field Marsh (this picture was taken in partial darkness and the eyes show reflective light from the camera flash).

<u>Black-crowned Night Heron</u>

When running in the early mornings just before sunrise or at dawn, I often saw Black-crowned Night Herons standing hunched over on the rocks or docks along the Bay, waiting and watching for prey. They stood motionless for a long time and then suddenly thrust their bill into the water to catch a passing small fish.

As their name implies, Black-crowned Night Herons forage at dawn, dusk, and at night. They roost in trees during the day. They are a medium-sized, stocky, short-necked heron with a black crown and back, gray wings and white under parts. In the breeding season, they have two or more long white plumes which extend from the back of the head.

Fig 3-26 – Black-crowned Night Heron at Crissy Field Marsh.

<u>Killdeer</u>

In the fall and early winter of 2003, several Killdeer called in the sand dunes at Crissy Field with their high, drawn-out "Keeee" and "Kill-dee" signals.

Killdeer are handsome birds with olive-brown backs and a white breast slashed by two black bands. They are plovers which are closely related to sandpipers and they are often seen with those species. Like sandpipers, they forage on small aquatic prey by picking or probing. Although Killdeer are technically in the family of shorebirds, they are unusual shorebirds as they often nest and live far from water. They like to lay their eggs in gravel, making no nest, and their eggs are well-camouflaged in this environment. The Killdeer gets along well with man, taking advantage of whatever habitat man provides or preserves, whether it is a field, unpaved road, or rooftop. It also appreciates the water's edge, and is often found on the shores of ponds, lakes, and marshes.

Fig 3-27 – Killdeer at Crissy Field Marsh.

<u>Western Meadowlark</u>

In mid-February of 2004, several Western Meadowlarks walked in the tall grass growing on the Crissy Field former airfield. When they had their backs to me, their pale gray-brown backs blended in so well with the grassy field that I could barely distinguish them, but when they turned around, I saw the yellow throat and belly, and black V on the breast.

The Western Meadowlark is a year-round resident in this area, so the birds I saw in 2004 could have stayed to breed in the tall grass. However, in subsequent years, people let their dogs roam in the grass, and coyotes lived in the Presidio bordering Crissy Field. Several times in the very early morning I saw a coyote wandering over the tall grass. After 2004 I did not see any Western Meadowlarks at Crissy Field.

<u>Brewer's Blackbird</u>

While standing outside the Warming Hut, I watched a female Brewer's Blackbird enter through the door of the Warming Hut. As I was curious, I followed her inside to see where she would go and how she would get out again. This Brewer's Blackbird seemed to know exactly where she was going. She turned left after the entrance and continued walking another 20 feet to where there were indoor tables and chairs to accommodate people who had bought food and drink at the counter. She walked around the tables and chairs for some time looking for crumbs, and then turned around and retraced her steps, turning the corner to go out the door of the Warming Hut. This seemed like a regular routine that she followed.

The Brewer's Blackbird is a robin-sized bird. The male is solid black with yellow eyes. Its head appears to have a purple iridescent shine in certain light. The female is all gray-brown with dark eyes. The Brewer's Blackbird has shown extreme adaptability. Although it is essentially a bird of open agricultural country in the west and central part of the country, in many urban areas it can be seen foraging in parking lots and parks.

THOMAS BREWER (1814-1880)

Audubon saw the Brewer's Blackbird for the first time in the summer of 1843 and named it for Boston ornithologist Thomas Brewer, who was one of the leaders in the mid-19th century study of birds in the United States. Trained as a medical doctor, Brewer abandoned this career to become an editor and partner in a printing firm. Birds were Dr. Brewer's lifetime passion. As a teenager he shared his observations made in the field with Audubon. At the age of 26, Brewer published an updated, inexpensive text of Alexander Wilson's "American Ornithology". Thomas Brewer, Spencer Baird of the Smithsonian Institution, and John Cassin of the Philadelphia Academy of Natural Sciences co-authored the massive three volume "History of North American Birds" in 1874 to 1884. Brewer's particular interest in the study of birds was in nesting and eggs.

Great Blue Heron

I often saw Great Blue Herons standing in the tall grass in Crissy Field, or wading in Crissy Field Marsh.

Fig 3-28 - Great Blue Heron standing at the edge of Crissy Field Marsh.

Fig 3-29 - Great Blue Herons in Crissy Field Marsh.

In the spring of 2018, I noticed a Great Blue Heron flying into one of the Eucalyptus trees forming a line along the edge of the field by the St. Francis Yacht Club. When I looked at the spot where the Heron had landed, I saw a nest high up in the tree. This area was extremely crowded with people, especially later in the day, and on weekends when people set up nets on the grass and played volleyball. However, all this activity below them didn't seem to affect the herons in raising their young.

Fig 3-30 - Great Blue Heron nest in Eucalyptus tree at start of Golden Gate Promenade.

In his *Life Histories of North American Marsh Birds* [Ref 3-20], A. C. Bent said about the Great Blue Heron: "It is a stately bird, dignified in its bearing, graceful in its movements and an artistic feature in the landscape...In its native solitudes, far from the haunts of man, it may be seen standing motionless, in lonely dignity, on some far distant point that breaks the shore line of a wilderness lake, its artistic outline giving the only touch of life to the broad expanse of water and its background of somber forest. Or on some wide, flat coastal marsh its stately figure looms up in the distance, as with graceful, stealthy tread it wades along in search of its prey. Perhaps you have seen it from afar and think you can gain a closer intimacy, but its eyes and ears are keener than yours; and it is a wise and wary bird. But even as it takes its departure, you will stand and admire the slow and dignified strokes of its great, black-tipped wings, until this interesting feature of the landscape fades away into the distance. A bird so grand, so majestic, and so picturesque is surely a fitting subject for the artist's brush."

Great Blue Herons are the largest heron in North America. Their average lifespan in the wild is 15 years, and the oldest recorded Great Blue Heron was 24 years old.

The Great Blue Heron feeds mainly on small fish less than half the length of its bill. Shellfish, insects, rodents, frogs, reptiles, and small birds are also occasionally eaten. It has two principal fishing techniques: still hunting and stalking. Still hunting is probably the commonest method used. Standing motionless with its neck extended at an angle of about 45 degrees to the water surface, in shallow water where fish are moving about, it waits patiently until a fish comes within reach, and then strikes with a rapid thrust of its bill. It can stand perfectly still in this position for a long time. The second way the Great Blue Heron fishes is by wading around slowly in shallow water, watching in the water until it drives a fish out from its hiding place. Then it stops and strikes with its bill.

Great Blue Herons normally nest in colonies in woodlands within a mile or two of their main feeding area and relatively inaccessible to humans and land predators. The main concern for the location of the rookery is to obtain security for the eggs and young. They choose a more or less inaccessible site and nest near the tree tops. Parents brood their young only during the first week, but one adult remains at the nest almost continuously for another two weeks, with the male watching the nest during the day while the female hunts for food, and reversing the roles at night. After the first month, the pair spends most of its time outside the colony, returning only to feed the young and stand watch for short periods.

If the food supply is not adequate to feed all the nestlings, only the strongest will survive. The feebler in the nest progressively weaken and are often accidentally pushed out by the stronger ones in the nest as they start moving about and exercising their wings. Once a nestling falls out of the nest, the parents will no longer continue to feed it. Mortality among the nestlings is high. An adult Great Blue Heron is a match for anybody, but a nestling is more defenseless when the adults are away from the nest. Also, a heavy rain or cold weather at the time of hatching can take a heavy toll among the young.

The Great Blue Heron can adapt to almost any wetland habitat in its range. It may be found in fresh and saltwater marshes, mangrove swamps, flooded meadows, lake edges, or shorelines. It may be seen in heavily developed areas as long as they hold bodies of fish-bearing water. With its variable diet, it is able to spend the winter farther north than most herons, even in areas where most waters freeze, but it must be careful not to get caught in an area that becomes completely frozen over. Sometimes an adult Great Blue Heron will be caught by a sudden winter storm and freeze-up, in which it cannot get to its regular food supply. In this case, it will often choose to wait out the freeze until it can get at its food at its favorite feeding spot again. Sometimes, the wait is too long.

The Great Blue Heron migrates by day or night, alone or in flocks. Populations along the Pacific coast may be permanent residents, even as far north as southeastern Alaska. Today, the adult birds have few natural enemies. The most serious threat is the draining of marshes and the destruction of its feeding habitat.

Chapter Four – Coastal Trail West of the Golden Gate Bridge

DURING THE SUMMER OF 2001, I took an online Ornithology course from Northern State University in Aberdeen, South Dakota. The course was taught by Dr. Dan Tallman, who encouraged me to look for smaller birds, and to take binoculars with me so I could identify the smaller birds. While taking the course, I discovered and was entranced by the part of the California Coastal Trail which runs on the west side of the Golden Gate Bridge through the Presidio to Baker Beach. This route is a round-trip distance of 3.6 miles and is a portion of the Coastal Trail, which stretches from the Golden Gate south for more than nine miles to Fort Funston.

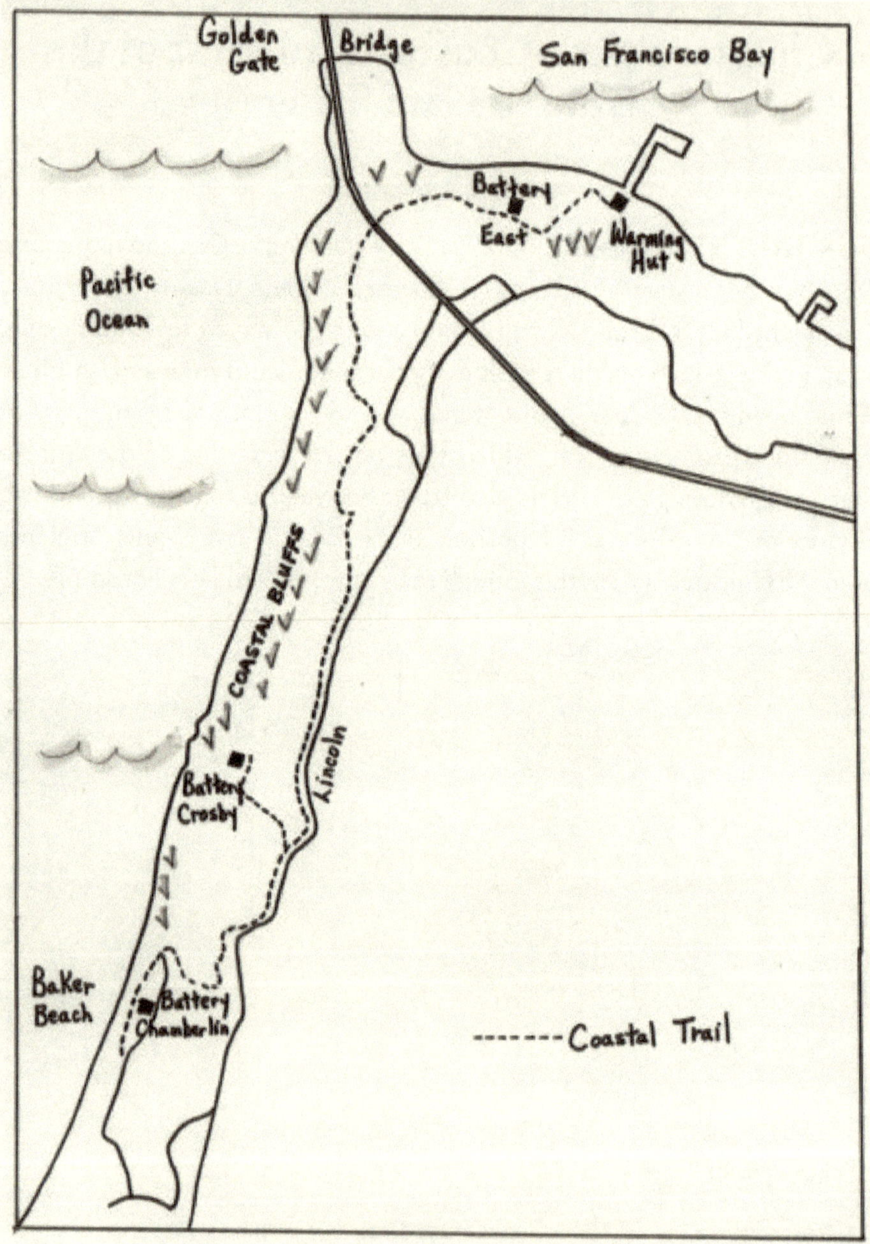

Fig 4-1 - Map showing the location of the Coastal Trail from the Warming Hut to Baker Beach.

At the back of the Warming Hut, wooden stairs climb up onto a bluff. The path goes through a brick tunnel and emerges on the east side of the Golden Gate Bridge. It then goes underneath the Golden Gate Bridge and follows the coastline. Along most of this part of the trail, there are magnificent views across to the Marin Headlands and out to the Pacific Ocean.

The Coastal Trail here winds through coastal bluffs covered with a coastal scrub of native plants and wildflowers. Wildflowers in the early spring include the vibrantly orange California Poppy, wild Easter Lilies, a wild Rose Bush whose pink roses smell heavenly, and Wild Radishes. The Wild Radishes have tiny flowers colored from white to deep purple

I always stopped to smell the roses on the wild Rose Bush at the top of the wooden steps. Although these roses did not always look their most beautiful, they had a strong rose smell. Wildflowers grow along the Coastal Trail almost year-round, but are most spectacular from March to mid-July. The winter rains start the wildflowers blooming in February. By mid-July a lot of the wildflowers have gone to seed and the picture becomes less colorfully green, and more brownish.

Fig 4-2 – Roses on the Wild Rose Bush have a lovely rose smell.

Fig 4-3 – Wild Radish flowers.

The Coastal Trail goes through the Presidio of San Francisco and contains numerous "batteries" or old coastal defense fortifications. The Presidio of San Francisco has had a long, diverse military history. It was founded as a military post by the Spanish in 1776. In 1822, it was under Mexican rule. In 1846 the United States acquired California, and the Presidio came under the control of the United States Army, who built a major Army hospital (Letterman Hospital), a pioneering airfield (Crissy Field), and an extensive coastal defense system. During the Civil War, advances in artillery had shown that masonry forts could not stand up to heavy bombardment, and therefore a new type of coastal defense system was built, consisting of earthwork batteries built to protect and hide large guns. The remains of many of these batteries can still be seen along this part of the Coastal Trail.

In 1994, the Golden Gate National Recreation Area acquired the Presidio from the Army and in 1998, management was given over to the Presidio Trust.

At 1.3 miles, a trail breaks off from the Coastal Trail to Battery Crosby, which was in service between 1900 and 1943. Stairs lead up to gun emplacements now filled with weeds and flowers. There are wonderful views of the Golden Gate from the top of the battery. Then the Coastal Trail goes past wooden stairs leading down to the east side of Baker Beach and continues further, eventually descending to Battery Chamberlin. Battery Chamberlin has a restored "disappearing" gun designed to drop out of sight after discharging so that artillerymen could safely reload it. Below Battery Chamberlin, Baker Beach is a wide expanse of sandy beach with heavy pounding surf from the Pacific Ocean.

Fig 4-4 – Batteries to Bluffs Trail.

Fig 4-5 – Coastal batteries along the Coastal Trail.

Fig 4-6 - Path to Battery Crosby.

Fig 4-7 - Baker Beach.

SERPENTINITE COASTAL BLUFFS

The serpentinite coastal bluffs along the northwestern shore of the Presidio are a sensitive ecological area. Surrounded by nonnative vegetation, they support a rich diversity of native plant species. These plants struggle to survive in their much-reduced habitat and some of them are federally designated as threatened. A fragmented band of serpentinite rock crosses San Francisco, emerging on the Presidio from Inspiration Point to the coastal bluffs and containing the only intact remnant of serpentinite bluff habitat in the San Francisco Peninsula.

Serpentinite, the California State rock, is a rare rock type with unusual characteristics. It is developed only in subduction zones, where one tectonic plate is subducted under another. These rocks are now at the earth's surface because the region experienced uplift after subduction ceased. Because serpentinite rock is derived from mantle material, its chemistry is different from most rocks in the earth's crust. It is mostly composed of a mineral called serpentine.

Serpentine is low in potassium and calcium, both of which are plant nutrients, and it contains high levels of magnesium, chromium, and nickel that are potentially toxic to plants. Over hundreds of thousands of years, plant species evolved mechanisms allowing them to survive in serpentine soils, and some of these plants are found only in these unique habitats. The National Park Service and the Presidio Trust are eliminating some nonnative Eucalyptus and Monterey Pine trees in order to create more habitats in the coastal bluffs for the endemic species to establish themselves. Over time the falling leaves and needles, as well as the shade produced by these nonnative trees, has had an impact on the grassland environment. With time, after some of the nonnative Eucalyptus and Monterey Pine trees are removed, the native species, which are adapted to the low-nutrient serpentine soils, are expected to compete favorably with the weedy non-native plants.

The birds along this part of the Coastal Trail are more coastal shrub and forest birds, including hummingbirds, chickadees, nuthatches, kinglets, thrushes, robins, waxwings, wood warblers, towhees, sparrows, blackbirds, finches, ravens, hawks, juncos, bushtits, and wrens.

This part of the Coastal Trail is extremely beautiful at all times and in all seasons. In places it is very wild and I believe it is at its most comforting when there were few people along it. On numerous occasions I stood in awe of its majesty and natural beauty. On one such occasion, a cold, white fog hanging low over the ocean poured in horizontally, except where it was blocked by a stand of sheltering Monterey Cypress. The milky fog looked like blowing snow and for a moment I imagined I was back in my hometown of Winnipeg, Manitoba, Canada in the middle of a snowstorm. Standing in this natural wonderland, I felt alone, but not lonely. I felt at peace with myself and with the world. It was like being transported to a surreal place and time.

<u>White-crowned Sparrow</u>

In late June of 2001 I saw numerous White-crowned Sparrows, including immature birds whose white stripes were not yet clear, along the Coastal Trail. This large, seven-inch-long, handsome sparrow has pearly gray under parts and buff sides. The adults have white and black stripes on the crown, while the immature birds have brown stripes on the crown. White-crowned Sparrows mate for life. They eat bugs, spiders, insects, fruit and fresh leaves.

The sparrows I saw foraged on the ground in groups of four to six birds. I saw an unoccupied nest in a low bush about four feet off the ground along the Coastal Trail path.

Fig 4-8 – White-crowned Sparrows.

These White-crowned Sparrows were a local breeding nonmigratory subspecies called *nuttalli*, as opposed to the *gambelli* that breeds in Alaska and northwestern Canada and the *pugetensis* that breeds on the coasts of Washington, Oregon and British Columbia. Most subspecies are migratory, but the central California form, "Nuttall's White-crowned Sparrow", resides year-round in a narrow strip of fog belt along the coast, usually nesting within a few hundred meters of the ocean. The nonmigratory *nuttalli* are joined in California in winter by the two other breeds.

White-crowned Sparrows are numerous along the Coastal Trail and I almost always saw these sparrows foraging along the side of the path or heard their "tseet" calls as I went by. They often sang over and over from the top of a bush, and I stopped to listen to their repeated songs. One day I stopped to listen to a White-crowned Sparrow singing very loudly in a tree. The song begins with one to three clear whistled notes and ends with three buzzy notes. The first two notes may be descending, rising, or at the same pitch.

The repeated songs of a given bird are usually very similar, but those of different birds often vary slightly. Morning and evening song periods usually involve 15 to 20 minutes of uninterrupted song, and as each song is of two second duration and the interval between songs is nine to ten seconds, the total output during such a burst may be 100 or more songs. In *Life Histories of North American Birds*, Roland C. Clement said he had counted 194 consecutive songs. [Ref 4-1].

The White-crowned Sparrow is a well-studied songbird because it is so conspicuous, abundant, and widely distributed. The ventriloqual nature of the White-crowned Sparrow's song is referenced in *Life Histories of North American Birds* as follows: "Amelia R. Laskey mentions a ventriloqual song of the immature as follows: 'At first the songs, coming at intervals, seemed to emanate from shrubs some 15 feet behind the bird, but as it came closer I could see its bill open and close. It was a lengthier song than the adults give in spring, and the bird erected its crown feathers as it sang.'" [Ref 4-2]

Two subspecies of the White-Crowned Sparrow – *nuttalli* (inhabiting a narrow band along the California Coast from northwestern California to Santa Barbara County, California) and *gambelii* – (inhabiting Alaska, the northern mainland of Canada, eastern British Columbia, and southwestern Alberta) are named for two great naturalists and ornithologists.

THOMAS NUTTALL (1786-1859)

The nuttalli subspecies of White-Crowned Sparrow is named for Thomas Nuttall, one of the most knowledgeable botanists and ornithologists of the 19th century. Nuttall was born in Yorkshire, England and came to America in 1808 at age 22. Within months of his arrival, he became engaged in field work for Benjamin Smith Barton, a well-known botanist who had just published the first textbook on North American plants. In 1825 Nuttall became a professor of natural science at Harvard University and director of their botanical gardens. In 1834 he resigned from Harvard at the age of 48, after Nathaniel Wyeth brought him a collection of plants from the Rocky Mountains and asked him if he wanted to join an expedition to the Columbia River. Nuttall could not turn down this offer to do what he enjoyed the most, namely field biology.

Nuttall proceeded to St. Louis, traveling with a young fellow naturalist, John Kirk Townsend. Nuttall found new and curious plants on this trip across the continent to the Pacific Northwest. Everything he saw fascinated him.

Nuttall's contributions, both professional and personal, to the natural science field were many and varied. Although his primary interest was in botany, he wrote papers in geology, botany and zoology. He was intrigued by everything he saw in nature. He also acted as a mentor to younger ornithologists and naturalists. Hundreds of American plants were first collected and described for science by Nuttall or his companions. Nuttall shared his specimens and field notes. After Nuttall's Pacific Coast trip, he gave new and rare Western American bird specimens from the Nuttall-Townsend collection to John James Audubon. These specimens were a source for Audubon's drawings. Nuttall also shared his observations respecting the habits and distributions of these new and rare species with Audubon. Nuttall's generosity and sharing of ornithological and other scientific information demonstrated his noble nature. (Ref 4-3)

Nuttall's passion for his work often seemed odd to those around him. For example, Henry Breckenridge wrote about their trip with fur traders up the Missouri in 1811: "There is in company a gentleman...Mr. Nuttall, engaged in [botany]...to which he appears singularly devoted, and which seems to engross every thought, to the total disregard of his own personal safety, and sometimes to the inconvenience of the party...To the...Canadian boatmen, who are unable to appreciate the science, he affords a subject of merriment; 'le fou' [the fool] is the name by which he is commonly known." (Ref 4-4)

Nuttall's enthusiasm for field biology to the exclusion of other things led others to sometimes label him as eccentric. For example, on one trip in dangerous Indian territory, the fur traders checked Nuttall's rifle and found the barrel clogged with dirt. He had used it to dig up plants.

John Kirk Townsend described the 48-year-old Nuttall after his second trip up the Missouri in 1834. They had reached Oregon when a storm on the Columbia River soaked Nuttall's plant samples: "Mr. N.'s large and beautiful collection of new and rare plants was considerably injured by the wetting it received; he has been constantly engaged, since we landed yesterday, in opening and drying them. In this task he exhibits a degree of patience and perseverance which is truly astonishing; sitting on the ground, and steaming over the enormous fire for hours together, drying the papers, and re-arranging the whole collection, specimen by specimen." (Ref 4-5)

Another revealing description of Nuttall's passion for natural history is given by Richard Dana, a former student of Nuttall's at Harvard University, who had gone to sea on a ship that gave Nuttall a ride back to Boston in 1834. Dana described Nuttall in his novel "Two Years Before the Mast" as follows: "...Professor Nuttall of Cambridge. I had left him quietly seated in the chair of Botany and Ornithology in Harvard University, and the next I saw of him, he was strolling about San Diego beach, in a sailor's pea-jacket, with a wide straw hat, and bare-footed, with his trousers rolled up to his knees, picking up stones and shells...[the] crew called Mr. Nuttall 'Old Curious' from his zeal for curiosities; and some of them said he was crazy, and his friends let him go about and amuse himself in this way." (Ref 4-6)

Thomas Nuttall greatly advanced the biological sciences. He published a book on the flora of North America called "Genera of North American Plants". He also published "North American Sylva", a multi-volume, lavishly-illustrated set of books accounting for all the trees in North America, with an emphasis on those along the Pacific Coast.

While a professor at Harvard, a colleague suggested he should publish a handbook of North American birds. The only bird books at that time were those by Alexander Wilson and John James Audubon. These books were too large to use in the field and too expensive for the average American. Nuttall proceeded to publish America's first field manuals on American birds. In 1831 he published land birds and in 1834 he published water birds. These manuals were continuously republished in updated form until the 1890's.

Nuttall also wrote many papers on varied biological subjects. Two of his major papers published as a result of his 1834-1836 trip to the Pacific Ocean were "Descriptions of new species and genera of plants in the natural order Compositae", detailing the diverse array of plants found in the sunflower family, and a second paper on new and rare plants which were of some economic or horticultural importance.

From 1836 until 1841 Nuttall worked at the Academy of Natural Sciences in Philadelphia, making short trips and writing up the hundreds of new species he had found. When his uncle in England died, leaving his estate to Nuttall but stipulating in the will that Nuttall must spend at least six months of each year in England, Nuttall returned there.

Nuttall has a direct link to modern-day ornithology. The Nuttall Ornithological Club, centered at Harvard University, started its main publication, "Bulletin of the Nuttall Ornithological Club", in 1876. Today, this journal is known as "The Auk". Published by the American Ornithological Society, it is one of the preeminent scientific journals about birds.

WILLIAM GAMBEL (1821-1849)

William Gambel was the first trained naturalist to spend an extensive amount of time on California soil. He arrived in 1841 and stayed through the end of 1843, visiting many parts of the state. Prior to this time, naturalists in California were part of naval expeditions or brief stays. Gambel was fortunate to train under and assist Thomas Nuttall, one of the top field naturalists in American history.

In 1841, Gambel joined a party on the Santa Fe Trail, continuing on through Colorado and California, collecting and eventually gaining employment under several Naval officers with whom he sailed along the California coast, continuing to collect as he went. By the time Gambel returned from California to Philadelphia, he was well-known to natural scientists. He published a series of papers peaking with his list of 176 species seen on his Western trip. Much of his information was incorporated into John Cassin's book on the birds of the Pacific Coast.

Gambel studied medicine over the next three years, receiving his medical degree. He was made Assistant Curator of the Philadelphia Academy of Natural Sciences. He subsequently married and then left the Academy due to conflicts with his supervisor, John Cassin. Gambel planned to begin a medical career in California where the Gold Rush was on. In 1849 he joined a group of settlers heading across the country. At one stage he decided to go with a slower-moving party whose pace afforded him more time for field collecting. This party reached Nevada at the end of a very dry fall, losing most of their cattle and horses along the way. They started to climb the east edge of the Sierra after the first snows. (This was not the famous Donner Party who had crossed the Sierra Nevada Mountains a few years earlier.) Gambel was one of the few survivors in his ill-fated group to make it across the mountains. He reached Rose's Bar on the Yuba River. There, while helping a group of sick gold miners, he caught typhoid fever and died on December 13,

1849. Although Gambel's life spanned only 28 years, he had accomplished much as a Western explorer, naturalist, and ornithologist during this time.

American Goldfinch

In the summer of 2001, I saw breeding American Goldfinches along this part of the Coastal Trail. Goldfinches breed later than most warblers because they are strictly seedeaters and they wait to breed until seeds are plentiful at the end of summer. I saw a breeding adult male American Goldfinch in late June eating thistle seed. He was a bright yellow bird with a black forehead and black wings with white markings. When he flew away, I went over to the bush where he had been feeding and was surprised to discover how prickly this plant was. I noticed the goldfinch had separated the outer covering of the seed and discarded it while it was eating.

I also saw four or five female goldfinches eating weed seeds from a bush. They had well-defined wing bars and were less brightly-colored yellow and more grayish than the male. Later that summer, in mid-August, I heard a fledgling calling and saw it sitting with fluttering wings in a bush, being fed by a male American Goldfinch.

Fig 4-9 - American Goldfinch. Courtesy of Chelsi Burns, USFWS.

The male American Goldfinch looks different at various times of the year, and also the male and female look different. During the summer months, males are obvious with their black caps, tails, wings and their bright lemon-yellow bodies. Females are less brilliant, with their olive-yellow coloring and lack of a black cap. Males lose their black caps during the winter, although some black coloring may appear on their foreheads. The face and throat of the male retain some yellow, but the crown, nape, back and scapulars turn buff brown. The wings are primarily black, but the lesser coverts and tips of the greater covers are dirty white, creating two distinct wing bars. The female in winter plumage has similar coloring although she has no yellow on her head or throat. Both the male and the female go through two molts a year, one in the spring and one in the autumn.

American Goldfinches constantly give calls in high, strong, and wavy flight, with the upward component often accompanied by contact calls. Individuals stay in touch with a very sweet, high-pitched "chee-ree-wee-wee". The male's song is heard throughout late spring and the breeding season.

American Goldfinches leave southern Canada and the northern Great Plains during the winter and go to the moderate southern states from California to Florida. They are year-round residents along the East Coast, mid-western states and along the West Coast. Those American Goldfinch who do migrate may be considered as relatively short distance migrants. The extent and direction of migration by individuals may vary annually, with birds moving in flocks. There is speculation that due to the availability of thistle and sunflower seed at feeders, and to global warming, the range of the American Goldfinch has moved, and will continue to move, further north.

Feeders could be sustaining goldfinches through the winter in places where they never would have survived on their own. However, this hypothesis has not been scientifically proven. (Ref 4-7) Although adult goldfinches migrate south for the winter in harsher climates, first year immature goldfinches may not. Thus, many juvenile goldfinches perish before the end of winter. The popularity of bird feeding has made food available where little or none could be found before.

American Goldfinches are gregarious at all times and usually feed in groups. They are not known to cache food or defend sources of food. However, the esophagus expands to hold extra food that can be transported to the nest, or used to meet metabolic demands under adverse weather conditions or when roosting.

The American Goldfinch is almost exclusively granivorous and consumes little insect matter, even when feeding nestlings. It eats the seeds of many annual plants. Most grasses flower in late spring and seed in early summer, and the American Goldfinch has specialized to exploit this seasonally abundant food supply. It begins courting in mid-summer. Nesting begins in July and extends into September, corresponding with weed seed abundance. As goldfinches court, mate, build nests, and incubate eggs, the seeds begin ripening. The birds do not necessarily wait for mature seeds, and a goldfinch will greedily thrash a thistle for a meal of unripened seed. Young goldfinches and seeds develop together.

Audubon commented: "In the month of August, ...whenever a thistle was to be seen along either bank of the New York canal, it was ornamented with one or more goldfinches. They tear up the down and withered petals of the ripening flowers with ease, leaning downwards upon them, eat off the seed, and allow the down to float in the air." (Ref 4-8)

American Goldfinches are very agile when feeding. They approach food plants with a hovering flight before landing and sidling towards the tip of the stem or branch. They are well adapted to clinging to plants blowing in the wind, or to hanging from seed heads, often in an upside-down position.

American Goldfinch prefer open countryside where mature trees are widely spaced and where small shrubs, young trees and thistle blend with grasses. The American Goldfinch has probably benefited from the European settlement of North American with its accompanying clearing of forest and introduction of agriculture. It is, however, adversely affected by the move towards clean farming and the eradication of weeds. A less rigorous maintenance of "weed-free" environments would benefit this species. The Coastal Trail is an ideal habitat for these birds.

Bushtit

Several times over the summer of 2001, I heard flocks of Bushtits in the trees and bushes along the Coastal Trail. They were difficult to locate in the leafy trees because they were so small and were constantly moving, but when I noticed any movement, I focused my binoculars to see them. I saw one that looked like a small, round, gray ball of fluff with eyes. I was fortunate enough to see one up close without binoculars. It was sitting low in a tree watching me. As soon as we made eye contact, it quickly flew off. It had pale, light yellow eyes, so it was a female Bushtit.

Bushtits are among the smallest North American birds. They are similar in body shape to a chickadee, with a round body, short neck and short bill. They are plain gray-brown above and whitish below washed with gray, buff, or pinkish hues. They have short wings, long tails, and a tiny stubby blackish bill. Females can be distinguished by their light-colored eyes, while males have dark eyes. They make constant ticking and lisping sounds to keep in touch with each other as they fly from place to place.

Bushtits are highly gregarious and have a complex social system. Outside of the breeding season, they travel in flocks of six to 60 birds, created by family groups joining together. Flocks remain stable and may contain the same individuals from year to year. Foraging flocks travel rapidly through the brush gleaning insects and spiders. They maintain contact with each other through high-pitched contact calls. At times, they forage so rapidly that other birds, such as chickadees and wrens that occasionally join them in a mixed-species flock, are left behind.

Bushtits roost together among dense branches and huddle closely together on cold nights. As nesting season begins, the large winter flocks break up as pairs form and establish their nesting territories, usually within the flock's winter range. Flocks of Bushtits, made up of birds that have completed or have not yet begun nesting, can still be seen during breeding season.

Fig 4-10 - Bushtits

<u>Raven</u>

I often heard the deep-throated croaking of two Ravens high in a Monterey Cypress tree along the Coastal Trail. The largest member of the Crow family, Ravens average 24 inches tall, with a wingspan of 43-56 inches. Their coloration is all-black with a metallic shine of purple or violet that is noticeable in certain lighting conditions. The bill is large and stout.

Later that summer at the end of July, I heard the characteristic croaking of a Raven which was not quite as deep as usual. The croaking was given repeatedly in a series of three or so croaks at a time. Using binoculars, I located the source of the croaking at the top of a high Monterey Cypress tree. This was a young bird sitting in the nest or high in the tree, calling to a parent. When I looked up, another Raven was circling the area.

Fig 4-11 - The Common Raven is a large, black majestic bird. Courtesy of Lee Karney, USFWS.

Anna's Hummingbird

Numerous Anna's Hummingbirds are found along the Coastal Trail. I could always locate them because they sat on the stem of a bush and buzzed. Anna's Hummingbirds sing more than any other hummingbird. The males are green above and grayish below, and have an iridescent rosy-red crown and gorget extending to the side of the neck. The magnificent red throat feathers are only visible at a certain angle, thus allowing the male Anna's Hummingbird to hide when he needs to, and to show off when it suits him.

In mid-August as I came down the steps from the Coastal Trail, an Anna's Hummingbird perched on the railing and looked at me. I was wearing a light pink t-shirt with colorful prints on it that could be mistaken for flowers.

When I looked away from the hummingbird, it darted right up close to me several times and then moved away again. It had a patch of red on its chin and was otherwise greenish, and was a female Anna's Hummingbird.

Fig 4-12 – Anna's Hummingbird is the most common of all California hummingbirds. Courtesy of Robert McMorran, USFWS.

Anna's Hummingbirds are year-round residents in the coastal scrub, largely because of the abundant and often available food plants, such as Indian Paintbrush—a plant with long-blooming, bright scarlet flowers—and Bush or "sticky" Monkey Flower, which has sticky green leaves and salmon-colored flowers that bloom almost year-round.

When courting the female, the male tries to impress her by dive bombing her. He flies very high up in the air and then dives straight down towards her. When he reaches the bottom of the dive, he makes a loud cheep sound and pulls up right in front of her with his bright red gorget flashing in the sun. (He is careful to position himself with the sun behind the female so as to give her the best possible effect of his brilliant red throat.)

The time the male and female spend together is very brief, and then the female is totally responsible for the construction of the small deep-cup nest of soft fibers lined with hair and feathers, and for the caring of the young. The male and female Anna's Hummingbirds occupy separate habitats during the breeding season, with the male defending the food territory and the female defending the nesting territory.

Concerning the hummingbird's preference for sweets over color, A. C. Bent provides the following information about the Ruby-throated Hummingbird from Althea Rosina Sherman [Ref 4-9]: *"This taste for sweets is very well known to many observers who have supplied hummingbirds with sugar and water placed about their gardens in artificial flowers. Miss Althea R. Sherman, for example, who has experimented in feeding hummingbirds during seven summers, estimated a single bird consumed 'two teaspoonfuls of sugar daily' .Experiments made by Miss Althea R. Sherman (1913) to test the supposedly erroneous theory which had been published that hummingbirds show a preference for red flowers, indicated conclusively that hummingbirds visited the bottles she placed about her garden if they contained syrup, whether or not they simulated a flower in shape or color. The birds associated even an untrimmed bottle with food, just as they soon came to recognize Miss Sherman herself as a supplier of food."*

ALTHEA ROSINA SHERMAN (1854-1943)

Althea Sherman was one of several well-known women ornithologists whose hours of field observations and meticulous notes were later appreciated by A. C. Bent and incorporated in his "Life Histories of North American Birds". Althea's homestead in National, Iowa was near the watershed between the Mississippi and Turkey rivers. As farmers plowed up the land and converted the marshes to agricultural use, bird diversity decreased. Althea, by keeping her land as wild as possible and by gradually buying up nearby abandoned lots, created an oasis for birds. Although she admitted it looked run-down, she loved her Iowa homestead, because it was a place the birds liked. A visitor called it a "tangle of bushes and native and cultivated trees". [Ref 4-10] *Today, however, we recognize the importance for the diversity of species of letting areas remain in or return to their wild state.*

On Thanksgiving Day in 2001, I went from Aquatic Park all the way to Baker Beach from 7:30 to 11:30 am. It was a beautiful day. It had rained the night before and in the morning the air was fresh. The storm systems to the West generated very high waves along the Coast. The *San Francisco Chronicle* commented on the unusually large waves at Ocean Beach. The entrance to the Coastal Trail was blocked off due to tree cutting. However, seeing as they weren't working on Thanksgiving Day, I went under the yellow tape and walked up the stairs. They had cut down a lot of trees and created a mess. It looked like a clear-cut forest. However, I read the sign saying they were removing the non-native Eucalyptus trees that tend to take over and displace native trees and shrubs. Once they had removed the Eucalyptus trees, they would replant native scrub and native California Hazelnut trees. Along the Coastal Trail, I saw red-washed Purple Finches and beautiful White-crowned Sparrows.

<u>Black Phoebe</u>

By Baker Beach, I saw several Black Phoebes. They are slate black overall except for a white belly, under tail coverts and outer tail feathers. Black Phoebes are primarily flycatchers. They perch on a fencepost or other observation spot, periodically fly out to catch a flying insect, and then return to their original spot. This type of behavior is known as "hawking". Their song is two notes or phrases, with the second one down slurred – "Phoe–bee", usually repeated. Black Phoebes are year-round residents in California, Arizona, New Mexico, west Texas, and Mexico. They build a mud and grass nest always under something, on a bridge or cliff, often directly over, and always near water.

Fig 4-13 - Black Phoebe.

<u>Ruby-crowned Kinglet</u>

On the steps to the start of the Coastal Trail, a tiny Ruby-crowned Kinglet was flitting in a tree. It came down to a branch near me and looked at me for a while before flying off.

Ruby-crowned Kinglets are one of the smallest birds, measuring only 4.25 inches and weighing about seven grams (a House Sparrow weighs about 20 grams). However, for their size, they lay one of the largest clutches of eggs of any North American songbird, averaging nearly eight eggs per clutch, with as many as 12 eggs recorded in a single nest. Winter food sources are primarily spiders and insects and their eggs, as well as small amounts of weed seeds and fruits, including the berries of wax myrtle, poison ivy, and red cedar. The Ruby-crowned Kinglet is olive green above with two bold white wing bars. There is a broken white eye ring, and the under parts are dusky white.

Ruby-crowned Kinglets flick their wings constantly, as often as once per second. Males can display a scarlet crown patch (the reason for the "ruby-crowned" part of their name), when they are excited by a potential mate, rival or predator.

Kenn Kaufman states: "This tiny bird is often hard to see in summer, when it lives high in tall conifers. During migration and in winter, however, it often flits about low in woods and thickets, flicking its wings nervously as it approaches the observer...The song of the Ruby-crown is jumbled and loud, all out of proportion to the size of the bird." (Ref 4-11)

Fig 4-14 – Ruby-crowned Kinglet. Courtesy of Donna A. Dewhurst, USFWS.

<u>Fox Sparrow</u>

In the bushes just before the underpass, I watched a Fox Sparrow singing and then feeding with several White-crowned Sparrows. It was the Sooty (Pacific) subspecies and was sooty brown with large brown spots on its breast. The Fox Sparrow is a big sparrow with a sturdy, stocky build. It flew to the ground and foraged by scratching in the soil, making a forward jump and then scratching back with both feet at once. This bird was on migration or wintering. During the breeding season it inhabits the coniferous forests of northern Canada, Alaska and the western United States in the Rocky Mountain regions. During the winter the Fox Sparrow migrates to woodland thickets and grassy pastures of the southern United States.

Fig 4-15 - Fox Sparrow.

The Coastal Trail goes underneath the south side of the Golden Gate Bridge. Over the Christmas holiday season of 2003, the trail was closed due to a heightened security alert. However, by late January, it was open again and I could resume bird watching and appreciating the ever-changing natural beauty of the area.

<u>Red-shouldered Hawk</u>

One day I saw a Red-shouldered Hawk sitting high up in a tree next to the wooden steps leading up to the Coastal Trail. The Red-shouldered Hawk preys on small mammals, birds, reptiles, amphibians, and crayfish, and drops on its prey from its perch. As I went by the Wild Rose Bush, I noticed a chirping and flurry of birds. These birds were hiding there from the hawk.

I watched the hawk through binoculars. It initially faced away from me and I saw its grayish back. It had horizontal gray and white striping on its tail. When it turned its head and directed its attention directly down at me, I saw how relatively large its eyes were, as it keenly observed me. I felt uncomfortable under the scrutiny of those eyes that can see eight times better than those of a human. This feeling was in spite of the fact I knew the hawk would not hurt me. I could barely imagine how intensely terrifying a hawk must appear to a small, defenseless bird. I walked further down the steps and looked up at the hawk. From directly below, its belly looked solid rufous or cinnamon-colored.

Fig 4-16 - Red-shouldered Hawk. From Pixabay.

<u>Rufous Hummingbird</u>

Halfway up the wooden steps leading to the Coastal Trail, I stopped one day for several minutes to watch for birds. Suddenly, a male Rufous Hummingbird flew in and landed in a bare bush about three feet away. It was all bright orange including its back, and was even brighter orange on its chin. It sat and looked at me for a while. This bird was in the midst of its annual migration.

The Rufous Hummingbird is an amazing little bird. It has the longest known avian migration proportional to its body size, and can travel over 4,000 miles from breeding grounds in Alaska and northwest Canada to wintering sites in Mexico. It travels up the Pacific Coast in spring and returns by the Rocky Mountains in late summer and fall.

The Rufous Hummingbird has the northernmost range of any hummingbird species, breeding from northern California north and east through Idaho, Oregon, Washington and Montana, and north through British Columbia and Alberta to southern Alaska and the Yukon. Breeding this far north gives it a short breeding season, but Alaskan populations experience the longest day-length of any hummingbird.

Fig 4-17 - Female Rufous Hummingbird on twig. Courtesy of Chelsea McKinney, USFWS.

San Francisco Alligator Lizard

The vegetation on the path from the Coastal Trail down to Battery Crosby was renewed in the spring of 2004 and this seemed to make a difference to the bird life there. As I walked down this seldom-frequented path, I saw numerous American Goldfinches and White-crowned Sparrows feeding on seeds on the ground. They all accepted my presence and went about their business. A small lizard was resting on a pile of cut timber. It was a San Francisco Alligator Lizard about six inches long from its head to the tip of its tail. It was appropriately named, as it looked like a miniature alligator. There were several more of these lizards along the side of the Coastal Trail path. These lizards were identified by name on a sign along the trail to Baker Beach.

Fig 4-18 – Sign identifying some birds and animals found in the Central Coast Dune Scrub.

Pygmy Nuthatch

In early summer of 2004, I had a very up close and personal encounter with an engaging Pygmy Nuthatch. Coming up the stairs behind the Warming Hut, I heard a bird repeatedly singing "Too-whit, too-whit, too-whit". It sat on a tree branch and then flew back and forth several times to the railing within a few feet of me. It had a brown crown with the dark cap just below its eye, white cheeks, a buff belly, and was a plump little bird. I was not sure why this bird in particular approached me and seemed to study me for several minutes. Possibly it was just as curious about me as I was about it.

The Pygmy Nuthatch is resident in the Presidio and breeds there. It is abundant, feeding on insects, spiders, and pine seeds. The Pygmy Nuthatch is the smallest of the nuthatches—only about four inches long. It is found in forests, especially mature stands of conifers. It caches its seeds for later use, a precautionary measure also used by several other bird species. Nuthatches get their name from their habit of placing large seeds and nuts in crevices of trees and then prying them open with their bills. This species nests in cavities in snags or stumps and breeds from mid-April to mid-August. It tends to guard its territory.

Interestingly, no records exist of Pygmy Nuthatches roosting alone. They always huddle in a group, sometimes with more than 100 birds in a single cavity. The Pygmy Nuthatch is unique among songbirds in that it uses three energy-saving mechanisms for keeping warm on cold nights: it uses a protected roost site or hole in a tree; it huddles with other nuthatches; and it lets its body temperature drop (called hypothermia).

Fig 4-19 - A Pygmy Nuthatch grasping onto its food. Courtesy of Lee Karney, USFWS.

Brown Pelican

In June of 1999, the newspaper said the water off the coast of San Francisco was several degrees cooler than normal due to El Niña. This made for very good feeding for pelagic or seabirds, such as Cormorants. It also kept temperatures in San Francisco cooler than normal. Along the waterfront, I saw large flocks of 15 to 20, and sometimes as many as 40 to 50 Brown Pelicans, soaring very low close to the water and close to the shore. The pelicans flew mostly in formation, one behind the other, going along the coastline westward towards and then underneath the Golden Gate Bridge.

At the end of August, 2004, I saw numerous Brown Pelicans and watched one group of about 15 pelicans flying one behind the other, close to the water, under the south span of the Golden Gate Bridge. On the evening news it said there was a problem with Brown Pelicans this year in that they were starving and couldn't get enough food. This year had been a very productive year for births along the Pacific coast of Southern California near Los Angeles. However, the birds were impacted by the effects of a mild El Niño. The news also said there was a problem with Pelicans getting too close to fishing boats and getting hooks stuck in their bills.

El Niño is a phenomenon where there is a cyclical warming of East Pacific Ocean sea water temperatures off the western coast of South America that can result in significant changes in weather patterns in the United States and elsewhere. This occurs when warm equatorial Pacific waters move in and displace the colder waters, cutting off the upwelling process. The waters close to the surface are warmer and the fish go deeper for the colder water. Birds like Pelicans are not able to dive that deep to catch the fish.

Unlike White Pelicans, Brown Pelicans remain along the coasts and are rarely seen inland. They reside in all habitats on the Pacific, Atlantic, and Gulf coasts. They live in flocks of both sexes throughout the year. In level flight, they fly in groups, with their heads held back on their shoulders, their large bills resting on their folded necks. They may fly in a "V" formation, but usually go in single file, flying low over the water. Upon sighting prey, they plunge in, with wings half-folded, from heights of up to 50 feet, resurfacing to drain the water from their bills before swallowing the fish.

In the 1960s and 1970s, the numbers of Brown Pelicans were greatly reduced because of the overuse of pesticides like the synthetic pesticide DDT. These pesticides found their way into the ocean from runoff water and then were absorbed by fish, which carried the chemicals into the Brown Pelican's food chain. The Pelicans were greatly affected because their eggs became too thin to produce healthy chicks. Since the ban on the use of DDT, the Brown Pelican is recovering. However, they are still considered endangered. They face a fluctuating northern anchovy food supply, as well as increasing human and dog disturbance of their ground-built nests.

The Brown Pelican nests on islands off the coast of Mexico and after four or five months spent raising their chicks, they head north up the California coast as far north as British Columbia, following their food supply of anchovy, sardine, and mackerel.

Fig 4-20 - Brown Pelican with Alcatraz in the background.

California Towhee

In mid-September of 2004 just above the steep wooden steps leading up to the Coastal Trial, I watched a mixed flock of White-crowned Sparrows and finches feeding on the ground and noticed two larger, gray-brown birds, with long tails and buff coloring under their tails. These birds were California Towhees.

California Towhees are permanent residents and, except for the dispersal of juveniles away from nesting areas, they do not migrate and are quite sedentary. They apparently mate for life. During the breeding season, insects make up most of the towhee's diet while at other times seeds and some fruit are important. Most food is found on the ground, and California Towhees may forage by scratching the soil using both feet at once. They find water in dry habitats by drinking the dew from grass. The California Towhee enjoys scrubby habitats with leaf litter. The coastal sage scrub plant community along parts of the Coastal Trail was a preferred habitat for them.

Fig 4-21 - California Towhee. From Pixabay.

Townsend's Warbler

I saw a bird flitting about high up in an evergreen tree along the Coastal Trail close to Baker's Beach. It was foraging in the highest part of the coniferous tree and I waited for it to appear where I could get a good look at it through binoculars. It was a beautiful bird decked out in colors of black, white, yellow and olive-green. It had a yellow breast and a black ear patch going through the eye, bordered on top and at the bottom by bright yellow. It was a Townsend's Warbler.

Fig 4-22 - Townsend's Warbler in hand. Courtesy of Steve Matsuoka, USFWS.

The Townsend's Warbler forages in the top one-third of trees, gleaning insects from leaf surfaces and needles. A bird of the Pacific Northwest, it nests in coniferous forests from Alaska to Oregon. In September, it begins its migration south to winter in California and the highlands of Mexico and Central America. In winter, it is relatively common and easily seen on the coasts of Oregon and especially California. During migration the Townsend's Warbler often feeds in mixed species flocks with chickadees, nuthatches, and other warblers.

JOHN KIRK TOWNSEND (1809-1851)

The Townsend's Warbler is named for John Kirk Townsend, an American naturalist, ornithologist and collector. Born in Philadelphia, John Townsend became interested in natural history and bird collecting. In 1833, he was invited by Thomas Nuttall to join him on Nathaniel Wyeth's second expedition across the Rocky Mountains to the Pacific Ocean. During this trip, Townsend collected a number of birds new to science. On his return, Townsend wrote a detailed, vivid description of the Wyeth Expedition, entitled "The Narrative of a Journey Across the Rocky Mountains to the Columbia River (1839)", published in England under the title "Sporting Adventures in the Rocky Mountains" (London, 1840). Townsend supplied John James Audubon with many birds for Audubon's "Birds of America", as well as providing many of the descriptions for Audubon's "American Ornithology".

Townsend was 24 years old when Thomas Nuttall and Nathaniel Wyeth invited him to join the expedition to the west coast. He was the first ornithologist, along with the botanist Thomas Nuttall, to visit the Oregon Territory. At the beginning of the journey, while Wyeth had to wait in St. Louis to procure supplies, Townsend and Nuttall decided to walk to Independence. It took the men nearly a week to traverse these 240 miles of prairie. They encountered an abundance of wildlife along the way, including massive herds of buffalo, and vast numbers of Pileated Woodpeckers, Greater Prairie Chickens, Sandhill Cranes, Carolina Parakeets (now extinct), and Passenger Pigeons (now extinct).

Once they left Independence, it took them nearly five months to reach Fort Vancouver in the Oregon Country. In Fort Vancouver, Townsend immersed himself in studying the region's birdlife. He found most of the birds were different from those he knew in Philadelphia, yet they were similar. For example, the Towhees were strikingly spotted with white on the back and wings. The Fox Sparrows were a dark chocolate brown.

Townsend went on to the Sandwich (Hawaiian) Islands where he continued to collect species of birds and plants previously unknown to science. He sailed to Tahiti and Chili, not returning to Philadelphia until November of 1837. He had been gone for four years – six months on the journey west, over two years in the Oregon Country western wilderness, and one year on the return sea journey.

In many ways, the western expedition was the highlight of Townsend's ornithological career. He became curator of the collection of the Academy of Natural Sciences of Philadelphia, which was considered one of the principal ornithological collections in the United States, and grew the ornithological collection in stature and fine appearance. He was a master at bird taxidermy. However, the close and continual contact with the arsenic powder used to prepare and preserve bird skins led to his untimely death in 1851 at the age of 41.

On October 9, 2004 the Snowbirds, a Canadian group of performance-flying pilots flying military jets, were performing in an annual show for Fleet Week in San Francisco. Usually the Blue Angels, the United States Navy flight demonstration team, performed in San Francisco during Fleet Week, but this year they had another engagement. The Snowbirds flew farther out over the San Francisco Bay, as opposed to the Blue Angels, who at times flew very low over the City.

The birds in Crissy Field Marsh did not seem overly concerned about the noisy planes flying overhead. I watched three or four Marbled Godwits probe deeply in the sand with their long bills. As I watched them, two Killdeer landed in the middle of them, making their usual loud cries. In spite of their much larger size, the Marbled Godwits looked startled and moved out of the Killdeers' way. I also watched three Willets. One Willet cocked his head and looked up at the planes in the sky, but did not seem overly afraid.

On October 30, 2004, I went to the Coastal Trail at dusk. The clocks were to fall back for daylight savings the following day. At the top of the stairs, numerous White-crowned Sparrows fed on the ground and on low grasses. I stood and watched them and they didn't fly away. I saw a different bird alight on the railing by the path. It was robin-sized, but was gray-backed, with a whitish belly and spotting on its entire breast. It had a large round eye. It mostly stayed on the ground as it moved along. It was a Hermit Thrush, the only brown-backed thrush likely to be seen in North America in winter.

Feeding on one of the native plants at the top of the path leading up to the Coastal Trail, was a small, four-and-a-half-inch female Lesser Goldfinch. It was dull yellow below and had black wings with white bars. I knew it was a Lesser Goldfinch because its call, uttered several times, sounded like a cat's meow. In *National Geographic Field Guide to Birds of North America*, the call of the Lesser Goldfinch is described as a "plaintiff, kitten like tee-yee". (Ref 4-12)

On December 12, 2004, the water level in San Francisco Bay was high, and the surface was unusually calm and glassy smooth. I could easily see the birds sitting out on the water. Instead of looking down on them, it was like seeing them at eye level.

When I climbed the wooden stairs behind the Warming Hut, I noticed the Wild Rose Bush at the top of the stairs had many fragrant flowers and also some new buds in spite of the cold weather and the time of year. I stopped to smell the flowers on this Wild Rose Bush when I went by, as I always do.

Chapter Five – Marshall's Beach

MARSHALL'S BEACH IS to the west of the Golden Gate Bridge. The waves often pound in to the beach from the Pacific Ocean. I usually sat for a half an hour or longer at the top of the last series of steps leading down to the beach, absorbed in observing the birds - on the beach below, on the rocks, and in the ocean. At certain times of the year, I saw large migratory flocks of Willets and Sanderlings feeding on the beach. They flew in, landed on the beach, and followed the waves in and out, searching for food left behind on the sand as the waves receded. Some of the birds were aware of my presence as I sat on the steps watching them and they kept an eye on me, but as I didn't move, they continued going about their business.

I watched small groups of Surf Scoters swimming in the rough water, as well as two Black Oystercatchers flying around the large rocks. It was a thrilling experience for me to see such wild birds. I had great respect for them and admired how they survived in such a wild environment.

Fig 5-1 – Path leading down to Marshall's Beach.

On March 19, 2016, I went along San Francisco's northern waterfront as far as Marshall's Beach from 6:30 to 10:00 am. It was a foggy day, with the Golden Gate Bridge partially obscured. Several Surf Scoters were floating in the Bay to the west of the Golden Gate Bridge. I debated whether to continue to Marshall's Beach, but in the end, decided to go. I was so glad I went! A small motor-powered fishing boat went by and anchored off Baker Beach. I walked down the slippery path to the steps leading down to Marshall's Beach and sat down on the top step. The water level was high, and waves were coming in all the way up on the beach to the bottom of the cliff, so I did not expect to see any shorebirds on the beach.

I heard a bird call – a series of five to seven loud, clearly-whistled notes: "pip-pip-pip-pip-pip", and thought maybe there was a Whimbrel nearby. Then, I could not believe my eyes! I watched as a large flock of shorebirds flew around and around the large black rock that rises from the water a short distance from Marshall's Beach. I watched them circle the rock numerous times, and then the whole flock settled on its steep side facing me. It looked as though it was hard for them to balance on the sloping rock, but they had no choice, as the waves were up over the beach, preventing them from landing there. I wondered if they would stay on the rock until the tide changed and the area on the beach became available for feeding.

Fig 5-2 – Shorebirds flying around rock by Marshall's Beach.

On Saturday, March 26, 2016, I got up early and left about 6:30 am, with the goal to get to Marshall's Beach. It was clear with a little mist in the air. The sandy beach was exposed, and although waves still came crashing in, it was not like the week before during an El Niño storm when the water was right up to the base of the cliff.

As I sat on the last step above the beach, a flock of 20 Willets landed on the beach and started feeding. Some of the Willets found something small and round in the water to eat. While they ate, others just stood around. Then I noticed a slightly larger shorebird, with a downward-pointing bill and white supercilium. It was a lone Whimbrel among the flock of Willets. The Whimbrel kept aloof, and once I saw it strike out at a Willet with its bill. It seemed wary, and I noticed it kept watching me as I sat on the step. The Willets didn't seem to pay any attention to me, but the Whimbrel didn't seem interested in feeding as long as I was there.

The only other person at Marshall's Beach that day was a lone fisherman at the far eastern end of the beach. He had long waders on and was out in the water fishing.

Fig 5-3 – Lone fisherman at Marshall's Beach.

On Friday, April 6, 2018 there was a "Pineapple Express" rainstorm coming through the Bay Area and it rained heavily all that night. This weather came in a stream from the Hawaiian Islands. The paper said the system was from the remnants of a hurricane. The fog was very thick the following morning, and I could hear the wail of the foghorns. When I went out at 6:30 am, I couldn't see the Golden Gate Bridge at all because of the fog. Indeed, I could only see about 10 to 15 feet in front of me. I was alone at Marshall's Beach and I sat at the top of the steps for a long time. I had not brought my camera with me, as I was expecting it to rain heavily.

At least 100 Willets were gathered on the south side of the large black rock rising out of the water a short distance from Marshall's Beach. Groups of five or six Willets kept flying in and landing on the rock. Only a couple of them flew in to the beach to feed. Most of them just sat or stood on the rock out of the wind. Two Black Oystercatchers flew to the rocky beach to the left of Marshall's Beach and started eating the lichen on the rocks.

The following day brought a contrast to the windy, foggy prior day. The sky was blue, but the waves at Marshall's Beach were huge. Massive swells broke over the rock where the Willets had sat the previous day. A few Willets flew in and landed on the south side of the rock several times, but then had to fly off as a wave engulfed the rock. The two Black Oystercatchers flew to the top of the rock and then flew off as a wave approached and crashed over the top of the rock. A mass of white flotsam from the incoming crashing waves lay on the beach.

One day as I approached Marshall's Beach, I heard one of the Black Oystercatchers calling and saw it on the sand. Then it walked further up the beach to join the second Black Oystercatcher and they flew off together towards the rocks on the far eastern end of the beach by the Golden Gate Bridge.

Fig 5-4 – Black Oystercatcher pair on rocks by Marshall's Beach.

On another very foggy morning, I heard the "will-will" calls of shorebirds as I went down the trail leading to Marshall's Beach. I smiled to myself because that meant there would be shorebirds on the beach. Sure enough, there were about 20 Willets on the beach both to the right and left of the stairs where I sat. The surf pounded in and the Willets milled about rather than fed. They may have been temporarily grounded due to the heavy fog. They didn't seem interested in running out towards the water and then retreating before an incoming wave, while picking up things to eat the wave had brought ashore.

A group of Surf Scoters swam past. A huge wave went completely over the top of the Surf Scoters, but they came to the surface again and didn't seem disturbed. They were accustomed to being underneath a wave.

In November 2018, thirty Sanderlings were at Marshall's Beach. They were constantly on the go, running out as a wave receded to see if it had left anything in the sand, and then scurrying back up the beach as another wave came crashing in. Sometimes they couldn't move fast enough to get ahead of the incoming water and were forced to fly, showing their white wing underlinings. Several Whimbrels were among the Sanderlings.

Fig 5-5 – Sanderlings and Whimbrel at Marshall's Beach.

One of the Sanderlings found a tasty morsel and scurried away with it. He was pursued by other Sanderlings in the area, and had to twist and turn as he ran away from them. When he set his morsel down to try to eat it, another Sanderling ran up to him and he had to pick the food up again and carry it to a new spot. The other Sanderling soon gave up the chase when a new wave came crashing in, deciding to run after the wave as it receded in order to scour the wet sand the wave had left behind.

On the morning of December 9, 2018, I sat on the top step above Marshall's Beach. A Willet flew onto the beach, flashing its white underwing coverts. When it ran after an outgoing wave, it was limping and favoring one leg. It was lame and had difficulty running after a retreating wave and then getting out of the way of the incoming water. I felt sorry for it and wondered how it was going to survive. However, it could still fly.

Then it did something which seemed strange to me. It hobbled along the beach closer and closer to where I sat, finally taking shelter behind a rock right below me. I could just see its head projecting from the rock below me. It appeared to be watching me. What was it doing? Was it trying to find a safe place to hide and rest? It stayed there for about ten minutes. I sat very still. I didn't even want to move to take its picture.

The incoming tidal waves started spreading further up onto the beach, encroaching behind the rock where the Willet was resting. The Willet moved away from the shelter of the rock and limped onto the beach. Here it started limping after a retreating wave and then hurrying back up the beach. Sometimes it had to fly to avoid the incoming water as it wasn't able to walk fast enough. It then moved further along the beach and joined a group of Sanderlings who were feeding. I felt heartened by the courage of this Willet trying to do the best it could to survive. Watching these birds live their lives gave me a great respect for them.

January 6, 2019 was a stormy, rainy, windy day. The rain stopped for a while on the way out to Marshall's Beach, and I sat down on the step. I heard the Black Oystercatchers chattering and saw the two of them fly off together. The waves crashed onto the beach. I was surprised to see 30 to 40 tiny Sanderlings in a group chasing the retreating waves, which came up almost to the rickrack at the base of the cliff. There was an open spot of sand in the rickrack, and the Sanderlings retreated to this spot when a wave came in. But as the tide came in, the waves encroached further and further up the beach. Soon there would be no place for the Sanderlings to escape the incoming water.

I watched several Surf Scoters riding over the top of a wave and disappearing down the other side. The rain started coming down heavily and I left the beach.

Early in the morning of January 27, 2019 I saw much sand on the shoreline at Marshall's Beach, unlike the previous few weekends of high tides and stormy weather, when the waves crashed in and the water came up almost to the base of the cliff. I went down the steps and walked along the sand on the beach.

Almost at the far eastern end of the beach, I noticed one lone Sanderling. I did not see any other shorebirds the whole time I was there. I first noticed the lone Sanderling as it actively pursued a retreating wave, using a rapid sewing-machine-like motion to feed on the wet sand the wave had just washed over. I watched it for fifteen minutes. The Sanderling then stopped looking for food and stood at the edge of the water. Then it did something I did not expect. It turned towards where I was standing high up on the sand and started walking towards me. It stopped quite high up on the sand and looked at me, both straight-on and sideways. We both stayed like for this for several minutes. As the tide was slowly coming in, I thought I had better retreat along the beach towards the steps. As I looked behind me, I saw the Sanderling walking higher up on the sand towards the rocks. Was it going to take shelter and hide up among the rocks at the base of the cliff? I had seen groups of 20 to 30 Sanderlings feeding along the beach here. This Sanderling looked very healthy. Was it okay that it was alone?

Sometimes I became so focused on watching the shorebirds at Marshall's Beach that I didn't notice how cold my hands were, until they became so cold that I couldn't feel them. Then I would put on the thin gloves I had with me and walk back up the path from Marshall's Beach, having an appreciation for the types of conditions birds had to live through in the wild.

On the morning of March 17, 2019, the waves crashed in all the way up on the beach to the base of the cliff. Twenty Willets were on the large black rock. They flew towards the beach and then circled back and landed on the large rock again. They flew low to the water except when a large wave rose up prior to crashing down, and they had to fly above the crest of the breaking wave.

I watched them do this fly-by three times. They obviously were hungry and wanted to land on the beach to feed, but it was too dangerous with the waves crashing in and water rushing all the way up the beach to the base of the cliff.

Out in the water, a male and female Surf Scoter rose with the large waves, going over the top of them, and coming down on the other side.

Fig 5-6 – Whimbrels at Marshall's Beach.

Fig 5-7 - Marshall's Beach and rainbow.

SECTION II – BIRDS IN NATURAL WONDERLANDS

IN EVERY WALK WITH nature, one receives far more than he seeks.

John Muir

If you truly love Nature, you will find beauty everywhere.

Vincent Van Gogh

Chapter Six – Mercer Slough

FROM THE FALL OF 2002 to the spring of 2003, I lived on the east side of Seattle where I discovered Mercer Slough, a large nature park close to a highly urbanized area. Mercer Slough is the largest wetland expanse remaining on the east side of Seattle that remains connected to Lake Washington. It is named for Aaron and Ann Mercer who settled there in 1862 and built a cabin, later filing a land claim in 1869.

When the level of Lake Washington was lowered eight to ten feet to build the Ballard Locks ship canal in 1916, the lake bottom was exposed. By this time there had already been farming by the Winters family and others along the edges of what was then a branch of Lake Washington. With the new soil exposed, the farm was expanded. The Winters family was the major land owner. They had a bulk farm for growing irises, daffodils and azaleas. In 1927 they built the Winter's House, a three-story Spanish style home for the substantial sum at the time of $32,000.

During the 1930s, agriculture boomed in the Mercer Slough. In 1943 the Winters family retired, selling their property to the Riepel family, who in turn sold a significant portion of the land to Endre Ostbo who operated a nursery there specializing in rhododendrons. In places in Mercer Slough, these large fragrant flowers still bloomed abundantly.

In the 1960s many of the smaller farms around Mercer Slough were abandoned, possibly as part of the larger trend in America away from agriculture and towards industrialization after World War Two. In 1983 the last Riepel moved and the property and Winter's House were abandoned for five years. Then in 1988, a Park Bond Issue passed which created funds for the City of Bellevue, in partnership with the Trust for Public Land, to buy the Mercer Slough property and the Winter's House. The City also set out to create a restored wetland park and habitat preserve out of Mercer Slough by buying all the surrounding old farms they could and managing the land as a unit. Bellevue was able to obtain 367 acres of Mercer Slough, which is the largest wetland expanse remaining on Lake Washington.

Mercer Slough is used by the public for trail walking, bird watching, and canoeing. It has over five miles of bark trails, with boardwalks built over the wetter areas. The trails can be entered behind the old Winter's House, which is preserved and serves as a visitors' center.

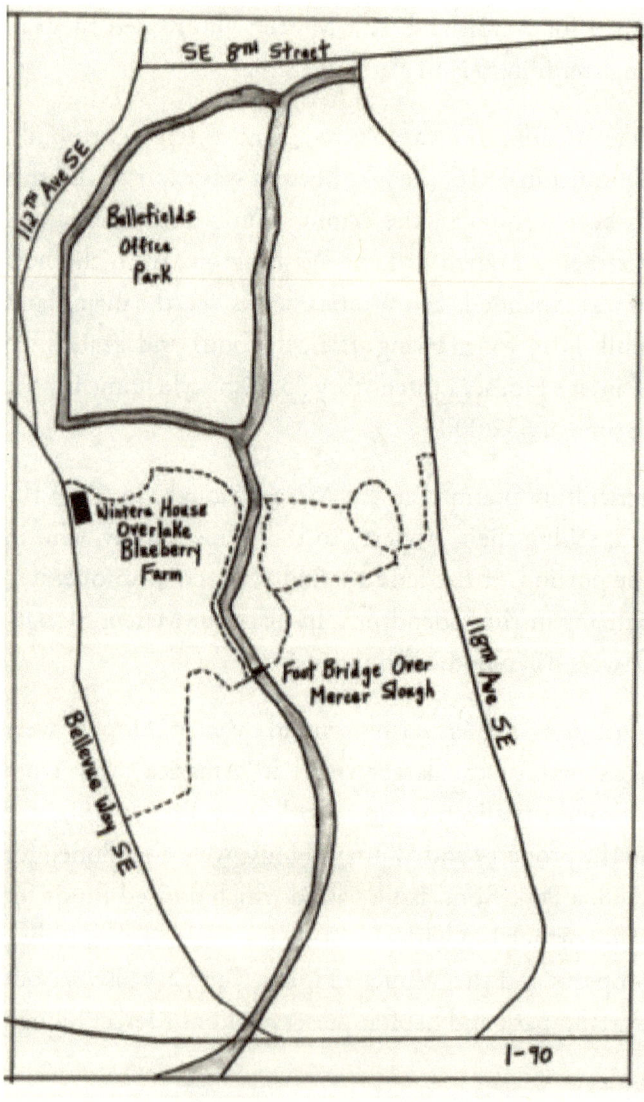

Fig 6-1 – Map showing the trails around Mercer Slough.

An active blueberry farm lies adjacent to the area. The blueberry fields of the
Overlake Blueberry Farm cover sixteen acres. The harvest season starts in July
and ends in October.

Fig 6-2 – Blueberry fields adjacent to Mercer Slough. Courtesy of Richard L.
Hicks.

Mercer Slough is one of the most diverse ecosystems in the urban Puget
Sound region. Its wet, mucky soils and the plants that thrive in them, mark
this area as a wetland. The plant community is specialized to survive in the
nutrient-poor and highly acidic conditions typical of bog peat systems. Some
of the areas in the slough are very boggy with peat soil. Indeed, the peat has
been measured at 70 feet deep in some places and is suspected of being even
deeper in other places.

Mercer Slough could be considered as a scrub-shrub wetland. However,
because it is so large, it has varied habitats, including upland forested areas
and wet meadows. While walking along the trails in the slough, I saw ducks,
hummingbirds, kingfishers, woodpeckers, vireos, chickadees, bushtits,
kinglets, thrushes, waxwings, wood warblers, towhees, sparrows, blackbirds,
finches, wrens and grosbeaks.

<u>Downy Woodpecker</u>

On one of my walks through Mercer Slough, I watched a male Downy Woodpecker as he went from branch to branch of a small tree, test-drilling the wood trying to find wood-boring insects. He had a short, chisel-shaped bill, a white back, white patches on his face and a red patch on the back of his head. On the way back, I saw the female. She had no red patch on the back of her head.

Because of its small size, the Downy Woodpecker can forage not only on trunks and major limbs of trees but also on minor branches and twigs, often climbing about acrobatically.[Ref 6-1] *It often forages along small twigs or weed stalks, hunting down vast numbers of small insects and larvae that infest trees and lie hidden in cracks along the branches, twigs, and tree trunk.*

Fig 6-3 – Male Downy Woodpecker.

The Downy Woodpecker is the most common North American woodpecker, occurring over the greater part of the continent from the Gulf States northward. It prefers the open woodland that covers a large part of the United States, preferring forest edges and areas around openings in the denser forests, leaving the densest forests for the larger woodpeckers.

Downy Woodpecker pairs will often return to the same nesting area every year of their adult lives, sometimes occupying separate sleeping holes in the trunk of the same tree. They nest in a cavity the birds drill themselves in a branch eight to 50 feet above the ground, generally in dead or dying wood, but sometimes in a solid branch. The entrance, one and quarter inches in diameter, is just large enough to admit the bird's body, and is perfectly round unless some bits of soft wood chip off. The cavity is roughly gourd-shaped, turning downward and widening soon after penetrating the wood, and extending to a depth varying normally from eight to 12 inches. Generally a few chips are left in the bottom of the cavity.

Downy Woodpeckers are mostly permanent residents, even in the northern parts of their range. They rely on their roosting holes where they sleep alone through the long winter nights and into which they may retreat in the daytime in very inclement weather.

A. C. Bent comments [Ref 6-2]: *"The ornithologists of a century ago show unanimity in their characterization of the Downy Woodpecker. Audubon (1842) remarked it 'is perhaps not surpassed by any of its tribe in hardiness, industry, or vivacity'. Wilson (1832) says 'the principal characteristics of this little bird are diligence, familiarity, and perseverance' and speaks of a pair of birds working at their nest 'with the most indefatigable diligence'. Nuttall (1832) shares Wilson's opinion using his exact words – 'indefatigable diligence' in his own account of the building of the nest.*

The Downy Woodpecker sits very still as it digs out a grub from under the bark of a tree, or from the wood under the bark, or as it dislodges a bit of bark in its hunt for a cocoon or a bundle of insects' eggs. We hear the gentle taps of its bill, and when our eyes, led by the sound, catch sight of the bird, perched on a branch or the trunk of a tree, we understand why it has been called industrious. It is concentrated on its work; it works patiently, seriously, like a carpenter working earnestly with his chisel, spending a full minute, sometimes more, to secure a bit of food."

<u>Spotted Towhee</u>

I watched a Spotted Towhee along the path bordering the blueberry farm. It had very distinctive coloring with a dark hood and very colorful bright-rust flanks, with white wing bars and white spots on its back. I heard a "meowing" sound and saw the Spotted Towhee in the undergrowth beside the path, where it was scratching noisily through dead leaves.

The Spotted Towhee was formerly lumped together with the Eastern Towhee as "Rufous-sided Towhee". It is a ground-dwelling bird and builds its nest on the ground in the weeds or under a thick bush. It hunts on the ground for the different seeds it feeds on, pushing aside the leaves and weeds to get at the seeds with its feet and bill.

Fig 6-4 – Spotted Towhee.

Frederic W. Davis comments on the food habits of this species in the Life Histories series as follows [Ref 6-3]: *"When feeding on the ground, the towhee usually progresses by 'kick' foraging, scattering the ground debris with its feet to expose potential food as it goes. When insect larvae and other food are plentiful on top of the substrate, the birds resort to visual or peck foraging without scratching the debris aside. In late May or early June, the birds are often seen in highbush blueberry eating the blossoms. Arboreal foraging predominates during the first week or two of June, and throughout the month the towhees frequent a variety of deciduous trees to glean larvae from the foliage. Fruits of the aromatic wintergreen, blueberries, and huckleberries are consumed not only by the adults, but are fed in quantity to the nestlings."*

Wood Duck

In the water of Mercer Slough, I saw two gorgeous male Wood Ducks as well as three females. The females flew from trees on either side of the slough banks into the water. The male Wood Ducks were in bright breeding plumage and had red eyes.

Many naturalists think the Wood Duck is the most beautiful duck in North America. It is a strictly North American species. Its summer range extends a short distance north of the United States-Canadian border, and in the winter, it does not migrate far south of the United States. Wood Ducks nest in trees. Preferred nesting sites are holes in hollow trunks or large branches of trees resulting from broken limbs, fire scars, lightning and logging damage, and the work of large woodpeckers. Nests are usually found close to water, although females sometimes select trees some distance from water. When the young are about 24-hours old, they use their sharp claws to climb up the inside of the nesting cavity to its entrance, and then they jump and flutter to the ground, generally landing unharmed. The female then leads them to the nearest water, where she teaches them how to obtain their food and avoid predators.

Fig 6-5 – Male Wood Ducks.

Audubon (1840) says [Ref 6-4]: *"If the nest is placed immediately over the water, the young, the moment they are hatched, scramble to the mouth of the hold, launch into the air with their little wings and feet spread out, and drop into their favorite element; but whenever their birthplace is at some distance from it, the mother carries them to it one by one in her bill, holding them so as not to injure their yet tender frame. On several occasions, however, when the hold was 30, 40 or more yards from a bayou or other piece of water, I observed the mother suffered the young to fall on the grasses and dried leaves beneath the trees, and afterwards led them directly to the nearest edge of the next pool or creek...They are excellent divers, and when frightened, instantly disappear, disperse below the surface, and make for the nearest shore, on attaining which they run for the woods, squat in any convenient place, and thus elude pursuit."*

Song Sparrow

Several Song Sparrows called continually. One sat on a tree branch facing away from me. It looked completely gray from the back. When it turned, it had brown streaks on the side of its head with also some white streaks and a whitish throat. Its underparts were whitish and it had streaking on the sides and breast, with a central dark spot on the breast.

Fig 6-6 – The Song Sparrow is a medium-sized American sparrow. Among the native sparrows in North America, it is easily one of the most abundant, variable, and adaptable species. Courtesy of Grayson Smith, USFWS.

The Song Sparrow is a maestro among sparrows, singing at least 20 different melodies with thousands of variations. Aretas A. Saunders wrote to A. C. Bent (Ref 6-5): *"I have 885 records of the song, no two of them alike...Each individual Song Sparrow sings a number of different songs. It commonly sings the same song over a half dozen times or so, and then takes up a different song. The number of songs per individual varies from six to 24, the latter being an unusual bird...Quality is usually sweet and musical...The song has three parts: strongly rhythmic introductory notes, a central trill, and a final series of rather irregular and indefinite notes."*

Donald J. Borrow (1961) writes [Ref 6-6]: *"A Song Sparrow apparently has an inborn tendency to sing songs of two general types, but it learns its phrases by listening to other nearby Song Sparrows. As a result, the songs of different birds in a local population contain similar notes and phrases (but usually arranged differently), while the songs of birds in separated populations contain different phrases. The farther away two populations are, the less likely they are to use similar phrases in their songs."*

MARGARET MORSE NICE (1883-1974)

Margaret Morse Nice was the expert on the life of the Song Sparrow. She was the real founder of the science of ethology, or the scientific study of animal behavior, according to Konrad Lorenz, the well-known ethologist. Lorenz wrote the following in the introduction to Nice's posthumously-published autobiography "Research Is a Passion with Me": "Her paper on the Song Sparrow was, to the best of my knowledge, the first long-term field investigation of the individual life of any free-living wild animal." (Ref 6-7)

Margaret Morse Nice kept notes on birds at the age of nine. She subsequently married and raised a family, but at age 36, she began her serious bird field studies. One day a month she took an all-day walk to observe birds. She said: "It is an inspiring experience to have a day for wandering – to be free and alone with nature for a whole long day; to feel unhurried, to be able to search carefully for birds, to be unmolested by considerations for other people." [Ref 6-8]

Margaret launched her Song Sparrow study by banding a male she later named Uno. She began to record data about the lives of Song Sparrows and made several original discoveries concerning this common species. She found that male Song Sparrows began to sing in mid-February and that each male had a different song, which clearly defined his territory. When the females arrived, the males stopped singing and began courtship. In care of the young, male Song Sparrows were exemplary parents. They were the sole incubators of the eggs, and after the nestlings hatched, they helped care for the young. She found evidence, from banding records, that some individuals of the euphonia subspecies were resident in regions where most of their kind were migratory.

4M was the most legendary Song Sparrow that Margaret banded and studied. He was banded in his second year and returned to raise new families each spring for eight years, reaching the age of nine and a half years, quite a long lifetime for a Song Sparrow. He also sang more than any bird Margaret observed. He started singing in late January or early February and continued into July, starting up again at the end of September and continuing through October. He portrayed "the picture of abounding energy and joy in living." On May 11, 1935, Margaret rose at dawn to record the total number of songs 4M could give in a day. At that time over eight years old, 4M produced an incredible 2,305 songs to Margaret's amazement and delight. (Ref 6-9)

When her "Population Study of the Song Sparrow" was published in 1937, Margaret received overwhelming praise for it, both in North America and abroad. French ornithologist Jean Delacour wrote that it was "perhaps the most important contribution yet published to our knowledge of the life of a species." (Ref 6-10)

In her obituary in the "Auk", Milton Trautman praised her "tremendous ability for concentration during long periods of time, patience in observing and recording data (including minute details), consuming interest in behavior, and determination to publish as much as possible of what she observed." (Ref 6-11)

Later on, Margaret began to publicize some of her ideas about conservation. These ideas were born out of the time she had spent observing birds and their habits and needs in the field. Her views on ecology were ahead of her time. She implored that weeds, shrubs, and vines should be left along roadsides and fence rows to provide bird habitat. Her book ended with a plea to leave space for wild creatures, forests for beasts and birds, swamps for wildfowl, and prairie for wildflowers. As early as 1944 she spoke out against the use of lead shot in waterfowl hunting. She was at the cutting edge of ecological conservation as well as bird behavioral study.

Margaret Morse Nice found deep satisfaction in her ornithological work as she believed "the study of nature is a limitless field, the most fascinating adventure in the world...We who love nature, who see and try to understand and interpret, are following the true goal. We have a talisman against the futility of the lives of many people." [Ref 6-12]

Black-capped Chickadee

One day in mid-November, I was at Mercer Slough about 3 pm. It was pouring rain. I didn't see many birds (even the Mallards were resting along the bank), except for Black-capped Chickadees. The chickadees completely ignored the rain. They "dee-deed" to each other, and acrobatically combed through the branches. I watched one hanging upside down. They never stopped moving. Their black caps, white side of face, and light chestnut sides looked very clean. They were most appealing and I watched them for some time. It became dark by 5 pm in mid-November, so maybe these birds had to gather as much food as they could while still light out, despite the heavy rain.

Black-capped Chickadees appear to be cheerful little birds that are constantly active—hopping, clinging, or hanging upside down from tree branches. They eat insects, seeds, and berries. They make a variety of musical sounds. The best-known is the "chickadee-dee-dee" that gives the bird its name. This sound is used to challenge or scold an intruder or to express alarm at something that frightens it. The

Black-capped Chickadee's song is two or three whistled notes: "pheee-bee" or "pheee-beebee". It may sing at any time of the year, but does so most often in the early part of the nesting season.

Fig 6-7 – Black-capped Chickadee. Courtesy of Pixabay.

The Black-capped Chickadee nests in holes in rotting wood of dead stumps or the dead parts of live trees. Often, they get through the hard outer coating of a post or stump into the decaying interior by initially choosing a hole made by a woodpecker in search of a grub. They then work industriously to deepen and enlarge this cavity with their small but strong beaks, sometimes making a hole which is nine or more inches deep. They are smart enough to carry the chips away, scattering them far and wide.

In the winter, Black-capped Chickadees collect in small loose flocks of eight to twelve birds. The flock flits through the woods from tree to tree. The birds scatter out a good deal, but they keep continually calling to one another, thus indicating the direction in which the flock is moving. As the flock moves along, each bird minutely examines the bark, branches, and twigs, searching for tiny bits of food like spider's eggs, cocoons, and other dormant insect life. The flocks usually contain too many birds to represent only a single family.

It is interesting to note that in these social relations, Black-capped Chickadees establish an order of dominance or "pecking order". Each bird is known to the other according to its rank, with a bird's rank determined by its degree of aggressiveness. All the birds in the flock are subordinate to the most aggressive bird and the lowest in rank is subordinate to everyone else. The rest are graded between the two extremes. The higher-ranking bird fights, chases, and threatens a subordinate bird who gives way to it. [Ref 6-13]

<u>Accipiter</u>

On a cloudy and windy day towards the end of November 2002 the birds kept well-hidden in Mercer Slough and I discovered why. I heard a bird in a marshy area by a tree and made a pishing noise to draw it out into the open. Suddenly, a crow-sized bird exploded out of the bush and burst down the path, twisting and turning as it flew. This bird had been sitting in the bushes, waiting for prey. It was an accipiter – either a Sharp-shinned or a Cooper's Hawk.

Accipiters are hawks that hunt in the woods instead of soaring overhead. The female hawk is always larger than the male. Because I saw this bird from the back, it looked all-black. Accipiters feed mostly on birds and small animals. Ninety to 97 percent of the prey taken by Sharp-shinned Hawks are birds. Avian prey may range in size from warblers and Song Sparrows to American Robins. Accipiters hunt by stealth, moving from perch to perch in dense cover, listening and watching, and then putting on a burst of speed to overtake their prey. Most prey is taken while "still-hunting" from ambush, or by stealthy approach flights that take advantage of landscape features such as hiding behind shrubbery to take their prey by surprise. The final phase may entail a twisting, circuitous flight at high speed and low levels through dense vegetation.

I had been a witness to their great speed and agility when the accipiter I saw burst out of the bush and sped down the winding path between the trees. Naturally, this little devil of the woods is dreaded by all the smaller birds, who have learned to keep out of sight and remain silent when one of these hawks is nearby.

<u>American Robin</u>

A few days later, I was at Mercer Slough on a warm, sunny day about 4 pm, just before dark. At the start of the path, I saw many American Robins sitting high in the trees and calling. I was happy to see them as their presence seemed to make other birds more comfortable.

American Robins are the largest thrushes in North America. They can be both forest and town birds, adapting well to the changing conditions man imposes on the environment. Robins love taking sun baths. On one very hot day when I had been trying to keep in the shade, I had observed an American Robin taking a sun bath in a sunny spot on the path at Mercer Slough. It lay on the ground, spread out its wings and lay in the sun for about ten minutes.

Fig 6-8 – American Robin. Courtesy of Pixabay.

The American Robin's breeding season is from early April to as late as September. The female robin makes the cup-shaped nest, taking from two to six days to build it. She makes an average of 180 trips a day, with mud or grass, during the peak building period. The males sing, mostly in the morning, and most frequently during the period of courtship. Males will also sing when the young are in the nest and at night, but caroling generally decreases after pair formation. The familiar "cheerily" is the carol song. In addition to their singing, American Robins make a variety of calls. Male robins stop singing in July, and, except for a brief time in September when the shortness of daylight fools them into thinking it is time to breed again, they do not sing again until the spring. Their other calls continue throughout the year. Female American Robins do not sing, but give alarm calls during the breeding season.

Although American Robins are typically thought to feed exclusively on worms, they eat many kinds of soft foods. Invertebrates such as earthworms, beetles, and caterpillars provide about 40% of their diet, but the other 60% consists of fruit, including blackberry, raspberry, wild cherry, sumac, wild grape, and blueberry.

Northern Flicker

One day as I sat on a bench under a tree, a larger-than-a-robin-sized bird flew into a branch at the very top of the tree. I recognized it as a Northern Flicker with its black bib and black spots. There was another flicker on an adjoining branch and the two were mates as one was a female without the red malar or "moustache" along each side of the male's throat. The two flickers were conducting a display and singing "wicka-wicka-wicka" to each other.

Fig 6-9 – Northern Flickers (female on the left and male on the right). Taken 5 April 2007. Courtesy of David Margrave (in the public domain).

Fig 6-10 – Red-shafted Northern Flicker.

Suddenly the two Northern Flickers flew away and were replaced on the branch by a large hawk with thin pale-white barring on the underside of its tail and a light-colored breast. I felt annoyed that this hawk should have disrupted the peaceful serenity of the birds' enjoying the good weather together.

Northern Flickers are woodpeckers, and are the anteaters of the bird world. They eat more ants than any other bird. Flickers are the only woodpeckers that frequently feed on the ground. The tongue of the Northern Flicker extends nearly three inches beyond its beak. The flicker explores the ground, often scratching away leaves or rubbish, to locate the ants' nest, digs into the nest with its long bill, and as the ants come pouring out, it laps them up in quantities, or else it inserts its long, sticky tongue deep down into the nest to get the young and eggs. Flickers also eat berries and seeds, especially in winter, including poison oak and poison ivy, dogwood, sumac, wild cherry, grape, bayberries, hackberries, and elderberries, as well as sunflower and thistle seeds.

In his life history of the Northern Flicker, A. C. Bent incorporated the field notes of others as follows: "Miss Althea R. Sherman (1910) made some very thorough studies of the nesting habits of the Northern Flicker at National, Iowa, in some boxes so arranged on her barn that she could observe the home life of the birds at close range...Some of Althea's observations on the young are as follows: Until the young are about 11 days old, they lie in a circle in the nest, their long necks stretched over each other, then for nearly a week they press against the side of the nest. At 17 or 18 days of age, their claws having acquired a needlelike sharpness, they begin to cling to the wall of the nest, and when three weeks old they are able to climb to the hole and be fed while the parent hangs outside." (Ref 6-14)

"Professor Beal (1911) has shown that 61% of the flicker's food consists of animal matter and 41% vegetable matter. About 75% of the animal food, or 45% of the entire food, consists of ants....If it had no other beneficial habit, the flicker would deserve protection for the good it does in keeping in check these injurious and annoying insects." (Ref 6-15)

It was nearing dusk and the sun was setting as I left the marsh. Later that evening, I thought about how pitch black it must be in the marsh at night with absolutely no lights.

<u>Steller's Jay</u>

One sunny but chilly day at the end of November, a Steller's Jay sat high in a tree. It was preening below its breast, which was an incredible color of light blue-green aqua. I could see the more traditional Blue Jay colors as it preened.

The Steller's Jay is a large jay which lives from Alaska along the coast to central California, and through the Rocky Mountains and high mountain areas of Central America to Nicaragua. It is usually nonmigratory throughout its range, except for high mountain populations which move to lower latitudes during the winter. Like other jays, it eats a wide variety of foods, including seeds, berries, and nuts. It has a distinctive crest with a dusky head. The under parts below the breast are greenish-blue turning bright blue under the tail and at the vent. The primary wings are sky blue while the rump and tail are bright blue. Overall, it is a very attractive bird.

GEORG WILHELM STELLER (1709-1746)

Georg Wilhelm Steller was born in Germany and went to Russia, where he worked at the St. Petersburg Academy of Sciences. He was appointed as naturalist on the explorer Vitus Bering's Second Kamchatka Expedition to chart the Siberian coast of the Arctic Ocean and to search for an eastern passage to North America. In July 1741 the expedition landed in Alaska, staying only long enough to take on fresh water. During this time, Steller described a number of North American plants and animals, including a jay later named Steller's Jay.

On the return journey, the expedition was shipwrecked on what later became known as Bering Island. Here, Vitus Bering and almost half the crew died from the effects of scurvy. The remaining members of the crew survived the winter by eating the large, slow-moving animals (giant relatives of the manatee) which were then abundant around the island. Steller named them Sea Cows because of their beefy taste. Once European settlers heard about its good taste, the Steller's Sea Cow soon afterwards was hunted to extinction.

Over the winter, Steller studied the fauna of Bering Island and later wrote "De Bestiis Marinis". The Steller's Sea Lion (the largest kind of sea lion), and Steller's Eider are also named for him.

Once spring came, the remaining crew constructed a new vessel from the wreck of the old, and sailed to the Kamchatka Peninsula. Steller was recalled to St. Petersburg, but caught a fever on the return journey and died in Siberia in 1746 at the age of 37.

<u>Hooded Merganser</u>

A Hooded Merganser pair made a resplendent sight as they swam together along the stream in Mercer Slough. The male had a large white extended fan-shaped head patch. The female had a striking tuft of feathers all over her head. I didn't know which of the pair was the more magnificent. The male was a combination of black, white and reddish brown. The head, neck, and back were black; the chest, breast, and belly were white; and the sides and flanks were tawny or reddish brown. The male's most distinguishing feature was his crest, which was fully erect, revealing a conspicuous white patch bordered by black. The female was dark, grayish brown with a gray neck, chest, sides, and flanks. She had an equally large crest, which was brown and tinged with cinnamon. Together, they made an absolutely stunning couple.

Fig 6-11 – Hooded Merganser pair.

Hooded Mergansers are often seen along rivers and in estuaries during the fall and winter. They prefer shallow waters and feed mostly on small fish, which they pursue in long, rapid underwater dives. In order to locate its prey by sight, the Hooded Merganser can change the refractive properties of its eyes to enhance its underwater vision. In addition, the nictating membrane (which is the third eyelid that some birds have) is very transparent and probably acts like a pair of goggles to protect the eye during swimming. [Ref 6-16]

Hooded Mergansers nest in holes in trees and compete heavily for nest sites with others of their own species as well as with different species such as Wood Ducks, Common Goldeneyes, and Common Mergansers. The eggs from two different species are often found in the same nest. Although a Hooded Merganser probably does not lay more than about 13 eggs, up to 44 eggs were found in one Hooded Merganser's nest. These larger clutches resulted when more than one female laid eggs in the same nest [Ref 6-17]

Once the female begins to incubate the eggs, the male leaves the nest site and is gone for the remainder of the breeding season. Hatching in Hooded Mergansers is highly synchronized, with the eggs usually hatching within four hours of each other. The ducklings are precocial (covered in down, mobile, and able to feed themselves). They remain in the nest another 24 hours and then the female leaves the nest, calling for them to follow her to a nearby pond. The female alone cares for the ducklings. After 70 days they can fly, and the female leaves them and prepares for her fall migration. Hooded Mergansers have only one brood per season. If something happens to her nest before the male has left the area, the pair may breed again, but once the male has left, if something happens to her nest, the female has lost her chance to raise any young for that breeding season.

On Christmas Eve in 2002, it rained steadily and was very quiet at Mercer Slough about 2 pm. I saw a Great Blue Heron in the blueberry farm by one of the man-made creeks. I also saw Buffleheads in the slough. They were extremely skittish and flew further down the slough when they caught sight of me.

I also saw two tiny Ruby-crowned Kinglets. Their red crown wasn't apparent, but the white eye ring, tiny size, big head, white wing bars and olive coloring were unmistakable. The way the birds never sat still but constantly searched among the trees and bushes was typical of their constant flickering behavior. One of them came very close to me in its purposeful meandering, and stopped to look at me. This was a great thrill for me to see such a beautiful, tiny, wild thing stopping to look curiously at me.

Marsh Wren

I did not have a chance to visit the Mercer Slough again until May of 2003. At the end of May, I saw a Marsh Wren with its tail bent away back, a whitish streak above its eye, and a plain beige breast. It made constant "chip,chip,chip" or "click,click,click" noises, holding its tail in a bent position all the time.

Fig 6-12 – Marsh Wren. Courtesy of Pixabay.

Marsh Wrens are known for their loud, persistent gurgling song. The "song" can barely be described as such. Wilson (1832) evidently did not admire the vocal powers of the Marsh Wren, saying: "it would be mere burlesque to call them by the name of song" for "you hear a low crackling sound, something similar to that produced by air bubbles forcing their way through mud or boggy ground when trod upon." (Ref 6-18)

Dr. Charles W. Townsend (1905) wrote: "The song begins with a scrape like the tuning of a violin followed by a trill with bubbles, gurgles, and rattles, depending no doubt on the skill or mood of the performer, at times liquid and musical, at other times rattling and harsh, but always vigorous."

Only the male Marsh Wrens sing. They sing while clinging to the reeds or moving among them. Males learn their songs from adults and begin imitating songs at about 15 days of age. Song learning and imitation continues throughout their adult life. [Ref 6-19] *Unmated males sing continuously all day and often at night throughout the breeding season, and mated males only decrease singing if they help feed nestlings. The high rates of singing continue for mated males because they are trying to attract a second female, as Marsh Wrens are polygamous, with males having more than one mate.*

<u>Common Yellowthroat</u>

In several places in Mercer Slough, I heard the distinctive song of a bird repeatedly singing "witchitey-witchitey-witchety" very fast all together. I heard this bird song on various visits to Mercer Slough in May of 2003, but did not see, nor was I able to identify, the bird making this song.

On the first day of June, I was watching the Marsh Wren when two people with binoculars approached and asked me if I was seeing anything interesting. They turned out to be very knowledgeable bird-watchers –

especially the lady "Jan", a Master Birder who led outings with the Seattle Audubon Society. Jan invited me to join them. She was extremely adept at sighting and identifying birds sitting in the trees.

I tried to describe the song of the bird I had heard repeatedly singing "whitchitey-witchitey-witchety", but had not seen. Jan said the bird was probably a Common Yellowthroat. She "pished" several times and a bird flew down in the bushes several feet away. Jan whispered it was very near and when she pished quietly one more time, it appeared very close to us for a few seconds and then flew away. All three of us got a very good look at this male Common Yellowthroat. Jan said it was a neotropical migrant and bred in this area in the summer.

Fig 6-13 – Male Common Yellowthroats wear a black mask. Courtesy of Dr. Madeline Kalbach, USFWS.

The Common Yellowthroat is a warbler of wet thickets and is far more frequently heard than seen. It is a small songbird with a plain olive green back, wings and tail. It has a yellow throat and upper chest, a whitish belly, and yellow under tail coverts. The male has a distinctive black mask. The Common Yellowthroat is common in thick vegetation from wetlands to prairies to pine forests, and is frequently found near water.

<u>Black-headed Grosbeak</u>

In mid-June of 2003 I heard a bird singing a robin-like warbled song, but it was softer, sweeter, and less hurried than an American Robin's song. Later, I saw a Black-headed Grosbeak eating a caterpillar, and I realized this was the bird who had been singing the lazy robin-like song. As my viewpoint was looking up at it sitting in a tree, I could see it had a yellow spot and white on the belly.

The male Black-headed Grosbeak is slightly smaller than an American Robin. It has a pure orange breast, collar and rump with a black head. Its upperparts are black with white wing bars and wing patches. Its bill is very large and triangular-shaped. The Black-headed Grosbeak breeds in southwestern Canada and the western United States from the eastern foothills of the Rocky Mountains to the Pacific, migrating to Mexico in the winter. It is frequent in the Puget Sound area from mid-May to mid-September, inhabiting deciduous forests and thickets.

The Black-headed Grosbeak interbreeds somewhat with its eastern counterpart, the Rose-breasted Grosbeak, along their mutual boundary in the prairies of North America. This situation arose when the treeless prairies, which once formed a barrier between the two species, became dotted with towns and homesteads, providing suitable habitats for both species. The Black-headed Grosbeak is a rather still and secretive bird throughout the summer. Like the Rose-breasted Grosbeak, the males of the species, despite their bright colors, share incubation with the females. However, they are not conspicuously marked above; the brightest coloration is on the breast and belly, which is concealed as they incubate.

Their food is varied. Heavy seeds are easily cracked open with their huge beaks. However, their diet consists mostly of insects with lesser quantities of fruit. The Black-headed Grosbeak is one of the few birds able to eat Monarch butterflies, despite the noxious chemicals those insects contain from eating milkweeds in the larval stage. They eat

large numbers of Monarch butterflies in Mexico in winter. [Ref 6-20]
*Black-headed Grosbeaks also consume harmful insects and are highly
valuable to farmers.*

<u>Swainson's Thrush</u>

In the forested areas of Mercer Slough, I often heard a bird singing over and over, but could not locate it. Its song was a rising series of echoing flute-like notes which rose higher and higher and gradually faded away. I would stand in the path amongst the trees and listen to the song for a long time, wondering how something could make such a beautiful, haunting sound.

In June I had heard these birds constantly singing in the trees in Mercer Slough, but had not been able to see one close up. During the first week of July I finally saw one who was sitting singing on a branch above me, so I had a good look at its underside. It was a light gray-brown bird with a white belly and very light spots on its upper breast. Viewed from below with the sun shining down, its tail looked almost white. It was a Swainson's Thrush, which looks similar to the more cinnamon-brown colored Hermit Thrush and to the Veery, whose song is downward, instead of rising.

The Swainson's Thrush is a very shy, furtive ground living bird. It is heard much more often than seen. Certain places in Mercer Slough met this bird's preferred habitat of damp coniferous forest edges or willow thickets found along creeks and sloughs (called riparian thickets). The Swainson's Thrush sings on its nest, and I believe the birds I heard singing over and over were sitting on nests. I was never able to see one of their nests, although it sounded like they were singing close by the path.

Fig 6-14 – Swainson's Thrushes are great songsters. Courtesy of Dr. Madeline Kalbach, USFWS.

The Swainson's Thrush diet consists of a variety of insects, spiders, and berries. It breeds throughout the southern and middle reaches of the northern boreal forest from Newfoundland to eastern Alaska, as well as down the Rocky Mountains to Arizona and along the Pacific Coast to the Mexican border. It winters in central Mexico and South America. The female Swainson's Thrush builds the nest by herself over a period of about four days. They build their cup-shaped nests from two to 20 feet off the ground and the female incubates the eggs for 11 to 14 days.

<u>Blueberries</u>

At the end of July, the weather was hot and dry and the blueberries in the Overlake Blueberry Farm next to the Mercer Slough were starting to ripen. Some were still green while others were large and dark blue. Blueberry seeds had spread outside of the farm in numerous places and there were blueberry bushes growing in places within the Slough.

I had noticed several people carrying buckets walking down the path and wondered where they were going. Mercer Slough was normally wet and you would not want to step off the elevated boardwalk and walk across it. But by the end of July, the water had dried up and the ground was dry. I noticed several well-trodden paths leading from the boardwalk and conjectured these paths had been made by people going to blueberry patches outside of the private farm. Sure enough, when I stepped down about a foot from the boardwalk, the ground was firm beneath my feet. The path ended at a space where there were numerous blueberry bushes growing. Although I had no pail with me, the large ripe blueberries looked so tempting that I started picking them and eating them off the bush. They would not have been sprayed with insecticides, so they didn't need to be washed before eating them. The blueberries tasted so sweet and delicious with their firm dark blue skins. I heard several people talking close by as they picked the blueberries, but I couldn't see them, as the blueberry bushes were so dense. I must have eaten a good basketful of blueberries. I felt like a bear eating wild blueberries this way. On an adjoining bush to the one where I was picking, I noticed several finches sitting and watching me.

Although numerous birds were in the marsh, noticeably absent by the end of July were the songs of the Swainson's Thrushes and Marsh Wrens, so frequently and constantly heard in the spring and throughout most of July. I didn't know if these birds were still around and just keeping quiet, or if they had already departed for places further south.

Cedar Waxwing

The blueberries continued to ripen through mid-August. I watched a Cedar Waxwing pick a very large round ripe blueberry off one of the bushes and fly into another tree to eat it. It took about five minutes before it got it down its throat. The waxwing bobbled the large round blueberry around, almost dropped it, and then caught it again several times. It finally positioned it correctly, tipped its head back, opened its beak very wide, and got the blueberry down.

Cedar Waxwings specialize in eating fleshy fruits high in sugar content. They are highly social all year long and flocks wander widely in search of temporarily abundant sources of fruit. In the summer, they live in open woodlands, fruiting trees, orchards, and suburban gardens. In the winter they may be found in wooded or semi-open areas where berries are abundant. Cedar Waxwings tend to be nomadic, moving about irregularly depending on food supplies. Breeding and wintering areas can change from year to year.

Male and female Cedar Waxwings are similar in their appearance. Their plumage is beautiful and unusual. The Cedar Waxwing is a sleek, crested, buff brown bird with a narrow black mask that extends over the face to end behind each eye in a point. Its belly is pale yellow. The plumage of the Cedar Waxwing appears exceptionally fine, as if it is made of soft velvet. Added to this attractive plumage are two extra special features: a yellow band at the tip of the tail, and a small, red, wax-like appendage at the end of each secondary feather.

Fig 6-15 – Cedar Waxwing. Courtesy of Pixabay.

A. C. Bent says about the appearance and demeanor of the Cedar Waxwing: "When we become well acquainted with the waxwing we look upon him as the perfect gentleman of the bird world. There is in him a refinement of deportment and dress; his voice is gentle and subdued; he is quiet and dignified in manner, sociable, never quarrelsome, and into one of his habits, that of sharing food with his companions, we may read, without too much stress of imagination, the quality of politeness, almost unselfishness....His plumage is delicate on coloring – soft, quiet browns, grays, and pale yellow – set off, like a carnation in our buttonhole, by a touch of red on the wing." (Ref 6-21)

Cedar Waxwings wait to nest until the fruit is ripening, often in mid-summer. They only defend a small territory against intruders and birds may nest very near to each other, forming small colonies. A group of Cedar Waxwings will often pass food items back and forth to each other, while sitting perched closely together, until eventually one of them will eat it. This behavior is also part of the courtship display, when the male hops sideways towards the female, passing a piece of fruit to her; she hops away and then hops back towards him and passes it back to him. This can go on for some time.

Cedar Waxwings can store a large number of berries in their crop, and they then can regurgitate one at a time to feed to the nestlings. W. E. Shore of Toronto, wrote an amusing account of their delivery to A. C. Bent as follows: "Having set up a camera at a nest in an apple tree, I retired to the blind to wait and was surprised to find that within 15 minutes both parents were back in the tree, but apparently empty-mouthed. However, one bird hopped to the side of the nest, and the two well-feathered young shot their heads up and opened their bills, an action which I considered overly optimistic. But they apparently knew their business, for, as I watched through binoculars, the adult gave a slight jerk of his head, and to my surprise a ripe, unbroken cherry appeared in its bill. This was promptly dropped into the bill of a young one, and again the head jerked, and another cherry appeared. This happened seven times; then the bird flew off, and the mate came to the nest and went through the same performance. The whole thing so resembled a magician producing cards out of thin air with the time-honored twist of the wrist and jerk of the hand that I could almost hear the word 'Presto' emanating from the solemn-faced birds as they continued to produce cherry after cherry." (Ref 6-22)

The Cedar Waxwing is sometimes accused of eating so many berries at one time that it becomes 'drunk' and lolls about on the ground, unable to fly. The assumption is the berries have fermented and the effect is similar to having drunk too much wine. However, George H. Lowery, Jr., has a different explanation for the observed behavior: "Sometimes Cedar Waxwings eat so many berries at a time that digestion must be accomplished rapidly in order to make room for the continuous intake into the esophagus and stomach. Occasionally a bird is found prostrate on the ground, seemingly 'drunk' from having consumed too much berry juice. But I am inclined to think another explanation is more plausible. These stupefied birds always have their throats packed beyond capacity with berries or fruit, which surely must exert undue pressure on the adjacent blood vessels. The possibility exists that the pressure against the internal carotid artery, which carries blood to the brain, causes a temporary blackout until digestive action allows some of the food in the esophagus to move down into the stomach and thereby relieve the congestion." (Ref 6-23)

One final observation about the behavior of the Cedar Waxwing is its tameness. Albert W. Honywill, Jr. (1911) gave a striking instance of this trait in a wild bird he met in Minnesota: "On August 4, 1908, four young birds were found that were not quite able to fly. While arranging them to be photographed, one of the old birds came and fed them. The old bird appeared to be fearless, and fed the young

*ones blueberries and wild cherries while I held them enclosed in my
hands, and even tried to get to its young when I pushed it gently
aside.*" *(Ref 6-24)*

Chapter Seven – Burnaby Lake and Still Creek

FROM MARCH 2016 TO November 2017, I lived in Burnaby, a suburb of Vancouver, Canada. I began jogging/walking to Burnaby Lake.

Burnaby Lake is the focal geographic feature and namesake of Burnaby Lake Regional Park, which occupies 770 acres of land and is home to a large variety of wildlife. At least 70 species of birds make the lake and surrounding areas their home, and about 214 species of birds visit throughout the year. Burnaby Lake is a glacial lake formed about 12,000 years ago, at the end of the Pleistocene ice age.

The lake was named by Colonel Richard Moody after his private secretary, Robert Burnaby. (Ref 7-1) In March 1859 Colonel Moody began to survey the site of New Westminster as the capital city for the new Colony of British Columbia. He was particularly intrigued with the possibility that a fresh water lake existed north of the town. In a letter to Governor James Douglas, Moody wrote: "I now learn from the Indians that a lake does exist... Burnaby and Blake immediately volunteered their services to explore and also to trace the mouth to Burrard's Inlet and to report generally on the countryside north of the town. After a considerable reluctance on account of the weather, I have let them go with four days' provisions in light marching order, not even tents, two Indians, a Canadian Voyageur attached to Parson's survey party and my own trust Corporal Brown R.E. They have been away now three days in the most deplorable weather. The rain was in torrents all last night and it is streaming down still in tropical torrents – nothing would gladden my eyes more than to see them back."

Robert Burnaby and the rest of the party did return safely and the official hydrographic chart produced in 1860 featured two discoveries: Burnaby Lake and the Brunette River.

Still Creek, Eagle Creek, and Deer Lake flow into Burnaby Lake, while the lake empties into the Fraser River through the Brunette River. The lake is said to act as a settling pond for incoming pollutants from Still Creek, thereby protecting the outflowing Brunette River. Large amounts of sediment, peat moss, decomposing plants, and water lilies make the lake unsuitable for swimming. Because many storm sewers drain to the lake and the Brunette River, the Caribou Dam at Brunette River controls the rate of water outflow to prevent flooding downstream during times of heavy rain.

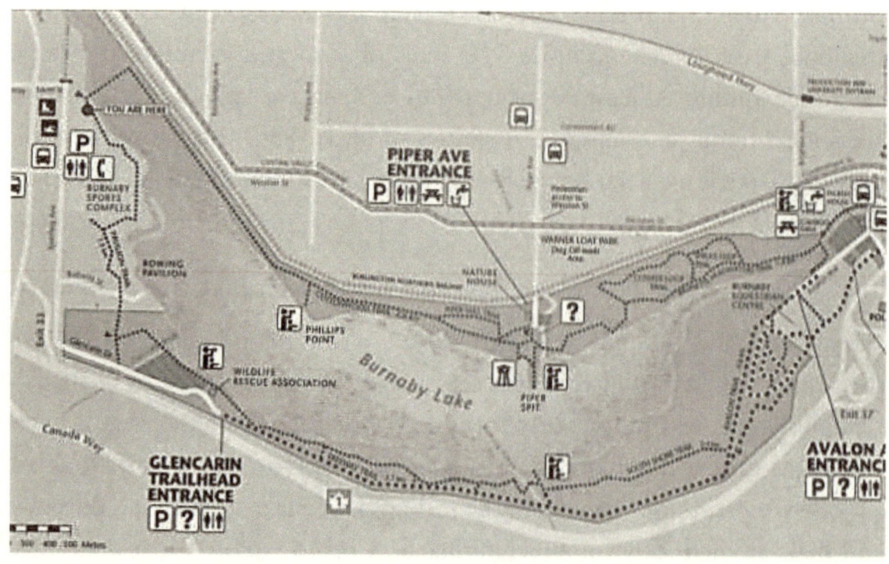

Fig 7-1 – Map showing the walking/jogging trails around Burnaby Lake.

Different birds use Burnaby Lake in different seasons for different reasons. Nesting and breeding birds use all the different habitat types found at Burnaby Lake during the summer. Over-wintering birds frequent the lake in the fall, winter, and spring. Some birds stop at the park during their migrations, and some birds are resident.

There is a trail loop around Burnaby Lake. The loop is approximately ten kilometers. On the north side of the lake, there is a place called Piper Spit, where many birds congregate.

Fig 7-2 – Piper Spit boardwalk jutting into Burnaby Lake.

On April 6, 2016 I went to Burnaby Lake in the morning. At Piper Spit, I saw many male and female Red-winged Blackbirds.

Fig 7-3 – Female and male Red-winged Blackbirds.

There were also many Green-winged Teal at Piper Spit. They are small ducks. The female Green-winged Teal has a lime green wing patch on her side. Both the male and female are beautifully colored.

Fig 7-4 – Green-winged Teal.

I counted 40 to 50 Long-billed Dowitchers at Piper Spit. Initially, they were all resting with their bills tucked into their scapulars, so I was unable to see their long bills. Then, I saw the long bill on one which did not have its bill tucked back. I asked a man who was watching the birds with a scope if he knew what kind of birds they were, and he answered they were Long-billed Dowitchers. He said he had never seen so many at Piper Spit, where he usually only saw a few.

Long-billed Dowitchers are medium-sized shorebirds with very long thin bills and long thin legs. They prefer fresh water at all seasons. They breed in the far north on wet, hummocky tundra. Even in coastal regions, migrants and wintering birds tend to occur on freshwater habitats. (Ref 7-2)

Fig 7-5 – Long-billed Dowitchers at Piper Spit.

<u>Sandhill Cranes</u>

I saw two Sandhill Cranes at Piper Spit.

Fig 7-6 – Sandhill Cranes beside boardwalk at Piper Spit in spring of 2016.

In June 2015 these Sandhill Cranes had had a baby, but it had not survived. George Clulow, a Past-President of the British Columbia Field Ornithologists, commented on the Sandhill Crane chick as follows: "A quick search of the literature shows that this new arrival is the first record ever of breeding Sandhill Cranes at Burnaby Lake, and anywhere else in Burnaby for that matter....Once the chicks leave the nest, both parents protect and feed the young....Sandhill Cranes are monogamous and tend to maintain pair bonds over many seasons, especially if they successfully breed together." (Ref 7-3)

Unhappily, the lovely Sandhill Crane chick did not survive for long. In an online forum for birdwatchers, there were unconfirmed reports of the chick's ailing health. The chick was not accepting food from its parents and was having trouble lifting its head. (Ref 7-4)

On 6 July 2015 George Clulow went to Burnaby Lake to confirm the reports of the chick's disappearance: "Sure enough, the two parents were there, occasionally bugling quietly, but no chick was in sight. Given the birds' extreme attentiveness to their young, the conclusion has to be that the youngster is dead. It was apparently showing some respiratory distress yesterday which got progressively worse during the day. The chick was nowhere to be seen this morning. A sad ending but there is hope for next year." (Ref 7-5)

Fig 7-7 – Sandhill Cranes with chick. Courtesy of Colin Clasen.

Fig 7-8 – Sandhill Crane and chick. Courtesy of George Clulow.

Fig 7-9 – Sandhill Crane chick preening. Courtesy of George Clulow.

Fig 7-10 – Sandhill Crane chick walking with parents. Courtesy of George Clulow.

Fig 7-11 – Sandhill Crane chick with parents. Courtesy of George Clulow.

On 28 August 2016 at Piper Spit, I saw a lone Sandhill Crane standing on the arm of the walkway which juts out. He seemed to be eating something in the cracks between the wood. When someone started to walk out towards him, he uttered a loud croaking and flew to the shore of the lake. He continued to utter this loud melancholy croaking and calling for twenty minutes. It was disturbing to see this solitary Sandhill Crane continuously loudly calling with no-one answering it. Was it calling for its mate? Eventually, it went back to the wooden boardwalk and resumed poking its long beak into the cracks between the boards.

The Sandhill Crane has a widespread breeding distribution in British Columbia. Sandhill Cranes are opportunistic foragers, feeding on both animal (primarily invertebrates) and plant foods. Typical breeding habitats include isolated bogs, marshes, swamps, meadows, and other secluded shallow freshwater wetlands surrounded by forest cover. Nesting wetlands are usually secluded, free from disturbance, and surrounded by forest. In coastal areas, brackish estuaries are used for rearing broods. Nests consist of large heaps of surrounding dominant vegetation, usually built in emergent vegetation or on raised hummocks over water. One of the most important habitat characteristics for Sandhill Cranes is an unobstructed view of surrounding areas and isolation from disturbance. Typical foraging habitat includes shallow wetlands, marshes, swamps, fens, bogs, ponds, meadows, estuarine marshes, intertidal areas, and dry upland areas such as grasslands and agricultural fields. (Ref 7-6)

On the morning of 6 May 2016, I went along the south shore of Burnaby Lake. Just before the Wildlife Rescue Association, there were nest boxes – some larger and some smaller. A male and a female Wood Duck sat on the top of one of the larger nest boxes, while two Tree Swallows sat on top of one of the smaller nest boxes.

Fig 7-12 – Two Tree Swallows checking out a smaller nest box along the south shore of Burnaby Lake.

Tree Swallow

Among North American species, only the Tree Swallow regularly eats berries. They eat many berries (especially bayberries), allowing them to survive wintry spells when other insect-eaters might starve. Tree Swallow habitat is open country near water, marshes, meadows, and lakes. The male Tree Swallow arrives on the nesting territory before the female. Courtship involves the male showing the female potential nesting sites. Tree Swallows migrate north relatively early in the spring. Southward migration begins as early as July and peaks in early fall. They migrate in flocks by day. (Ref 7-7)

I saw quite a few Mallard and Canada goose families in May and June of 2016. Then they all seemed to disappear from the areas where I had seen them. I was not sure where they all had gone.

Swainson's Thrush

In June 2016 I heard many Swainson's Thrushes singing from the branches of trees all along the trail loop around Burnaby Lake. Once in a while, I saw a Swainson's Thrush singing high up in a tree. Their songs are beautiful – so light, musical, and airy. They are described as flute-like. The end of the song trails up higher and higher, with the last part too high for the human ear to distinguish. Swainson's Thrushes are lovely birds – oyster white bellies with light brown spots high up, gray backs, and very long legs. I stood and watched one standing and singing high up on the bare branch of a tree. It sang over and over. From below, its legs looked very long.

Swainson's Thrushes are forest birds, rarely found far from closed-canopy forest. Their breeding habitat is a mix of deciduous and coniferous forest. They are shy, but vocal birds that skulk in the shadows of their generally dark forest-interior habitat. They forage for insects and arthropods on or near the ground. On migration, particularly in the fall, they also eat small red-colored fruits.

Swainson's Thrushes are more likely to be heard than seen. They sing frequently in the summer with upward-spiraling, flutelike songs. Their whirling song has a ventriloqual quality that makes is difficult to track. They also sometimes sing quiet songs that can create the illusion their song is coming from a more distant location. They call frequently during fall and spring migration, when their soft, bell-like overhead "peeps" may be mistaken for the calls of frogs.

On their wintering grounds in Central and northern South America, Swainson's Thrushes inhabit closed-canopy forest and can often be found attending army-ant swarms.

The Swainson's Thrush is a common species that has gradually declined across its range, experiencing a loss of about 38 percent between 1996 and 2014, according to the North American Breeding Bird Survey. Problems on its breeding grounds include grazing, development, human activity, and invasions of nonnative plants. During spring and fall migrations, significant numbers of Swainson's Thrushes die from collisions with windows, radio and cell-phone towers, and tall buildings. Studies of bird deaths at communication towers in Minnesota, Illinois, and West Virginia, revealed that Swainson's Thrushes were killed in greater numbers than any other bird species. (Ref 7-8)

Swainson's Thrushes breed through much of North America's boreal, western lower montane, and Pacific slope forests, and migrate long distances to their wintering grounds from southern Mexico to South America. There are six subspecies segregated into two groups, the "russet-backed" coastal, and the "olive-backed" interior group, which meet and hybridize along a contact zone in British Columbia's Coastal Mountains. These two groups use different migratory pathways to reach their separate wintering grounds along the Pacific Slope of Central America, and in northern South America, respectively. (Ref 7-9)

Some interesting studies have been done concerning Swainson's Thrushes in British Columbia (Ref 7-10) Forty birds from two distinct groups of Swainson's Thrushes – one in Pacific Spirit Park in Vancouver, and another near the interior city of Kamloops – were fitted with penny-sized geolocators. The state-of-the-art technology recorded light intensity data just about every day for a year, as the birds migrated as far south as South America over the winter and returned to British Columbia for the summer of 2011. That information allowed researchers to determine where the birds went and where they stopped along the way, confirming what was long suspected.

"These two groups are taking very different routes," said Kira Delmore, than a zoology PhD student at the University of British Columbia and lead author of the paper published in the Proceedings of the Royal Society of London B

The two groups took different routes to different wintering grounds. The Vancouver birds travelled down the coast to Mexico and Central America, and the Kamloops birds flew across the Rocky Mountains and down the central United States to South America. Previous research suggested the migration routes were genetically-determined, and the results gathered in 2011 raised the possibility that migratory behavior plays a role in the process by which one species becomes two.

Although songbirds travel solo at night, in each distinct group the birds stopped at the same sites along the way. "All of the individuals from each one of our populations are actually stopping at the same sites on migration. For example, all of the birds from Kamloops stopped in Alabama before crossing the Gulf of Mexico," Delmore said. That information will help with conservation. "We know that habitat availability is going down and now we know where the birds really need to stop and where they really need to spend time on migration, so we can focus our conservation efforts on those areas."

Fig 7-13 – A Swainson's Thrush wearing a geolocator. Photo courtesy of Kira Delmore.

"Given that migratory behavior is under genetic influence in many species of birds, these results raise the question of what hybrids between these two subspecies would do," said Darren Irwin, associate professor of Zoology at the University of British Columbia and co-author of the paper. "One possibility is that hybrids would take an intermediate route, leading to more difficulties during migration. It so, the migratory differences might be preventing the two forms from blending into one."

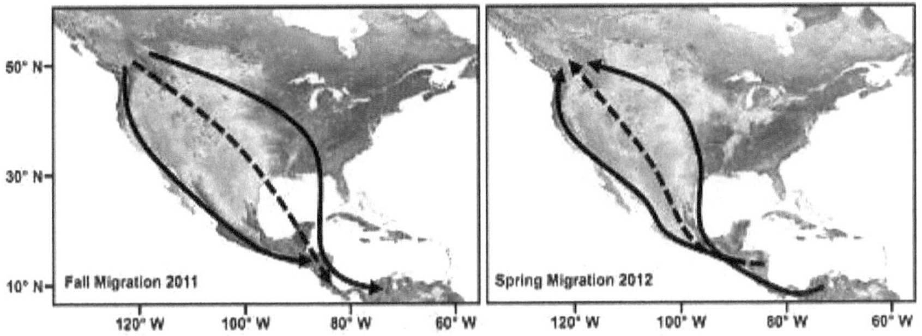

Fig 7-14 – Routes of parent sub-species solid black. Hybrid route indicated with dashed line, traversing areas with little insect life, vegetation, or water. Courtesy of Kira Delmore.

Indeed, a follow-up study [Ref 7-11] *showed that the mixed genes in hybrid birds drove them to select more difficult routes than their parent species. "Instead of taking well-trodden paths through fertile areas, these birds choose to scale mountains and cross deserts," said Delmore. Many of the hybrid thrushes chose intermediary migration routes situated between the paths of their parent populations, regardless of how challenging that route might be.*

In many cases, hybridization can cause separated populations to collapse into a single form. "In this case, where hybrids might well be surviving at lower rates, this may not happen," said Delmore. "The self-destructive behavior of hybrids could be helping to maintain the great diversity of songbirds we enjoy."

July 11, 2016 was overcast with a forecast for showers. I was the only person at Piper Spit. I discovered this was where all the ducks and Canada Geese were congregated at this time of year. I suspected they were molting as many feathers floated in the water by the boardwalk.

As I went through the woods on the trail around Burnaby Lake, I heard a variety of bird songs, including American Robin, Swainson's Thrush, Common Yellowthroat, Rufous-sided Towhee, and Northern Flicker. However, the birds all disappeared into the bush as soon as they saw me. At times I had seen many Tree Swallows flying around, but in mid-July, there were no Tree Swallows near the nest boxes.

<u>Rabbit</u>

On 16 August 2016 I went the full 10 kilometers around Burnaby Lake, taking the "Conifer/Spruce Trail", which diverges from the main trail on the north side of the lake. Not as many people take this path. There was a rabbit on the path. I stopped about 10 feet away and watched him. The rabbit hopped several times very quickly down the path and I saw that he had very long legs. Then he jumped several feet in the air, rolled on his back on the path, and righted himself. Did he have an itchy back? (I was bitten by mosquitoes several times as I stood on the path.)

Twice he bounded down the path straight towards me, stopped, and then bounded back. Was he trying to approach me? I was talking to him. Then he went to the side of the path, squatted down, and appeared to eat some vegetation.

Fig 7-15 – Rabbit on trail around Burnaby Lake.

<u>Black Bear</u>

Signs at the entrances to the trails around Burnaby Lake indicated there were bears in the area. At various places along the side of the path, the long grass was bent back and lying flat, as though something large had slept there. I often thought about and watched out for bears around Burnaby Lake, where the signs read "Caution – Bears in Area".

Fig 7-16 – Sign along Burnaby Lake trail.

On the morning of 5 August 2016 I drove to Burnaby Lake and did a slow jog/walk around the lake, starting on the south shore. On the straight road before Caribou Dam, I saw a man, carrying a full backpack, hiking far ahead of me. He looked like a serious hiker. He was walking at a medium pace, while I was walking quickly, and I gradually began to catch up with him. As I got closer, I knew he could hear my footsteps on the gravel, and at one stage, I dragged one of my feet, which made a shuffling noise. The man turned around to see who was "following" him. As I caught up to him and came side-by-side, he said in a friendly way: "I just wanted to make sure it wasn't a brown, furry thing behind me." I laughed, and said: "Well, at least it wasn't running after you." We walked together to the parking lot. He said he was going hiking on Burnaby Mountain that day as he wanted to get in some higher-elevation exertion.

I asked him if he had ever seen a bear on the paths around Burnaby Lake and he told me he had seen a bear on two occasions. Once he had seen a bear by the Wildlife Rescue Association building. He commented that when they cleaned the bird cages, there was often spilled seed, and the bears liked it there because there was something to eat.

I asked him if he had ever seen bear cubs in the area and he said the bear near the rescue building was a smaller black bear and was a yearling – the first year the bear had been on its own in the wild. I asked him what he had done when he saw the bear, and he answered "we just made some noise; the bear went into the bush; and we slowly went by".

On 30 June 2017 at 7:15 am I saw a black bear walking on a path near Burnaby Lake. The main walking path goes along Still Creek and then makes a right turn when it comes to a little stream. There are two small wooden bridges which cross this stream and lead to a lesser-used path parallel to the main path. I often took this lesser-used path, and had noticed a place where the long grass was bent flat as though something large had lain down there.

On this day I decided to take the lesser-used path on my way back and turned to go down it. I was walking, not jogging, and was listening to the birds. I took several steps down the path. There was something large and black walking slowly down the path towards me. The sun shone in my eyes, but I immediately thought: "Is this a bear?" I put up my hand to shade my eyes, and saw it was a fully-grown black bear. I stopped. The bear continued walking slowly down the path towards me.

I immediately turned around, retraced my steps down the path, and walked across the small bridge over the little stream. I was curious about what I had just seen, and wanted to make sure I wasn't imagining things. So once I had reached the main path, I stopped to see if I could catch sight of the bear from a relatively safe distance away.

Sure enough, I saw a full-grown all-black bear slowing walking straight down the path parallel to the main path. He looked well-fed and was more massive than me. He looked neither to the right nor the left, but kept looking straight ahead and slowly walking down the path. He did not see me watching him.

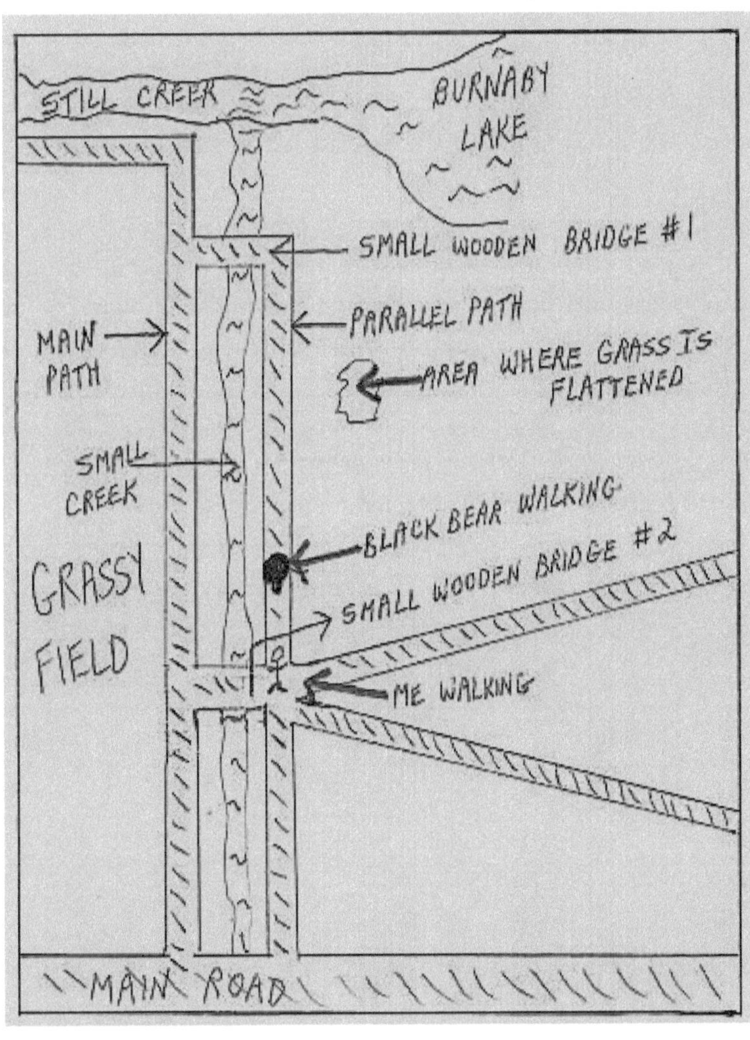

Fig 7-17 – Map of where black bear was walking on path at Burnaby Lake.

I wondered: Where had he come from? Where was he going? What would he do when he reached the road? Would he go off into the woods somewhere? Did he know where he was going? Had he trod this path many times before? Was he exploring new territory or was this place familiar to him? He was a big bear and would need to eat a lot every day. What would he eat? Where would the bear go and what would he do?

I had passed only two joggers and one walker that day on the trails around Burnaby Lake, but the place was getting busier, with more people and cars arriving.

In Kenn Kaufman's *Field Guide to Nature of New England*, it says: "If you encounter a bear while hiking alone, the best advice is to back away slowly, but not to run." (Ref 7-12)

At the end of August 2016, I saw a flock of Black-capped Chickadees, and with them was at least one Bushtit. The Bushtit looked like a round ball of fluff and was tan beige colored. I saw a Bushtit nest by the bridge over Still Creek. This nest remained intact through numerous fall and winter storms.

Bushtit nests are built by both sexes and are firmly attached to twigs and branches. They are a tightly woven hanging pocket, up to a foot long. The small entrance hole near the top leads to a narrow passage that opens into the nest chamber. Both parents may sleep in the nest at night

Fig 7-18 – Bushtit nest hanging from a tree along path by footbridge over Still Creek.

On 5 December 2016 it snowed heavily in Vancouver. This was the first time it had snowed in Vancouver in almost three years. The snow did not melt throughout December, and more snow fell in late December and again in early February 2017. On 2 January 2017 I drove to Burnaby Lake, hoping to go on the trails there. A small vehicle had driven over the paths and flattened the snow, so although the trails were slippery in some places, I could still enjoy the nature at Burnaby Lake. The snow was pristinely white and made a pretty picture. I wondered about the wildlife and how they were doing in the snow and cold, when most of their food supply would be frozen and covered in snow.

Fig 7-19 – Bridge over Still Creek on January 2, 2017.

I saw numerous small birds sitting on the snowy path. They did not fly away into the bushes when they saw me, as they usually do, but instead continued searching for food in the snow. There was a holly bush beside the path with a few red berries still remaining on it. I tore off a small holly branch with one red berry on it and was planning to take it home with me. However, when I thought about the small birds I had seen along the path, I put the branch and berry back on the ground, as some bird might have wanted it.

Fig 7-20 – Song Sparrow by side of trail at Burnaby Lake after heavy snowfall.

Fig 7-21 – Sparrows at Piper Spit after heavy snowfall.

Fig 7-22 – Spotted Towhee by side of trail at Burnaby Lake after heavy snowfall.

Fig 7-23 – Song Sparrow and Spotted Towhee by side of trail at Burnaby Lake after heavy snowfall.

Much of Burnaby Lake was frozen over and the ducks and Canada Geese were congregated where there was open water. Water was still flowing in many parts of Still Creek, and I saw several male and female Buffleheads swimming along in the creek. At Piper Spit there were numerous Mallards, Green-winged Teal, and Wood Ducks, as well as Canada Geese. Some of the Mallards climbed out of the open water onto the edge of the ice, and sat or walked on the ice.

Cold ice doesn't bother the feet of ducks, as they have mainly tendons, and very little muscle in their feet. The muscle that makes them move is further from the feet and is better insulated. Ducks also have a very clever circulation system, where warm blood going down to the feet goes closely past the cold blood coming back from the feet. This is called a counter-current heat exchange as heat is exchanged from the hot blood to the cold, meaning that the birds do not lose too much heat through their feet. There is also a suggestion that ducks make an anti-freeze compound in their feet called Ethylene Glycol, which stops the blood in their feet from freezing by lowering its freezing temperature.[Ref 7-13]

Fig 7-24 – Mallard walking on ice at Piper Spit.

At all seasons, the trails around Still Creek and Burnaby Lake were very beautiful and interesting places for a naturalist like myself.

Fig 7-25 – Trees along trail around Burnaby Lake.

Fig 7-26 – Trail around Burnaby Lake.

Fig 7-27 – Great Blue Heron at edge of Still Creek where it enters Burnaby Lake.

Fig 7-28 – Male Hooded Mergansers swimming in Still Creek.

Fig 7-29 – Trail around Burnaby Lake after heavy snowfall.

SECTION III – BIRD RESCUE

———

I ONCE HAD A SPARROW alight upon my shoulder for a moment, while I was hoeing in a village garden, and I felt I was more distinguished by that circumstance than I should have been by any epaulet I could have worn.

Henry David Thoreau

History repeats itself, but the special call of an art which has passed away is never reproduced. It is utterly gone out of the world as the song of a destroyed wild bird.

Joseph Conrad

═══════

Chapter Eight– Volunteering at WildCare

IN THE SPRING OF 2002, I volunteered at WildCare, a wildlife rehabilitation and nature education center in San Rafael, California, 13 miles north of San Francisco over the Golden Gate Bridge in Marin County. WildCare takes in rescued wild birds and animals that are injured, ill or unable to fend for themselves. They are a well-equipped wildlife hospital that cares for these birds and animals until they can be restored to the wild.

When someone brings an animal or bird, the intake person at WildCare records the date and problem on a numbered patient card. This card is updated daily and stays with the animal or bird as it moves from one stage of treatment and rehabilitation to another. The person who brought the animal or bird can check up on its condition by calling WildCare and giving the card number assigned to the patient.

Fig 8-1 – Sign at the entrance to WildCare in San Rafael.

Volunteers at WildCare have a minimum four-hour weekly shift. The spring and summer are known as "baby bird season" as many orphaned or injured nestlings and fledglings are admitted. I was a volunteer in the song bird room on Saturday afternoons from 1:00 to 5:00 pm. Volunteering was an interesting and educational experience.

WildCare has well-thought-out and communicated procedures, strict attention to disinfection, and knowledgeable and dedicated staff. When a bird first arrives in the song bird room, an examination is conducted, the bird's weight is recorded on its patient card, and an identification band is applied. Then the bird is placed in an appropriately-sized basket containing a perch, food, and water. Very young baby birds are placed in a heated incubator. Babies who are too young to feed themselves are fed using a syringe with a nutrient-rich mix called "mash". Baby birds are fed every 45 minutes from sun-up to sun-down. There are four shifts in the bird room in the spring and summer: 7:00 to 9:00 am, 9:00 am to 1:00 pm, 1:00 to 5:00 pm, and 5:00 to 9:00 pm.

I learned how to set up cages for various sizes of birds, putting the correct seed, mealworms, fruit and water in small dishes and jar lids. I also discovered how difficult it is to catch a bird from inside a cage in order to weigh it or to give it medications. The easiest birds to feed were the baby birds not yet fledged, who opened their mouths wide whenever presented with food.

Fig 8-2 – Baby Junco gaping. Photo by Alison Hermance of WildCare.

Fig 8-3 – Baby Goldfinch. Photo by Alison Hermance of WildCare.

Fig 8-4 - Baby Robins. Photo by Alison Hermance of WildCare

One memorable experience occurred on March 9, 2002, when a beautiful Varied Thrush with a diagnosis of Caught By Cat (CBC) was brought into the bird room. It had no damage to the feathers on its head, but more of the feathers and skin on its back were missing than remained. Eric, the technician on duty, cleaned its bare back and sides, put on a type of clear tape to prevent moisture from escaping, and gave it an antibiotic. The bird was very acquiescent and was probably in shock. I prepared a cage for it and when I left after my shift ended, the Varied Thrush was resting in the cage. Very few birds caught by cats or dogs survive, due to germs that enter their bodies through the open bites. I worried about this beautiful bird all week.

The following Sunday, the Varied Thrush wasn't in the bird room, and when I looked in WildCare's log, it said it had expired on March 12. When I inquired about the thrush, I was told a schoolboy had taken a picture of it, and the boy was going to make a presentation to his school class on how awful it is to let cats roam wild. Although this was one positive result, I still felt so sad for what had happened to this beautiful bird.

Fig 8-5 - Varied Thrush. From Pixabay.

The Varied Thrush is somewhat similar to the American Robin in shape and demeanor, but is orange-breasted with a dark breast band, orange eye stripe, and orange wing bars. The Varied Thrush is most common in the dense wet hemlock, fir, and spruce forests of the Pacific Coast, from southern Alaska to California. In the winter, it may migrate to lowlands or fly south to California parks, habitats it shares with robins. Varied Thrushes forage on the ground in dense thickets by flicking aside leaves and debris to expose insects, earthworms, and other small invertebrates as well as seeds, fruit, and acorns. The Varied Thrush has a moderate conservation importance rating because of its relatively small total range and its association with coniferous forests of the Pacific Northwest, a declining habitat due to the cutting of northwestern forests.

On April 20, the incubator in the bird room was crowded. Five baby finches were in their original nest, which was round and durably constructed of very small twigs. The mother had hit a window and broken her neck, so the nest and babies had been brought in together. The nest had a ring of poop all around the rim where the babies had turned around, but couldn't quite make it outside the nest.

Four Western Scrub-Jays, who were partially feathered and had long legs and large, beautiful eyes, were also in the incubator. The Scrub-Jays had not all been brought in at the same time, so were not all from the same family. Two of them were in a "nest" (a round bowl with Kleenex lining and several Kleenex folded up and made into a circular "donut"). A third one was getting in and out of the nest, and a fourth one preferred lying on the floor of the incubator beside the nest.

A few weeks later, I had an opportunity to feed some of the Scrub-Jays. Using tweezers, I picked up a mealworm from the dish in the cage and tried to encourage them to recognize this as food and to eat it. One Western Scrub-Jay in particular watched what I was doing, but it would not eat the worm. If I dropped it, the Jay carefully picked it up and returned it to the feeding dish. Scrub-Jays often serve as "helpers" at the nest, and I wondered if its behavior was related to this activity and it was trying to be helpful. The technicians generally discouraged spending too much time with the young birds or talking to them, but sometimes it was difficult for me not to do this, as it was so enjoyable for me to spend time with the birds.

Fig 8-6 - Western Scrub-Jay. Courtesy of Gary Kramer, USFWS.

The californica or coastal subspecies of Scrub-Jay is darker blue than the interior subspecies. Behavior differs greatly between interior and coastal populations. (Ref 8-1) Coastal population Western Scrub-Jays are confiding, tame, and easily seen. Interior populations are more secretive and often are seen darting from bush to bush or are simply heard giving their harsh calls. Pairs of all North American subspecies hold territories year-round. The californica group is spreading northward in the Northwest.

In late April a tiny, fledgling Golden-crowned Sparrow was in the bird room. It was a master at finding places to hide. It hid behind the feeding dishes in the cage. When I lifted the netting off a corner at the top of the basket to refill the food and water dishes, it always escaped. It flew well and hid behind things - in cracks under the door of the bird room, and behind the stacked cages in a corner. However, I or one of the other volunteers eventually managed to locate and catch it with a net to put it back into the basket.

Fig 8-7 - White-crowned Sparrow at top looking down at Golden-crowned Sparrow.

I was not as good as some of the other volunteers at holding on to small birds in order to weigh them or to give them medications. Although I enjoyed volunteering at WildCare and they said they enjoyed having me, I won a recognition award that year for "Volunteer who was most likely to let birds out of their cages while feeding them or giving them meds".

I took a couple of baby bird seasons off from volunteering at WildCare, and when I returned in the spring of 2005, I changed my four-hour weekly shift from Saturday afternoons to Sunday mornings from 9:00 am to 1:00 pm. The technician on duty was named Vincent, and my shift supervisor was Darla Deme, an extremely kind, capable, and personable lady.

On May 1, 2005, the bird room was busy. All four incubators were full. In one hot incubator there were some "preemies" - very tiny babies who slept all the time except when they opened their mouths wide and gaped for food. Two Western Scrub-Jays were in a second incubator. One of the Scrub-Jays lay down in a corner behind the nest and opened its mouth when you held the mash-filled syringe up to it. The other Scrub-Jay looked much larger, but this may have been because it was under stress and was fluffed out. This Jay sat in the nest with its eyes open, refused to open its mouth, and had to be force-fed. It looked highly skeptical about its situation. Two Scrub-Jays were in a third incubator with a note on it saying these birds were not doing well, the cause of their illness was unknown, and not to put any other birds in with them. Two Starlings in a fourth incubator looked very scrawny, but one was hyper-active, standing up tall and watching everything that was going on.

Several baskets of Scrub-Jays in groups of two were on tables in the bird room. There was also a basket with a large Steller's Jay. A note on the basket said the Steller's Jay was very traumatized.

Fig 8-8 – Steller's Jay. Courtesy of Lee Karney, USFWS.

On the other side of the table, was a basket with four finches. Two of them were very young with wide, yellow lips, while the other two were older. They all had bird bands and the green-banded finch escaped twice from the basket when a corner of the netting over the top was lifted in order to feed the birds. Another volunteer and I caught it again using nets.

I did a lot of bird feeding, using various-sized plungers depending on the size of the bird's mouth. All the birds were fed bird mash. Separate dishes of water, bird seed, fruit salad, and worms were in the cages of the older birds. Few of the birds seemed to eat from the dishes.

Someone brought in a baby California Towhee. It had some rufous coloring on its underside and feathers stood up on its head. It had to be weighed. First, I measured the weight of the container without the bird in it. Then after resetting the weighing machine to zero, I gently placed the baby bird in the container and found the weight of the container plus the bird. Then after subtracting the weight of the container from the total, I could find out how many grams the bird weighed. I recorded this weight on a small card that would stay with the bird as it was moved from the incubator to a basket or cage. The bird would be periodically reweighed and its new weight recorded on the card. In this way, the gain or loss in weight was monitored.

It wasn't appropriate to put this little California Towhee into the incubators with the Scrub-Jays or the Starlings. The temperature in the incubator with the preemies was too high for the baby Towhee. Darla and I moved the two Scrub-Jays out of their incubator and into a basket with a warming pad underneath.

The California Towhee wouldn't stop cheeping. Once in the incubator, it stood up out of the improvised "nest" and kept cheeping. It was probably calling for its mother. Even when a towel was put over the incubator and it couldn't see outside, it still continued to cheep.

I was tired after my four-hour shift, but also felt I had done the best job I could.

When I volunteered the following Sunday on May 8, there were many birds in the bird room and I decided to stay later than my scheduled shift. There were five baskets of Scrub-Jays with two or three birds in each of them. The pair of Scrub-Jays that had been moved out of the incubator a week earlier were together in a basket and seemed to be doing well. They were sitting on a perch and the "nest" was no longer there. The one who had a lame left leg was sitting beside the one who had had the skeptical look on his face. The skeptical one looked less hostile now. The Scrub-Jays seemed somewhat interested in the food items of seed, worms, mash and bits of fruit in the basket.

A tiny Lesser Goldfinch was eating seed on its own. The Lesser Goldfinch was small indeed – only a few inches long.

A note on a basket with two Scrub-Jays said one of the Jays could not stand, and the other one was very traumatized. I fed them a couple of times during the morning. The one in the nest who could not stand looked very weak and it could not swallow the mash. When it spread out its wings, I could see the shafts where the feathers weren't fully developed. It also was not going to the bathroom. The note on the basket said to change the Kleenex in the nest when it became soiled, but both times when I came to feed it, there was nothing to clean up. I told Darla, the shift supervisor, that there was something seriously wrong with the bird. She immediately put it in a bowl of warm water and stimulated it to go to the bathroom. Then, wrapping it in a small towel, she put it in the incubator to dry off, and gave it some water as she thought it might be dehydrated.

When she took the Scrub-Jay out of the incubator 50 minutes later and brought it to the table, she seemed to know it wasn't going to make it. Its eyes were closed and its head hung down. Another volunteer pointed out it had a lot of bruising on its upper legs and body. I had noticed that its feet were all curled up. Darla looked up the bird's sheet, which said it had been caught by a cat (CBC), had fractures and pain in both legs, and probably had lung punctures. It expired on Sunday, May 8 at 3:00 pm. The other volunteer, Darla, and I were almost in tears. We just were not able to do enough to help this poor bird.

On July 17, 2007, I volunteered at WildCare from 8:30 am to 1:00 pm. I cleaned and put fresh food and water in large bird cages with numerous birds. Seven finches, three sparrows, three Western Scrub-Jays and a Steller's Jay were all in the same cage. I saw the Steller's Jay begging for food and being fed by a Scrub-Jay. The three sparrows were young and still had yellow around their mouths. There was a branch with leaves on it in the back of the cage and the three of them sat together on this branch hiding behind the leaf cover. Two of them escaped from the cage when I cleaned it. They flew to the windowsill, looking out at the real trees.

Someone brought in a bird which had been "hit by a car". Its head kept turning right around to one side. Someone in the bird room identified it as a grosbeak. It was orange, so it was a Black-headed Grosbeak, a bird that breeds in the western half of the United States and winters in Mexico. It was a beautiful bird – very orange, with a touch of yellow at the sides, and a black head. It was quite large – slightly smaller than a robin. I got a basket ready for it and put in a dish of water. Darla said to put some stones in the dish, so the bird wouldn't put its head in the dish and drown. We also made a donut from a towel. However, the bird was trying to walk around and kept tumbling on its side and back as its head was so turned around.

Before I left that day, I went to see the Black-headed Grosbeak. I removed the towel covering the basket and tried to keep the bird still with one hand, while applying pressure against its head to keep its head pointing straight. I could feel the pressure against my hand as it tried to turn its head to the side again. After about five minutes, the bird seemed tired and content to be in the donut with its head supported against the towel, so I covered up the basket with a towel again.

Fig 8-9 - Black-headed Grosbeak. Courtesy of Dave Menke, USFWS.

During the day, one of the Scrub-Jays had picked up a feather and stuck it outside the cage. I had picked it up and put it in my pocket. Victor, the technician on duty, was going to show me some examples of feathers showing stress bars or stress lines. Before I left for the day, I showed the feather to Victor and he said yes, this was an example of a feather showing stress bars. Stress bars are white lines running across the shaft of the feather, usually caused by malnutrition when the feathers are growing. A bird's feathers can be a great indicator as to its overall health. The growing of feathers requires a broad spectrum of nutrients and if how the bird is getting nutrients into its body is disrupted while the feathers are developing, feather stress bars are produced.

It was very busy in the bird room on August 7 from 8:30 am to 1:00 pm. Darla and I worked first in the room downstairs where birds needing medications are kept. She gave them medications (meds), while I cleaned cages and provided their food and water. The ledges on either side of the room were full of cages. On one side of the counter, two of the cages held six finches each; one cage held six sparrows; one cage had a Scrub-Jay; and several small cages contained a single bird. On the other side of the counter, were five small cages with a single pigeon in each one; plus a very large cage with two Scrub-Jays and a Steller's Jay. At the end of the counter a lone cage contained a single Scrub-Jay who had pox behind one eye.

The Scrub-Jays in the large cage had been there for a long time and were scheduled to go to the outdoor aviaries. The Steller's Jay was the same one who had been begging for food from a Scrub-Jay many weeks ago. That particular Scrub-Jay was out in the aviaries already. However, the Steller's Jay was doing very well on its own now. It liked to take a bath in the large round clear plastic dish.

Several cages of young birds who needed to be fed every 45 minutes were in the main bird room. A California Towhee stood up loudly calling for its mother. Darla said towhees are difficult to raise and that Francoise, a baby bird rehabilitator, would take the Towhee home that afternoon to raise it in foster care.

Two Scrub-Jays were in a cage in the main bird room. One of them was very tame. As soon as I opened the cage door to change its food, it came out and sat on top of the cage door. Although it was no longer getting hand-fed, it took my finger in its mouth a couple of times. I gave it a blueberry, but instead of eating the berry, it hopped to a perch with it, held it with a foot, and pecked at it. I was not worried about its escaping out of the cage. Once it did fly out, and then just sat there, looking uncomfortable, almost as though it didn't like to be out of its area and didn't know what to do. The second Scrub-Jay had been following it around copying everything it did a week ago, but this week the second Scrub-Jay kept to himself. Once I noticed the two briefly fighting.

I weighed all the finches and sparrows who were on a two-hour feeding schedule. The little birds get weighed every couple of days to make sure they are continuing to gain weight, until they are released out to the aviaries, and then eventually back into the wild. Victor said if all their weights were either up or stable, to change the sign to say "Feed every 3 hours".

It was fun weighing the little finches and sparrows and was easier than I had expected. They were incredibly light and soft to hold. It was so enjoyable for me to be able to hold these tiny creatures who only weigh about 20 grams. There is a correct way to hold them and you have to use just the right amount of pressure – enough so they can't wriggle away, but not so much as to hurt them. I had to "stuff" their little wings and heads into the box and make sure their toes were inside and not clinging to the rim. On one sparrow, I accidently closed the lid quickly when I thought it was all inside the box and I closed it on its head. I let out a yell, opened the lid and gently pushed its head back into the box. It didn't look any the worse for it.

The little fledglings were in large cages with five or six birds in each cage. They all had bands on their legs. The bands were different colors with numbers on them. When I weighed them, I matched the band color and number up with the number on their card and then recorded the weight and date, and initialed it. Sometimes two birds in the same cage were wearing the same color of band and it was hard to tell whom I had already weighed. A couple of times I caught the same bird twice and then put it back. When this happened, I noticed the bird had a hurt expression on its face as though it were saying "You already weighed me! Don't you know I had my turn already?" I had a lot of excitement and fun with the little birds that day.

On August 13, I volunteered at WildCare on a Saturday from 9:00 am to 12:30 pm, and again from 1:00 to 3:30 pm. Francoise, an expert in caring for birds, was in the bird room in the afternoon and she managed to have all the cages re-arranged and cleaned in about 30 minutes – I have no idea how she did it!

Victor demonstrated how to band a sparrow. He used a "palette" to spread the band apart. Then he exposed the leg and laid it on the palette. Then he withdrew the palette, squeezing the band shut.

I prepared a cage for a female Western Tanager – very yellow all over, but no red on the head. Western Tanagers summer in British Columbia and the northern and western states, and usually winter in the tropics. This bird was on migration. Victor told me it had hit a window. He said it had no head trauma, but sometimes the force can push water into the lungs. I put dishes of worms, fruit, and water in the basket, as well as a branch. Tanagers are mostly insectivorous and they also eat some fruit and many berries. We had peaches and grapes in the bird room that day. I then covered the basket with a thin towel. When I peeked into the basket a few times, the Western Tanager was sitting on the branch resting, with its big, black eyes open. It didn't move and it hadn't touched the food.

Fig 8-10 – Western Tanager. Photo by James "Newt" Purdue / USFWS Volunteer / USFWS. Taken at Red Rock Lakes National Wildlife Refuge.

On October 2, 2005 there were two Fox Sparrows at WildCare. They were dark, sooty brown with inverted Vs on the breast. One had been caught by a cat (CBC) and was missing a tail. The other had hit a window and was very quiet. There was also a Hermit Thrush, who was smaller than a Robin and about the same size as the Fox Sparrows, except thinner. The Hermit Thrush had long, skinny legs.

Two Western Scrub-Jays, ten Pigeons, a Fox Sparrow, and a Hermit Thrush were in one of the outdoor aviaries. The Hermit Thrush warily approached closer and closer as I stood still in the aviary. It eventually came up to a dish of worms at my feet and ate one. The Hermit Thrush was a beautiful bird. It had a cream belly with spots and a large, inquisitive, intelligent eye. It constantly flicked its wings.

Fig 8-11 – Hermit Thrush. Courtesy of Julia Butler Hansen, USFWS.

On Sunday, November 6, 2005 from 8:30 am to 12:30 pm, there were many birds in the med room downstairs, including three or four Hermit Thrushes, a Golden-crowned Sparrow, a female Black-headed Grosbeak, a finch with a bad eye, several Pigeons, and a Northern Flicker. The Northern Flicker was in a wooden box. Many of the smaller birds got .03 - .05 cc Clavamox, and the finch got a drop of Cipro in its eye. I gave the birds their medications this time.

A Golden-crowned Sparrow had died during the night. I found it dead in its basket when I went to give it meds. It had been at WildCare for several days. When I asked Darla why it would have died, she looked up its sheet and found it had been caught by a cat, stepped on by a dog, and probably had some serious internal injuries. Its weight when it first came in had been 32 grams. It had steadily lost weight and when Darla weighed it, it was only 18 grams. Its breast keel stuck out prominently.

A gorgeous Townsend's Warbler that had been caught by a cat was brought in. One of its wings seemed to be drooping and the bird bent forward instead of standing straight. Victor examined it and couldn't find anything wrong with its wings. Victor said sometimes birds have been through a lot in the wild and they are very weak and dehydrated by the time they arrive at WildCare, so I put some water in a syringe and gave it drops of water. It did get a little water down, but then just moved its head quickly back and forth to shake the water off. I tried giving it some worms but it just bit the end of the wriggling worm. I covered the incubator and left it alone. Victor phoned one of the song bird foster care people to come to pick it up.

I volunteered Sunday morning from 8:30 am to 12:30 pm on New Year's Day in 2006. WildCare is open every day, just like a hospital. At the end of December, 2005, several major storm systems with high winds and heavy rain had hit the Bay Area over a period of ten days. Victor said there had been two inches of water in the lower bird room the day before. When I arrived, there was no flooding, but later on during the morning, the high tide came in and the water in the creek was over the top of the pedestrian bridge outside the front door of the building. The water was a foot deep, too deep to cross over without wearing boots. Fortunately, there was a way out at the back of the lot behind the building.

There weren't many birds in the bird room at WildCare at that time of year, but in another ward, I saw two phalaropes. Red-necked Phalaropes are small, 8-inch-long, delicate shorebirds. They are normally pelagic, or at sea, in the winter. They nest in the high Arctic. In *Lives of North American Birds*, Kenn Kaufman says about the Red-necked Phalarope: "Despite their small size and delicate shape, they seem perfectly at home on the open ocean."

(Ref 8-2) These birds may have been blown in to shore by the high winds. When I questioned Darla about how they could be returned to their natural environment, she said there were always boats going out to the Farallon Islands, or whale-watching excursion boats could take them.

On August 6, 2006 many finches and sparrows were at WildCare. Three sparrows in one cage had found a hole in the netting, and sat up there to get fed. Three smaller sparrows in another cage would not be syringe-fed and kept wanting to escape. Once out of the cage, they were hard to catch as they found hiding places and hunkered down. One hid for over an hour. I looked everywhere for him. Then suddenly he flew up from somewhere and Victor caught him.

An Anna's Hummingbird had an injured wing that was supported with a splint. It held this wing straight out and wasn't able to fly. It drank from a tube and you could see its throat move as it drank. It had a very long, thin beak and its tongue went outside this beak when it drank. Darla said hummingbird nectar is 1/3 sugar to 2/3 water boiled for 20 minutes.

There was a lone Scrub-Jay in a cage and a note said to feed it with tweezers every two hours. It was a friendly bird and came over to greet me. I gave it sunflower seed kernels and pieces of corn from a corn on the cob. I tried to give it worms and pieces of cherry, but it didn't like these. Then it started stashing things at the back of the cage. One time it flew outside of the cage. It was so easy to pick up and didn't try to fly away. I hoped it would do well on its own in the wild.

In February 2007 I paid a return visit to WildCare after an absence of many months. In the outdoor courtyard, where birds that cannot be released to the wild are housed, there was an enclosure with a Spotted Owl. Darla said WildCare had received quite a few of these owls. As their old growth habitat further north was being destroyed, they moved south in search of territory. I hadn't thought a Spotted Owl would be as big as this bird, but they are 17 ½". This bird had been raised after being orphaned. It was quite a tame bird and was not considered releasable. It was strictly nocturnal. It looked appealing, sitting on its perch, with one eye half open.

Victor informed me that between November 1, 2006 and January 31, 2007, 68 Varied Thrushes had been admitted to WildCare. This number was more of one species than they usually saw of all bird species at that time of year.

The usual migration pattern of Varied Thrushes is known as eruptive migration and occurs in an approximately two-year cycle. According to naturalist Rich Stallcup of the Point Reyes Bird Observatory (PRBO), this year had probably been the largest known Varied Thrush migration in birding history. An abundance of food in their northern breeding range in the Yukon and Alaska had supported a population explosion. When the fall migration began, the birds had encountered a failure in the berry crops in Washington and Oregon, and they were forced to continue south to California.

National Geographic's *Field Guide to the Birds of North America* says about the Varied Thrush: "Numbers vary from year to year in the southern part of its mapped winter range" [Ref 8-3], consisting of Oregon and most of California.

Breeding in the Yukon and Alaska, Varied Thrushes are probably not as watchful of people, cats, and cars. Usually feeding on the ground, they are very susceptible to being caught by a cat. Victor said the thrushes brought in to WildCare had either been caught by a cat, hit by a car, or ran into a window.

Varied Thrush #3077 was brought to WildCare on January 20, 2007. This individual had been caught by a cat, and had significant bruising and infected wounds. It was hydrated and put on a course of antibiotics, but its wounds were too severe, and it was euthanized on January 31, 2007. The overall survival rate for Varied Thrushes brought to WildCare is about 40 percent. WildCare is able to save about 80 percent of those who are strong enough to begin treatment. Treatment includes the use of steroids, antibiotics, pain medications, sutures and fracture stabilization. Many have suffered feather loss that can jeopardize their ability to make the return migration. [Ref 8-4]

I was at the front desk at WildCare checking out six Varied Thrushes and Hermit Thrushes that were going to be released into the wild, when a lady brought in a gorgeous Golden-crowned Sparrow. She said she had rescued it from the mouth of a cat and it was hopping around on the ground but couldn't fly. Its left wing was completely fractured at the "wrist" and the bone was protruding. Victor said there was nothing he could do and he would have to euthanize it.

Very caring people work and volunteer at WildCare. Working in the baby bird room was a memorable experience for me. I loved working with all the birds up so close. Although it was sometimes hard physical work and emotionally demanding, it was also interesting and rewarding. On every shift I learned something new. I think a large part of the reason I liked being there so much is because I really liked the birds. Also, I came to admire many of the people I met at WildCare – people like Darla and Vincent—who were very kind and knowledgeable, and who had a lot of common sense when it came to helping wild creatures who were orphaned, injured, or sick.

People who love birds sometimes become involved in bird rescue and rehabilitation. This has been the case going back in history. Indeed, several well-known women ornithologists of the nineteenth century found themselves occupied in this activity. In particular, Amelia Lasky and Cordelia Stanwood wrote detailed, extensive notes about their avian rescue and rehabilitation activities.

AMELIA LASKEY (1885-1973)

Amelia Laskey published an astonishing 153 papers in ornithological journals. She applied to the United States Fish and Wildlife Service for a banding permit, and from 1931 to 1934 she banded 3,734 birds of 69 species [Ref 8-5]. She began at least three long-range bird life history studies on the Bluebird, the Tufted Titmouse, and the Cardinal, and also conducted a 30-year study of Mockingbirds.

Up until 1936 her bird study was done in her backyard and nearby area, but in 1936, she expanded her Bluebird study into the 2,000-acre Warner Park. This became her outdoor laboratory where she began erecting large numbers of Bluebird nesting boxes. At the height of her study she had close to 100 boxes and kept meticulous records of each box. Between the birds she looked after inside, and her outside bird studies, she was kept very busy.

Amelia's work in bird banding, nest watching and bird rehabilitation led to many important discoveries. One evening while observing birds migrating against a full moon, she observed that birds were crashing into an airport ceilometer light. She began watching for bird casualties at those lights and at television towers and kept this up over a period of 20 years. Her pioneering work led to the establishment of many new early and late fall migration dates, as well as an awareness of just how many birds were being killed by man-made structures during fall migration. (Ref 8-6)

Amelia amassed a large amount of data on the birds she observed and continued writing up this data for prestigious journals in the 1950's and early 1960's. By spending so many hours watching and banding species, she discovered previously unknown information about their habits and lives. At her death in 1973, she had left undone the final summarizing of her immense data on Bluebirds. However, to Amelia, "the most enjoyable part of a study is gathering the material first hand – the joy of watching the birds and trying to understand them." (Ref 8-7)

Amelia Laskey's bird banding station became an avian infirmary when local people began bringing her injured and young birds. She was not able to help the sick birds, but the stunned ones recovered quickly after a rest. Those with broken bones she put in a large flying cage with food and water, and they too recovered even though she did not use splints or tapes. "Nature's way of healing is far superior to my inexperienced surgery", she maintained. Interestingly, she had remarkable success in getting other species of nesting birds to adopt orphaned nestlings. Robins took in a Cardinal, and Cardinals looked after Mockingbirds, Bluebirds, and Robins. Amelia also raised many nestlings and fledglings herself. (Ref 8-8)

CORDELIA STANWOOD (1865-1958)

Cordelia Stanwood was an early naturalist and ornithologist who also became involved in bird rescue and rehabilitation activities. She raised a variety of young birds in her home. This kind of work took a great deal of time, as she commented on while describing her care of a Hermit Thrush nestling. She cleaned up after it, carried water to it, and fed it every 45 minutes from four in the morning until seven at night. She gathered fresh food, such as ants' eggs, earthworms, grasshoppers, strawberries, and mulberries. (Ref 8-9)

Cordelia Stanwood worked as a teacher for 17 years, but then became disillusioned with the work. After several years of discontent, she found her real calling and became a self-taught ornithologist in middle age.

In 1906 she began her remarkable field notebooks that were to chronicle the following 50 years of her outdoor work. In these notebooks, she not only recorded her observations, but also her feelings, at least towards nature and the natural world. Listening to purple finches "put me in a frame of mind that was almost ecstatic". It is apparent that her study of birds not only saved her mind but also her natural affections. She would sit beside a Hermit Thrush's nest and talk to it. She called a Black-throated Green Warbler mother a "delightful thing", telling her "I never did see anything half so beautiful as you, your nest, and your eggs." (Ref 8-10)

The high mortality among bird eggs, fledglings, and immature birds is reflected in Cordelia Stanwood's life study of the Hermit Thrush. She commented that, as is true with other ground-nesting birds, a comparatively small percentage of young reach maturity. Out of 14 nests containing a total of 47 eggs, only 19 fledglings left the nest. Others were subsequently lost after leaving the nest before they were able to fly well enough to perch well above the ground out of the reach of terrestrial enemies. [Ref 8-11] *Unfortunately, this high mortality rate can be applied to other species of birds.*

Cordelia's intense affection for the birds did not detract from her recordings of the minutest observations of bird behavior. Indeed, her personal attachment to birds seemed to yield better ornithological results than those of more emotionally-removed observers. Cordelia became a freelance writer. For over 40 years her work appeared in both scholarly and popular publications. A. C. Bent quoted her liberally, giving her full credit. Bent also used her unique photographs, which were another attempt on Cordelia's part to record the lives of the birds she loved. Cordelia would sit in blinds for hours to get pictures, putting up with mosquitoes and black flies.

Cordelia raised what she thought was a pet Crow whom she called Beppo. It was actually a Raven, but Cordelia never realized this, as ravens did not normally frequent the area where she lived at that time. Cordelia found it in the summer of 1918, took many photographs of it and wrote in her notebook about its very clever and sometimes annoying pranks, such as snatching clean clothes from the neighbors' clothesline. In May, 1919, Beppo disappeared. Days later, Cordelia found its body in the barn. Someone had shot it.

Cordelia Stanwood's incredible efforts in writing, observing, and photographing natural events were not sufficient to support her financially. In her experience "scientific bird work is intensely interesting, but unless one has a salaried position, it is not remunerative, while writing, unless one is talented, would never keep the scribbler out of the work house." [Ref 8-12] *However, in spite of her impoverished status, she kept writing in her field notebooks, while she sat outside on her campstool absorbing the sunshine and watching the panorama of nature around her, right up until the age of 87.*

Although she had been pitied by many people who did not really know her, Cordelia Stanwood had lived a life far richer and more useful than many women of her day could have imagined. In her unpublished book "Fir and Feathers", she wrote "One can never tell what delightful surprise is in store for him the moment he loses himself in the big out-of-doors....Interest and attention are keys that unlock new worlds to us."

Birdsacre or the Stanwood Wildlife Sanctuary, a 130-acre nature preserve and wildlife rehabilitation center near Ellsworth, Maine, is named for Cornelia Stanwood.

Chapter Nine – Oil Spill in San Francisco Bay

BECAUSE I HAD PREVIOUSLY volunteered at WildCare, I was eligible to take training offered in California on the protocols of caring for oiled wildlife. WildCare is one of the many California statewide collectives of trained wildlife care providers, regulatory agencies, academic institutions, and wildlife organizations that are part of the Oiled Wildlife Care Network (OWCN).

Following the devastating *Exxon Valdez* oil spill in 1989, California established the California Department of Fish and Wildlife's Office of Spill Prevention and Response (OSPR) in 1990. Subsequent California legislation in the 1990's resulted in the development of the OWCN, which was established in 1994. The OWCN is administered by the School of Veterinary Medicine at the University of California at Davis.

The OWCN is recognized as a world leader in oil spill response, rescue, rehabilitation, and research. Because quick and effective action is essential to saving lives during an oil spill, the OWCN is kept in a constant state of readiness for oiled wildlife events. During non-spill time, the facility in Cordelia, California is used by International Bird Rescue, a crucial participant in the OWCN, as an international training center for oil spill response and for non-oil related marine bird rehabilitation.

Once activated by the Department of Fish and Game, the OWCN rapidly mobilizes to rescue oiled wildlife during spills. Live animals are taken to specialized facilities and treated for several days prior to cleaning. Once cleaned, animals are cared for until they return to their normal condition, and then they are released back into the wild.

Education, and outreach to the public and scientific communities, are a vital piece of the OWCN's activities. As a recognized world leader in oiled wildlife response, the OWCN has helped develop national and international standards for oiled bird and mammal care. Staff members regularly consult with and educate responders from around the world.

In October 2006, I participated in OWCN's two-day Basic Skills Course held at the San Francisco Bay Oiled Wildlife Care & Education Center in Cordelia, about 30 miles east of San Francisco. This Center is a full-time bird rehabilitation center run by International Bird Rescue (IBR) - formerly called International Bird Rescue and Research Center (IBRRC) - in partnership with the California Department of Fish and Wildlife's OSPR and the OWCN. International Bird Rescue also runs a full-time bird rehabilitation center in San Pedro in southern California, and an as-needed oiled wildlife response facility in Anchorage, Alaska.

The Center is a 12,000 square foot facility. It is designed to accommodate 1,000 birds indoors during a large oil spill in the San Francisco Bay area and includes specialized areas for bird intake, holding, washing, drying, isolation and recovery, as well as for food preparation, radiography/surgery, and necropsy.

I never thought I would have to put the training I received in October 2006 into practice so soon, for an oil spill in San Francisco Bay.

On November 7, 2007, the *Cosco Busan*, a cargo ship travelling in heavy fog from the Port of Oakland to the Pacific Ocean, rammed into one of the piers of the Bay Bridge which links Oakland to San Francisco over San Francisco Bay. The impact ripped a hole in the side of the ship and 53,569 gallons of Intermediate Bunker Fuel Oil spilled into San Francisco Bay.

The bunker fuel spill was extremely toxic to marine life, and especially to the birds that floated and fed through the spill. The oil coated the feathers that kept the birds warm, causing the birds to get cold in the chilly Bay water. They spent most of their time trying to preen the oil out of their feathers, thus ingesting the oil. Weakened, the birds often beached themselves, where they would fall prey to predators, or die of poisoning from the ingested oil. When they got out of the water, they stopped feeding, even though they needed a constant supply of food to maintain their high metabolisms.

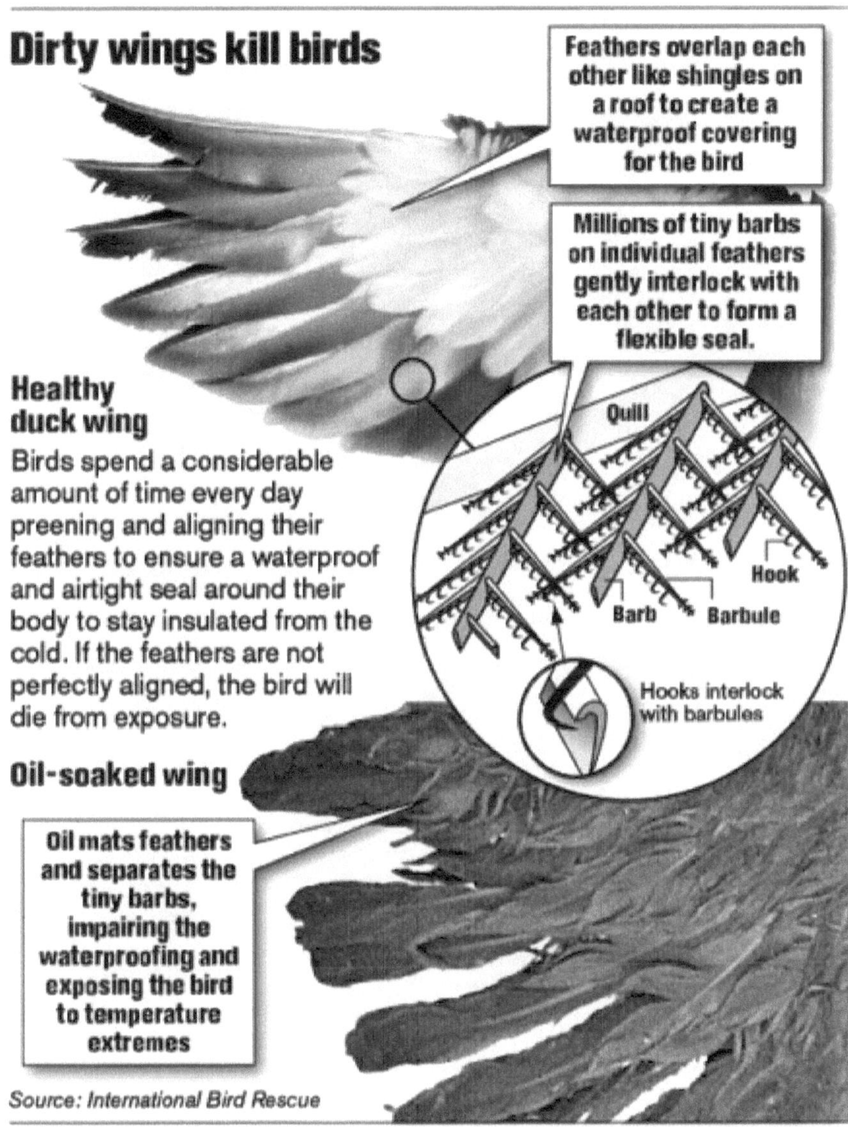

Fig 9-1 – Effect of oil on birds' feathers. Source: International Bird Rescue. Courtesy of John Blanchard, *San Francisco Chronicle*.

The oil was carried by the tide and currents to most of the areas around the Bay. Some of it was carried out under the Golden Gate Bridge, where currents spread it northward onto the beaches of Marin county and out to the Farallon Islands.

Fig 9-2 – *Cosco Busan* Oil Spill. Courtesy of California Department of Fish and Wildlife. Retrieved from *https://wildlife.ca.gov/OSPR/NRDA/cosco-busan*

The timing of the *Cosco Busan* oil spill in early November was especially disastrous for the migrating birds like Surf Scoters, Western Grebes, and other birds who fed in and spent their winters in and around San Francisco Bay. Many of these migrating birds had just arrived. When they arrived, they were at the lowest weight of their life cycle because they had just migrated from breeding areas thousands of miles away in the northern boreal forests of Canada and Alaska. They migrated to the Bay Area, where they expected to find a safe place to spend the winter with plenty of available food. Many Surf Scoters were caught in the oil. Around 80,000 of these diving ducks had arrived in the Bay Area by November. The Surf Scoter was the species most affected by the *Cosco Busan* oil spill.

Scoters are one of the most numerous waterfowl species wintering in San Francisco Bay, and San Francisco Bay scoters comprised an average of 39 percent of all those overwintering along the North American lower Pacific Flyway during the years 1988 to 2009. Long-lived waterfowl species with low reproductive potential such as scoters are particularly sensitive to changes in adult survival and may have the most difficulty recovering from oil spills. Additionally, many sea ducks show high winter site fidelity and pair on wintering areas. Thus, factors that affect survival rates in San Francisco Bay could have disproportionate effects on local subpopulations.

Beaches along the northern coast of San Francisco, including Aquatic Park, Crissy Field, and Baker Beach were closed due to the oil. Thousands of people, including fishermen, wildlife rehabilitators, nature lovers and volunteers, as well as government agencies, tried to clean up the mess along the shoreline.

Fig 9-3 - Oil boom along San Francisco's northern waterfront. Courtesy of U.S. Department of Commerce, National Oceanic and Atmospheric Administration, Damage Assessment, Remediation, and Restoration Program. *https://darrp.noaa.gov/oil-spills/remembering-cosco-busan-overview-2007-oil-spill*

On November 7, 2007, the day of the spill, I left the office where I worked in downtown San Francisco at 5:00 pm. I could smell the oil in the air. On Friday, November 9, the front-page headline of the *San Francisco Chronicle* read: "Heartbreaking!" and showed a Surf Scoter covered in oil. I had to try to do something. Because I had received training in oiled wildlife care, I was able to volunteer at International Bird Rescue.

Driving along Interstate 80 from San Francisco to Cordelia, I could smell the toxic oil in the air. Once at the International Bird Rescue center, I became part of the tremendous organization required to attempt to treat and release birds that were oiled. I volunteered at different times in the intake, pre-wash, and wash-and-rinse areas. I saw oiled Surf Scoters, Western Grebes, Horned Grebes, Eared Grebes, Greater Scaup, Common Murres, and Common Loons. Most of the Surf Scoters and Western Grebes were coated in oil from head to toe. It was distressing to see such heavily-oil-soaked birds.

I spent four days during the period from November 10 to 17 doing my small part in helping to care for and clean oiled birds brought to the International Bird Rescue facility in Cordelia. I worked from 7:30 am to 5:30 pm on November 10; from 8:00 am to 5:00 pm on November 11; from 8:00 am to 4:30 pm on November 15; and from 8:00 am to 4:00 pm on November 17.

Fig 9-4 - Oiled Eared Grebe resting on rock by Bob Dang. California Department of Fish and Wildlife, Office of Spill Prevention and Response, Natural Resource Damage Assessment.

,https://wildlife.ca.gov/OSPR/NRDA/cosco-busan

Fig 9-5 - Oiled Eared Grebe moving across water by Bob Dang. California Department of Fish and Wildlife, Office of Spill Prevention and Response, Natural Resource Damage Assessment.

,https://wildlife.ca.gov/OSPR/NRDA/cosco-busan

Fig 9-6 – Oiled Surf Scoter and oiled grebe. California Department of Fish and Wildlife, Office of Spill Prevention and Response, Natural Resource Damage Assessment.

,https://wildlife.ca.gov/OSPR/NRDA/cosco-busan

Fig 9-7 - Oiled Surf Scoter. *http://blog.bird-rescue.org/index.php/2007/11/2007-cosco-busan-san-francisco/*

The oiled birds who were lucky enough to be rescued went through a well-planned and well-coordinated process. They were rescued from boats using nets, or picked up off beaches. They were initially stabilized and given toxiban to help neutralize the toxic effects from the oil they had ingested. They were sent in handling cartons to the washing center in Cordelia. Here each bird underwent intake, where it was examined and documented, and blood and feather samples were taken. Its picture was taken as evidence for future litigation.

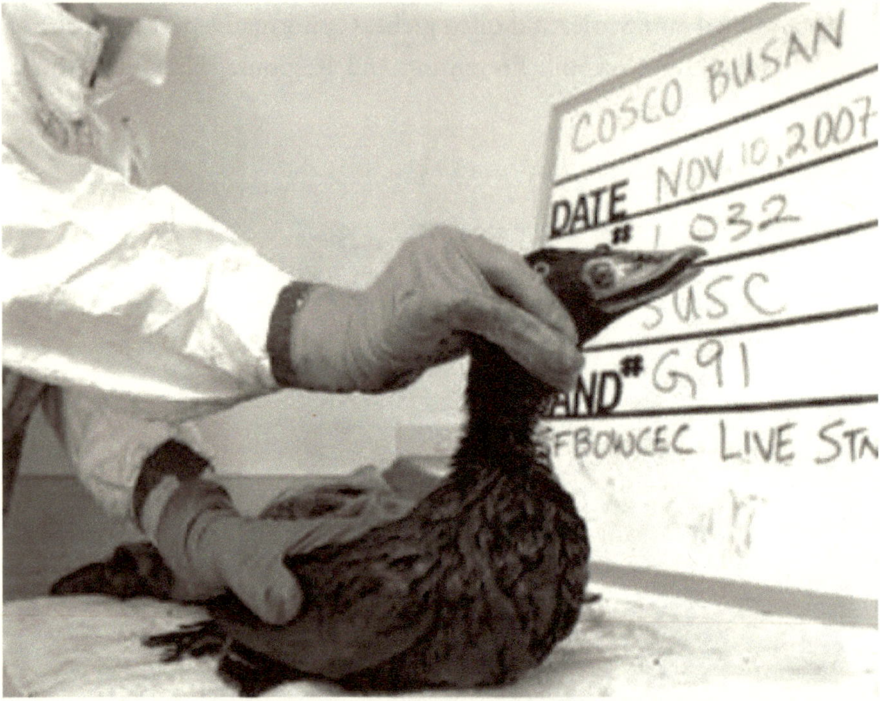

Fig 9-8 – Whiteboard holds rescue data for a photographic record of one of the Surf Scoters caught in the *Cosco Busan* oil spill. Courtesy of Dave Jones in *University News*, University of California at Davis.

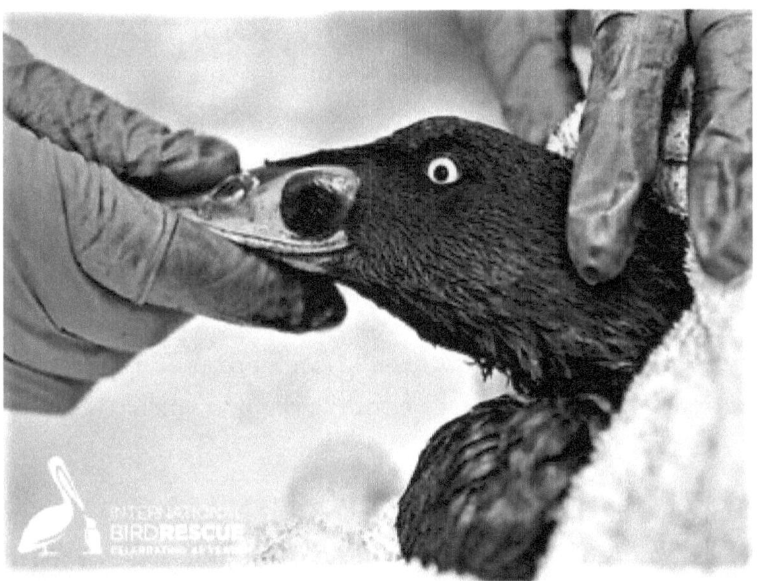

Fig 9-9 - A rescued oiled Surf Scoter from *Cosco Busan* spill is examined at the San Francisco Bay Center. Courtesy of International Bird Rescue. *http://blog.bird-rescue.org/wp-content/   uploads/2007/11/ oiled_scoter_exam_Cosco_Busan_2007.jpg*[1]

From the intake area, birds were moved to the "Hot Zone", an immense room which was kept hot, as the oiled aquatic birds had no means of insulation and could die from hypothermia. In the "Hot Zone" they were kept in pens, with often ten birds to a pen.

The huge room at the Cordelia facility was filled with about 40 pens. Ten heavily oiled Surf Scoters huddled together in some of the pens, while other pens held ten Western Grebes, or a single loon. The pens had netting bottom cage inserts to allow discharges to fall to the floor, and to prevent side effects when birds who were built to live in the water had to sit on a hard surface. The first day of my arrival at the San Francisco Bay Oiled Wildlife Care and Education Center, I helped to hose down the floor underneath all the pens. The contaminated water flushed into a drain inset in the center of the room.

---

1. *http://blog.bird-rescue.org/wp-content/%20uploads/2007/11/oiled_scoter_exam_Cosco_Busan_2007.jpg*

The people at the Center were dressed from neck to ankle in white Tyvek suits for protection from the toxic effects of the oil. Sheeting was placed over the top of the pens so the birds would be as little terrorized as possible by the sight of what they perceived as human predators. In order to build up the birds' stamina so that they could survive the washing process, they were alternately force-fed pediolyte, Ensure, and mash, by tubes connected to syringes of pediolyte or food. Volunteers worked in teams, with one person wrapping a towel around a bird and holding it, while the other person inserted the tube down the bird's throat, being careful to avoid the opening to the trachea or windpipe. Depending on the species' normal diet, the birds were also offered fish to eat.

Oiled birds remained in this stabilization area for several days in order to get the much-needed nutrition, hydration and medical treatment they needed to regain their strength before being subjected to the washing process. The oiled birds suffered from hypothermia. Many hadn't eaten in days and they were dehydrated and exhausted by the time they were captured. They needed to be stabilized before attempting cleaning.

Because cleaning was a stressful and life-threatening event for the bird, the goal was to wash each oiled bird only once, and it was crucial that the bird was healthy enough to handle the washing ordeal. The criteria used for sending a bird to wash and rinse were: it must be properly stabilized; it must have received appropriate medical treatments; it must be of sufficient weight; it must have good blood values including minimum values of packed cell volume and total protein; and it must be bright, alert and responsive.

A definite hierarchy was in place at the Oiled Wildlife Care and Education Center. This was necessary in order to prevent chaos. Everyone did the job they were asked to do. At one point, I asked a supervisor if one of the Surf Scoters could be washed as soon as possible because it was so heavily oiled. The tired person in charge responded that they were all heavily oiled.

For several days, I acted as the volunteer holding the oiled bird while it was being tube-fed. One afternoon, I and my co-volunteer heard a loon's wail coming from one of the pens. We both stopped what we were doing for a minute and froze. The sound was so wild and sad. The loon was probably wailing to let its mate know where it was.

During my second-last day of volunteering, I was responsible for locating birds whose recent blood work indicated they were strong enough to undergo washing. I was standing at the central counter in the "Hot Zone" room, feeling overwhelmed, when another volunteer approached me and asked if she could help. She said she was most interested in the oiled Common Murres as she worked with these birds on the Farallon Islands. We teamed up and began checking the temporary bands on each bird in a pen, comparing the band number to that on the list of birds whose blood work was good enough to send it for washing. We went from pen to pen, with the other volunteer picking up a bird and reading the number on its temporary leg band. Each bird we picked up had a number not on the list of those birds approved to go to the washing area. We both were feeling disappointed and frustrated as we were unable to locate any of the birds whose blood results indicated they were strong enough to be washed.

While we were checking the birds' readiness to get washed, I had noticed an unassuming man who was standing on the sidelines and watching everything going on in the room. This man appeared calm, cool and collected, and there was an aura about him. Only later did I become aware that this was Jay Holcomb, the Executive Director of International Bird Rescue, and the man most responsible for developing the protocols for treating oiled birds

On the following day, the wash room opened up and birds were getting washed. Once stable, an oiled bird went through a series of tub washes with a low concentration of Dawn dishwashing liquid. Large birds, such as loons, were washed by only the most experienced staff at International Bird Rescue. Volunteers with some experience handling wild birds could wash and rinse birds such as Surf Scoters and Western Grebes.

The washing area was very hot and humid with water everywhere. People involved in washing and rinsing wore rubber boots and plastic aprons. Badly oil-soaked birds were pretreated with a substance to help make the oil easier to wash off. A toothbrush was used to clean around the head, and the bird's head was kept out of the water at all times. Once the water in one tub became dark, the bird was moved to a new tub with clean water. The time to wash and rinse a bird varied depending on the size of the bird and the amount of oil on it. The average wash and rinse time was about 45 minutes.

Specially trained volunteers wash birds at the Oiled Wildlife Care facility in Cordelia following the Cosco Busan oil incident in November 2007. Photo credit: CA Fish & Game / D. Hamilton.

Fig 9-10.

Specially trained volunteers clean birds during Cosco Busan oil response in 2007. Great care must be taken to prevent further injury like bird dislocation and broken wings. Photo credit: CA Fish & Game / D. Hamilton.

Fig 9-11.

Birds were not washed at night. In the early years at International Bird Rescue (IBR), they washed birds all night long, until data analysis showed a marked increase in mortality of the birds washed after dark. IBR had found the birds' stress increased when their circadian rhythm was upset, just as with humans. Birds also needed plenty of rest, and leaving them alone to sleep at night reduced mortality.

Dawn blue-colored dishwashing liquid had been the choice degreaser of oiled wildlife since the late 1970s. Repeated research had shown that Dawn was the best because it removed oil without damaging a bird's plumage, irritating its skin, or posing additional health problems to the people involved in rehabilitation efforts. Additionally, Dawn was widely available. The discovery of the use of Dawn was the first major breakthrough in providing care to oiled injured wildlife. Proctor and Gamble now generously donates all of the Dawn detergent used by International Bird Rescue and other rehabilitation organizations throughout the world.

After washing, the birds were taken to a separate rinsing area where a special nozzle was used to completely rinse the solution from the feathers. Volunteers worked in teams of two, with one person holding the bird and controlling its bill if the bird had a sharp beak, while the second person rinsed off all traces of detergent. The rinsing process was just as important as the washing process because any detergent or solution left on the feathers could impair the natural waterproofing process. Specially-designed spa nozzles were used that propelled the water at sufficient pressure to remove all traces of detergent from the bird's feathers. [Ref 9-1]

On my last day of volunteering at International Bird Rescue, I was fortunate to work in the wash-and-rinse room. My reward for working at IBR was to hold a beautiful female Surf Scoter who was cleaned of oil. Her feathers were now soft and silky. After she was completely rinsed, I kissed her on the back of the neck. She smelled so clean. This was such a contrast from having picked up Surf Scoters who were covered in oil and who reeked of the toxic substance. I will never forget the feeling I had of how beautiful she was. I hoped she had a good life after she was returned to the wild.

After the wash and rinse process, the cleaned bird was placed in a protective net-bottomed pen equipped with commercial pet grooming dryers. As the bird rested comfortably, it began to preen its feathers back into place. The complete realignment of feathers in a tight overlapping pattern was necessary to create a natural waterproofed seal. After washing, each feather needed to be aligned properly so water could not seep through to the body. Each feather was made up of microscopic barbs and barbules that hooked together like "Velcro". Once hooked together, they became a tight waterproof barrier. Each properly aligned feather overlapped another, like shingles on a roof, creating a temperature-controlled barrier. Birds aligned their feathers by preening (combing their feathers) during which they distributed natural oils throughout the plumage. These natural oil secretions helped in the long-term maintenance of feathers by keeping them supple so alignment could be maintained.

In the drying area, the birds were tube-fed a nutritious food mixture to assure proper nourishment. They were given plenty of fluids and vitamins, and were allowed free access to food. When the birds were completely dry, they were placed in an outdoor warm water therapy pool where they continued to preen and bathe. They could rest on a ledge elevated above the water. They were closely monitored for their floating and swimming ability, general alertness, and progress towards waterproofing. They were re-dried and returned to the warm pool repeatedly until their waterproofing improved sufficiently that they could go into the cold-water pool.

In the outdoor diving pools, the birds were in their normal water-based environment and could continue to feed, preen, and behave normally. Once they were completely stable and healthy and their waterproofing was determined to be flawless, they were ready for release to the wild. An aquatic bird needed to be perfectly waterproof prior to release or it would not survive in the wild. Before release, the birds were banded with a stainless-steel US Fish and Wildlife Service leg band. This allowed for future identification and aided International Bird Rescue in its research.

Finally, once the cleaned birds were once again thoroughly waterproofed, they were taken in boxes and released far enough away so they would be unlikely to make it back to oil-spoiled sites until most of the surface oil had been cleaned up. Most of these birds would have been either on migration south or over-wintering on the Bay. Most were set free either to the north of San Francisco Bay in Tomales Bay in Marin, or to the south of Half Moon Bay, regions with the least chance of contamination. (Ref 9-2)

As a volunteer, I participated in almost all the activities at the International Bird Rescue center in Cordelia, from intake, stabilization, and matching blood work, to rinsing, and seeing cleaned birds. I can't explain in words how terrible I felt about seeing ten heavily-oiled Surf Scoters huddled together in a pen, reeking of oil, and scared to death. I also can't express how relieved I was to rinse off a bird who had just been washed, and to see its beautiful clean feathers reappear, with the down fluffing up on its breast.

As of November 27, 2007, only 215 of the birds that had been washed at International Bird Rescue had been released back to the wild. The official statistics for the *Cosco Busan* oil spill were 2,940 birds from over 50 species were collected alive and dead. Of the 1,084 birds collected alive, 421 were cleaned and released, while 653 died or were euthanized, giving a 40 percent release rate. Bird experts think that for every bird found dead or alive, about five to ten others go unreported because they sink at sea, get eaten by predators, or fly elsewhere to die. Oiled birds try to evade capture. Some oiled birds may be rescued and rehabilitated, but most probably suffer and die from hypothermia or from ingesting the toxic oil while attempting to preen their feathers. Wildlife biologists fear that more than 20,000 birds may have ultimately perished from the *Cosco Busan* disaster. They believe thousands of birds landed in the oily Bay and then left the area to die elsewhere.

Joe Eaton and Ron Sullivan are two avid birders who wrote the following in the *San Francisco Chronicle*: "For three days we had been bringing in birds without knowing whether they were still alive. We had seen armloads of foil-wrapped casualties being moved from one freezer to another. And we knew that the ducks, grebes, murres and loons that had made it to Cordelia alive were just the tip of the iceberg. For every bird rescued in a disaster like this, 10 to 100 die unseen. There's no adequate response to an environmental insult on this scale. But it's **our bay**, and **our birds**, and we – the research center crew; the beach patrollers; the drivers; the people who brought coffee, cake, pizza and sandwiches – do what we can." [Ref 9-3] [**the bolding is mine**]

This described how I felt about volunteering. San Francisco Bay was **my bay** and these were **my birds**, who had given me so many hours of pleasure simply by allowing me to watch them live their lives. I had to try to help them during this unspeakable unnatural disaster that was not of their doing. I volunteered because I felt I owed something to the beautiful creatures who gave me so much pleasure and whom I found so fascinating.

No-one will ever know how many migratory birds were killed as a result of this disastrous oil spill. Many of these species of birds were already in decline for unknown reasons related to their environments. The San Francisco Bay is a major migratory bird stopover and over-wintering spot. We have to better protect places like this and never take these valuable, pristine areas for granted. If we do not start taking seriously the negative impact we have on the natural environment, and looking for ways to minimize this impact, we risk continuing to lose more of these wondrous creatures who share the earth with us and whose lives are so amazing and fascinating. Once the point of no return occurs (and it is not clear exactly when this happens for a particular species), we will never again be able to see, enjoy and admire these beautiful creatures.

JAY BURCH HOLCOMB (1951-2014)

Current state-of-the-art protocols in the rescue and rehabilitation of oiled birds owe a great deal to Jay Burch Holcomb who is considered a giant in the field of bird rescue and rehabilitation. He helped to pioneer techniques to improve the survival rate of birds and animals rescued from oil spills, harmful algal blooms, and other marine disasters.

Jay was born in San Francisco in 1951 and moved to San Anselmo in Marin County when he was nine. For as long as he can remember, he was fascinated by wild animals and wanted to be of service to them. Wildlife rehabilitation did not exist in a formal way when he was young, but when he found orphaned, oiled, and injured wild animals, he did what he could to get them back into nature. He explained as follows: "As a kid of nine or ten, I just knew I was going to take care of wildlife. I'm a determined person. There were certain things I came into this world knowing. I like the innocence of animals, and the fact that they're straightforward. They're pure. You can have an honest relationship with them. I have a lot of respect for them, and I wanted to help them." (Ref 9-4)

After high school, Jay left the College of Marin and started working at the Marin Humane Society. There he discovered many wild animals that needed help, and he began rehabilitating them. His first experience with an oil spill was in January 1971 when two Standard Oil tankers collided under the Golden Gate Bridge and gushed 800,000 gallons of crude oil into San Francisco Bay. As Jay said: "There were lots of volunteers, but they had no expertise, no supervision. They picked up 7,000 live birds. Rooms were just packed with birds. And most of them just died. It was horrible." (Ref 9-5)

In 1978, Jay helped found the rehabilitation program at the Marin Wildlife Center, now called WildCare, where he worked until 1986, when he left to join the International Bird Rescue and Research Center (IBRRC) (now International Bird Rescue). Alice Berkner, the founder of IBRRC, said about Jay: "He had a tremendous amount of enthusiasm, and seemed to have a natural aptitude with animals as well as intelligence. Jay has got a terrific sense of humor. It's a valuable asset when you do crisis response." (Ref 9-6)

In 1989, Jay became the Director of International Bird Rescue (IBR). He had a reputation for working well with other people and agencies, and for making decisions on what's good for the birds and animals.

While IBR is based in California, they respond to oil spills all over the world. Their response team not only cares for the birds and animals, but also manages oiled wildlife rehabilitation efforts, including volunteer training and supervision, and media interaction. Jay and his staff teach local wildlife workers how to clean oiled birds, and also how to organize armies of volunteers, news media, and other crisis-related logistics. They often stay on site for months.

Jay's experience responding to oil spills, as well as his resourcefulness in devising methods to clean and rehabilitate birds, built IBR into one of the world's preeminent wildlife organizations. The group's team of wildlife specialists has led rescue efforts at more than 200 spills around the world. Jay's group crafted a volunteer-response and organization plan that is now standard among first responders. They have responded to large events such as the Exxon Valdez spill in 1989, spending six months in Alaska running three bird rehabilitation centers and two search-and-collection programs. The largest oiled wildlife rescue and rehabilitation effort ever mounted up to the year 2000 took place in South Africa when an iron ore ship, the Treasure, sank between the two largest breeding islands for African penguins. Over the ensuing week, 40,000 penguins were collected and half were oiled. IBR took a lead role in the management of the rescue team. Jay managed the rehabilitation facility that cared for 15,000 penguins. More than 90 percent of the penguins captured were eventually released back into the wild.

IBR has responded to oil spills in the United States, France, Norway, Spain, South Africa, Australia, Ecuador, Argentina, and New Zealand. Some of the most high-profile oiled wildlife response efforts include: the 2011 Rena spill in New Zealand; the 2010 Deepwater Horizon spill in the Gulf of Mexico; the 2007 Cosco Busan spill in San Francisco Bay; the 2002 Prestige spill in Galicia, Spain; the 1999 MB Erika spill in Brittany, France; and the 1989 Exxon Valdez spill in Prince William Sound, Alaska.

Jay mostly learned about wildlife care on the job. At an oil spill, he was invariably calm, focused, good-humored, and organized. His demeanor set the tone in situations that would otherwise be chaotic and overwhelming. He was always able to show people a better way. But at the same time, he was always learning. Every event was an opportunity to learn something new. (Ref 9-7) He believed the trickier part of IBR's mission was the logistics. Coordinating rescue efforts and training hordes of volunteers, with almost no advance warning, is endlessly challenging. He said: "You end up having this massive, out-of-control situation, and a lot of hysterical people, and your job is to say, 'OK, we can do this.'" (Ref 9-8)

After 40 years of quietly working to rescue thousands of oiled birds and animals around the world, in 2010 Mr. Holcomb became nationally known during the Deepwater Horizon oil spill, due to news coverage of bird rehabilitation efforts in the Gulf of Mexico. In 2011, IBR's efforts to save oiled birds during the spill were prominently featured in the Emmy Award-winning HBO documentary "Saving Pelican 895", which chronicled the step-by-step rehabilitation efforts of a single juvenile brown pelican. Jay was prominently featured in this documentary.

In 2010, Mr. Holcomb was named Oceana's Ocean Hero, and he also received the John Muir Conservationist of the Year award. He had previously received the 1996 National Wildlife Rehabilitators Association Lifetime Achievement Award.

Jay Halcomb passed away on June 10, 2014 of kidney cancer.

Early in 2012, Jay wrote the following: (Ref 9-9)

"Dear friends,

I was hard at work with the Deepwater Horizon oil spill in the Gulf of Mexico last summer when Oceana's Ocean Hero award was given to me, so I was not in the position to say much about it. I was really honored to receive it and I love what it stands for. Then in September 2010, I also received the John Muir Conservationist of the Year award. I realized that although these awards honored me, they were actually acknowledging the message of our work, recognizing animals and nature as important and worthy of our attention.

I am a wildlife rehabilitator; that's been my career and my life. All I have ever wanted to get across was the value, importance and beauty of animals, and to accept some accountability and responsibility for their welfare – especially when they are impacted by human activity. This desire was born out of watching and befriending animals as a kid, and by listening to disturbing things that people thought of them. Very early in my life, I became aware that I had a sense of purpose that I could not shake – nor did I want to – so I just lived as I was compelled to. At age five or so, I became aware of an intense desire to help animals but had no idea how to make it happen. I held that knowingness in my mind, knew it would happen, and basically allowed it to unfold in front of me. I spent the next 40 years or so working with companion animals and rehabilitating wild animals.

In a nutshell, that's how it happened for me. I want everyone to know these two awards are really a major win for wildlife rehabilitation and for the preservation of nature. I mean, I'm a coot, raccoon and gull (very common species) rehabilitator being recognized as a Hero and Conservationist of the Year in the name of the great John Muir? That in itself is extraordinary, because if you look at my achievements you will see they are all about helping 'common' individual wild animals – animals discarded as unimportant. I guarantee you this is exactly how they are held in the minds of most people. If that were not true, then we would not have endangered species and massive loss of habitat. That evidence is all around us and it points to our own attitudes. Early on, I became aware of the skewed outlook many people had about animals and nature. I have always felt all life is equal, and the keys to the kingdom, so to speak, are held in nature and in the simplest of animals. They should be revered, protected and adored, as they are the most misunderstood living things on earth, yet carry sacred knowledge we all want and strive to understand. Who are we? What's it all about? Just look at all of the religious figures and naturalists alike who went into nature and observed it to find the answers to all of their deepest questions and challenges.

The fact that two prestigious conservation organizations have recognized me, a simple wildlife rehabilitator who sees all animals as equal and deserving of our compassion, means they too consider wildlife rehabilitation a valid endeavor.

During the Deepwater Horizon oil spill, I was constantly asked by reporters, 'Why is it important to care for these animals?' I think it's obvious, but clearly not everyone does. Keep in mind that two highly respected environmental organizations, Oceana and the John Muir Society, just recognized a wildlife rehabilitator and his work in putting the common and simple animals on the pedestal by honoring me with these awards. That is why these awards are valid and important; they recognize a wildlife rehabilitator who has spent a great portion of his life caring for all animals, endangered to common, and sees the value in all of them.

In essence, my life has been living my message to the world; it always has been. The last 25 years have been a wild ride that took me all over the world, exposed horrible atrocities to me, and allowed me to touch and help wild animals – a privilege I have never taken for granted. IBRRC became an avenue for me to express myself and carry on my mission. I am beyond grateful to IBRRC's founder, Alice Berkner, for seeing something in me and bringing me on board in 1986, and for all that IBRRC has given me! You can be a great writer or painter, but without paper or canvas you are just a dreamer. My canvas has been IBRRC, and I will never forget that without it I would have been just another dreamer.

Another thing I learned from nature was to evolve myself, as nature does. I am doing that by letting go of the directorship of IBRRC, and am now the Director Emeritus and ready for whatever that brings. I don't know how it will unfold but I think the upcoming year will bring about great opportunities for IBRRC and me. I officially close this chapter and open a new one.

That's all for now. Power to the coots, the raccoons and the gulls...all the animals...even the starlings!

Jay Holcomb

Director Emeritus

International Bird Rescue Research Center (IBRRC

Fig 9-12 - Jay Holcomb. International Bird Rescue, *Every Bird Matters*, June 10, 2014, "Mourning the Loss of Jay Holcomb, Our Hero". *http://blog.bird-rescue.org/index.php/2014/06/mourning-the-loss-of-jay-holcomb-wildlife-hero/*

Fig 9-13. Jay Holcomb holding a Brown Pelican (note the correct way he holds the bird). *Jay Holcomb, 1951-2014 – A Tribute to International Bird Rescue's Jay Holcomb from International Bird Rescue.* *http://blog.bird-rescue.org/index.php/2014/06/jay-holcomb-1951-2014/*

International Bird Rescue's motto is "Every Bird Matters". The following story is pertinent to their work: "An old man was walking along the beach and saw in the distance a young boy who appeared to be dancing and gyrating at the ocean's edge. As the man got closer, he realized the boy was not dancing at all. The tide had gone out, beaching thousands and thousands of starfish. The boy was throwing one starfish after another back into the ocean so they might survive. 'Son, you can't possibly throw all of those starfish back. How can what you are doing possibly matter,' the old man asked. As the boy threw yet another starfish back into the safety of the ocean, he replied, 'it mattered to that one.'" (Ref 9-10)

This story captures the heart and soul of International Bird Rescue's work: it matters to every bird they save.

Chapter Ten – Ode to an American Goldfinch

———

ONE DAY IN LATE JULY 2005, I was walking home from work in San Francisco's financial district. As I turned the corner where Montgomery Street runs into Columbus Avenue, I saw two young girls about ten years old and an older girl in her late teens standing outside the Church of Scientology building. As I approached them, I noticed one of the younger girls was holding a shoebox without a lid. A constant, strident cheeping came from inside the box. I was curious as to what could be making this noise. At first, I wondered if the cheeping might be coming from a sparrow, but it didn't sound like a sparrow. As I went by, I looked inside the box and saw a small, pale yellow bird. I realized this was an uncommon wild bird to be living in the heart of the city. I stopped.

"Did you find a bird?" I asked.

"Yes," the older girl replied. "The girls found it on the ground on Sansome Street. They didn't know what to do with it but have decided to take it to a pet store nearby."

I asked: "Is it possible to return it to where they found it because its mother is probably looking for it? I volunteer at a wild bird rescue center called WildCare in San Rafael and they say you should just leave a baby bird alone, as its parents are probably close by."

"No, I waited in the area with them for a long time and we looked all over, and there were no other birds around."

The older girl said to the young girls: "You better put your hand over the top of the box so it doesn't fly away."

I felt drawn into this situation because of my love of birds and my belief I knew something about birds after all the reading I had done on their life histories and then volunteering in the Baby Bird Room at WildCare on Sunday mornings. Maybe I could persuade the young girls to give me the bird to take to WildCare.

I turned to one of the younger girls and asked: "Is the pet store where you are taking it a good one?"

"Oh yes, I got my hamster from there and he lived a long time. It is a few blocks away over there," she answered, pointing towards Chinatown. Then the two young girls started walking down Columbus Avenue with the box.

I shuddered at the idea of leaving a wild bird at a pet store. What would they do with it there? If I could only get possession of the bird, I could take it to WildCare where they would know how to take care of it. I said to the older girl: "Maybe I could drive to San Rafael and get it to WildCare before they close."

I started following the two young girls down Columbus Avenue, as this was the way I normally walked home. The two girls were already a half-block ahead of me. I had to catch up with them. Then I saw they had stopped at a red light. I hurried to get to them before the light changed. I reached them and we all waited at the red light.

My mind was racing. I thought I couldn't let them take this beautiful wild bird to a pet store as it belonged in the wild. How was I going to get the bird from the girls?

I said to them: "If you will let me have the bird, I will drive to San Rafael and take it to WildCare. I know they will take care of it very well there."

To my surprise, the girls agreed. They immediately handed me the box and we parted ways.

Now, I had complete responsibility for the welfare of this tiny gem. It kept up a loud cheeping every few seconds, probably a location call for its mother. I covered the top of the box as best I could with my hand.

I walked for several more blocks, thinking I had to get something better than this open shoebox to put the bird in. I thought maybe one of the restaurants would have a better box and arbitrarily went into the *Steps of Rome*. A friendly waitress came up to me and asked if it was a table for one. I explained I had a small bird someone had found and would she have a box for it. She looked at it and said "Oh, how cute!" A waiter also came over and smiled when he looked in the box and saw the bird. The waitress brought a small clear plastic to-go box with a hinged lid and I said this was the perfect thing. I put the little bird in the to-go box and closed the lid almost all the way, so it wouldn't be able to get out.

Now, I knew time was of the essence. The sooner I could transport this little bird to WildCare, the sooner he would be properly taken care of.

Before leaving work that day I had ordered a to-go dinner from a restaurant called *Capp's Corner*, so I had to pick up the meal first. It was only a block off the most direct route home. I arrived at the restaurant and explained to the hostess what had happened and where I was taking this wild bird. She asked what kind of bird it was and I said I wasn't sure. The owner of the restaurant was sitting at the bar. He saw I had a clear to-go box and asked if I had bought an appetizer for the meal. I showed him the bird inside the box and said I was taking it to WildCare in San Rafael. The hostess had my order all ready, as usual, and she said good luck with the bird.

I was carrying a full load – purse, briefcase, plastic bag with a complete dinner in it, and my box with the bird inside. I had my purse over my left shoulder, my briefcase over my left arm and the dinner bag in my left hand. My right arm and hand were reserved for my precious cargo. I walked as quickly as I could, while still being careful not to trip over anything as I didn't want to drop the box.

I arrived home, opened the door of the apartment, and called to my husband: "Ken, can you come here for a minute?" Ken took the dinner parcel, while I explained I had taken a young bird from a couple of girls who had found it and I needed to phone WildCare to see if anyone was still there and ask if I could bring the bird in that night. Ken took the box with the little bird into the bedroom while I sat at the kitchen table and phoned WildCare. Someone answered and I said I was bringing a bird in right away. They said someone was still in the Bird Room until about 8:30 pm that night. The whole time I was on the phone I heard loud strident cheeping every couple of seconds coming from the bedroom which is separated from the kitchen by a long hallway. It was amazing that something so small could make such a loud noise that carried throughout the apartment. Also, it was making this noise from inside a plastic box.

Ken came out of the bedroom and said he was falling in love with the bird after only spending a few minutes with it. He had set the box down on a table, and the little bird was looking all around and turning its head to follow him around as Ken moved about the room.

I was too excited and anxious to really enjoy being with the bird. I just wanted to get it to someplace where people knew how to care for it. I got in the car and put the box on the passenger seat, holding a space open with a finger to let air into the box. It was warm in the car. Traffic on the way to the Golden Gate Bridge was start-and-stop. I couldn't turn on the air conditioning in our 1994 Nissan Sentra because it didn't work well when the car was moving slowly or was stopped.

The little bird in the box on the passenger seat beside me just kept calling every couple of seconds during the whole 45-minute trip. I could hear it moving around in the box and trying to jump up, but it hit its head on the top of the box. I noticed the top of its head had a darker mark on it, but I thought the bird couldn't hurt itself because the box was soft plastic. Whenever it didn't call or I couldn't hear it moving around, I anxiously looked down at the bird to make sure it was still breathing. It was very aware of its surroundings and looked around everywhere.

I parked at WildCare, feeling relieved to have finally made it there. I knew from my experience as a volunteer that all new cases admitted, including animals and birds, were entered in a log book and given a number so they could be tracked during their treatment. The little bird's number was #4259. Because I didn't know what kind of bird it was and the technician on duty at the time was not one of the bird specialists, the species name was left blank.

I took the bird into the Bird Room where another volunteer was feeding the baby birds. The summer is baby bird season at WildCare and is very busy with orphaned baby birds and injured fledglings. The volunteer and I looked in the field guides and we decided the bird was probably a Ruby-crowned Kinglet because it was so small and was olive-colored. It didn't have the ruby crown, but only adult males would have it. The field guide said Ruby-crowned Kinglets eat insects. We put the little bird into one of the incubators and put water inside. The technician on duty suggested mashing up a few worms and giving them to the bird and she brought over a little dish of worms and mashed a few up. I had the incubator door open and the little bird came and sat on the edge and I spent a long time giving it pieces of mashed-up worms. It seemed to like them and ate a fair amount. Both the other volunteer and technician on duty said the bird was so cute.

When I stopped feeding it for a minute, the bird suddenly flew out of the incubator and around the Bird Room, finally landing on a lace curtain which covered the outside window. There are trees outside the window and I think it saw the trees and wanted to fly to them. I said: "You will be out there soon enough, little guy."

I got the net used to capture birds who get out of their temporary cages, caught it in the net, and put the bird back in the incubator. It was almost 8:30 pm and would be getting dark soon. I thought it would be okay to leave the bird overnight in the incubator. However, when I started to go away, I saw it suddenly became very thin —it had looked more fluffed out before. I looked into the bird's eyes and could see how very scared and hurt it was. I told it I would see it soon and I left. I felt certain the bird would be fine and I would see it again the next Sunday morning when I went in for my regular volunteer shift at WildCare.

The next morning, I called WildCare to see if they could confirm what species of bird #4259 was. I said I had brought it in the night before, and it was in the incubator. When the receptionist came back from checking, she said she was sorry but the morning technician, Cindy, had found the bird dead in the incubator when she came in. I said there must be some mistake because it had been so bright, alert and responsive when I left it the night before. I asked if I could speak to Cindy. The receptionist went to check again. She came back and said Cindy was busy giving morning medications but that #4259 was an American Goldfinch. It had expired during the night, and was found dead in the incubator in the morning. The receptionist said this happens a lot and there are often internal injuries which you cannot see. I was in shock. I was devastated. How could this be?

When I went to WildCare for my volunteer shift the next Sunday, I looked up #4259 in the log book. The reason for admittance written in the book was "orphaned", but above this someone had written the word "kidnapped" in pencil. I felt terrible. I talked to Victor, the Sunday Bird Room technician, about what could have caused the little bird to die. He said they often have no idea what birds have been through before they are admitted to WildCare. He explained that often when birds and animals have been outside for a long time, they are very dehydrated when they come in. I realized I should have given the bird some water. It wouldn't drink on its own. But I should have given it some with a syringe in the side of the mouth. Victor said not to give it a lot of water, but just a little water this way

Then Cindy came in to the bird room to show us something. I wasn't sure if she was the one who had written "kidnapped" or not, and I explained to her how I had found the bird. She said they tell anyone who finds a bird in a dangerous place, such as downtown San Francisco with its traffic, to bring the bird in. I felt a little better after talking with Victor and Cindy.

Still, it bothered me all the following week to have "kidnapped' written in the official record of #4259. I couldn't just erase it from the book myself, so the following Sunday when I came for my shift, I asked Victor, as a head technician, if he could erase the word. He did. I felt better as this is the only official record of what happened to this American Goldfinch. I will never forget this brave, darling little bird who did everything it could to survive and who deserved to live so much.

My everlasting mistake was to think I knew enough about birds to determine what was best for this little bird. I should have put some water in the shoebox, put a cloth cover over the box to keep it dark, kept an eye on the bird overnight, and taken it to one of the people associated with WildCare who are specialists in caring for small birds. At the very least, if I had done this, an expert in birds at WildCare would have been able to identify the bird as an American Goldfinch, and would have given this bird the proper care.

The diet for American Goldfinches consists of seeds. I thought I was doing the right thing by giving the bird pieces of mealworm (and it eagerly ate them), but I feel this is what killed the bird. The bird trusted me and took whatever I gave it. Also, this bird should not have been placed in an incubator. It had enough feathers to keep itself warm. It had enough sense to try to fly out of the incubator one time when I had the door open to give it food, and it flew towards the trees outside the window when it began to get dark. Then I had to go and re-capture it and put it back in the hot incubator. I should never have left this bird alone overnight. When I left the Bird Room, the last time I looked at the bird, it looked extremely thin and the look in its eye said it did not understand why I had captured it in a net and put it back into a hot incubator. I had betrayed it.

I only hope that it did not suffer overnight before it passed away, but in my heart, I know that it did suffer. I will never forget, nor forgive myself, for as long as I live, for making this mistake and unintentionally killing this beautiful bird due to my arrogance in thinking I knew a lot about birds.

I think about #4259 often. I now believe this bird fledged from the Transamerica Redwood Park, a downtown park beside the Transamerica Pyramid building. Although surrounded by steel and glass buildings, this small park has 50 tall transplanted redwood trees, ferns, flowers, and a fountain. The park is located a block away from where the girls had found the bird.

I should have thought carefully in order to understand what could have happened to this bird, and continued to think about what I should do to avoid making a mistake. Then I would have realized this bird was not newly-hatched, but it was a fledgling. It proved it could fly. It did not belong in a hot incubator meant for baby birds. I should have waited to rely on an expert's opinion as to its species, instead of deciding myself when I wasn't sure. Just because I volunteered in the Baby Bird Room did not make me an expert on birds.

I now know what I should have done, but it is too late.

Fig 10-1 – "Young American Goldfinch", taken September 19, 2014 at 7:39 am. Courtesy of CheepShot / CC BY (https://creativecommons.org/licenses/by/2.0)

Fig 10-2 - Female American Goldfinch resting on a pipe. Courtesy of Lee Karney, USFWS.

Chapter Eleven – A Stranded Loon

EARLY IN THE MORNING on October 31, 1999 while running along the San Francisco waterfront near Pier 39, I saw something that caught my attention as it looked very odd. Something was sitting on the sidewalk beside the large black boat anchors. The boat anchors were decorative only and were a distance away from the water where boats were docked. The seated object was dark gray in color, almost the same color as the boat anchors. At first, I thought the object was a dog. Then I recognized it as a loon.

Fig 11-1 - Boat anchors on walkway near Pier 39 where grounded loon was sitting.

The loon was grounded. It was a large bird, the size of a small Canada Goose, with a fairly long sharp beak. It sat flat on the pavement with its legs tucked underneath.

I was aghast, as I realized this loon was in deep trouble. I had once read a story in *Bird Watcher's Digest* [Ref 11-1] about a loon that literally carried itself to the doorstep of a facility of the Cornell University Ornithology

Program in order to be saved. It had accidentally landed close by on the ground and had struggled to walk to the door. One of the staff found it there and because of their ornithological knowledge, they knew what to do. They had bundled the loon up in a large towel and transported it in their truck to the nearest lake, where they set it free. Once in the lake, the loon was in its natural environment. It had enough room to propel itself over the surface and become airborne, so it could continue on its migration.

I had to figure out a way to help this loon. I cautiously approached it as it sat on the pavement.

A group of elderly Chinese ladies had gathered around the bird. They pointed at it and talked in Chinese. I said to one of them: "It needs to get to the water", and pointed towards the Bay. I said: "I don't have anything with me, like a bag or towel I can throw over it to take it down to the water". The Chinese ladies looked at me, nodded, and smiled. I had the impression they thought I wanted to put the bird in a bag and take it home with me. A vision of the smoked ducks I had seen hanging up in Chinatown restaurants flashed through my mind.

These ladies did not know what to do about the loon and after a few minutes, they left to continue on their way. Meanwhile, I could not walk away and leave the loon there. I stood beside it for some time, looking down on it and wondering what I could do.

From my readings about birds, I knew the legs of loons and grebes were placed towards the rear of their bodies, making it difficult if not impossible for them to walk on land. Loons took a long time to become airborne over the water, propelling themselves on their rear-placed legs to gather enough speed for takeoff. Loons might mistake wet pavement for waterways and set down there. If nobody found and rescued them, they were doomed, as they were unable to take off again. Knowing this, I realized this loon was in grave danger. I knew it could not fly away should a dog come after it.

This loon probably had been migrating at night and mistook the pavement for water. From the air, it may have thought the black boat anchors on a broad expanse of pavement were other loons sitting in the water

The loon watched me for a while and then looked away. I believe it realized it couldn't do anything about its predicament. It had a resigned look on its face as it looked off into the distance. It faced away from the direction of the water in the bay. I realized that from where it sat on the ground, the loon was unable to see how close it really was to the water, as the broad boulevard walkway was elevated several feet above the waterline.

The loon looked healthy and unhurt. I tried to think about how I could get this bird to the safety of San Francisco Bay. If I had a towel with me, I could throw the towel over it and carry it there, but all I had was my nylon running jacket. I finally made up my mind and acted.

Quickly and decisively, I walked behind the bird and bent down to pick it up. It turned its dagger-like bill towards me and scratched my bare lower leg in self-defense, but I managed to get it under my left arm, with my right arm supporting its legs and with its bill facing well below my face. I was surprised how large and leathery its webbed feet felt. However, its feet did not seem bloody or injured, so it must not have hurt them when it landed on the pavement.

In a low, gentle, soothing voice I repeatedly told the loon: "You're a gorgeous bird. You're so beautiful" as I hurriedly turned in the direction of the water. The bird was heavy and it kept twisting its head around. Once, its bill scraped my cheek. Then it seemed to settle down a little.

I found the gangplank down to the dock where some large boats were tied up. Fortunately, there was no rope across the gangplank. I said to one of the deckhands on the first boat: "We need to get to the water. Is this the way to the water?" He just looked at me quizzically as though he was trying to understand what I was doing. I didn't have time to explain so just kept going down the plank.

I took the loon out on the dock between the second and third boats and was about to set it down. Then I noticed the surface of the water at the end of this dock had an oily sheen from the large boats that tied up there. I didn't want to set the bird down in oiled water so I backtracked up the dock. At this point, having caught sight of the body of water, the loon started to struggle. It got its legs loose and was moving its wings. As I turned to go down the next dock towards the open water again, the loon stopped struggling. At the very end of this dock I set it down. It immediately stood up and jumped off the dock into the Bay.

The loon swam some distance away and then stopped and looked back, spreading its wings and rearing up out of the water. It also made a strange sound. I like to think it was saying "Thank you." I turned my head to look in the direction where the boats exit from the docks into San Francisco Bay, and the loon then also looked in this direction. I knew that it could make its way out into the Bay where it would have plenty of water to get airborne. It was safe in its own environment now, so I turned and walked back up the gangplank to the boulevard. A Chinese man and woman were standing on the boulevard and clapping. I guess they had watched the loon and me.

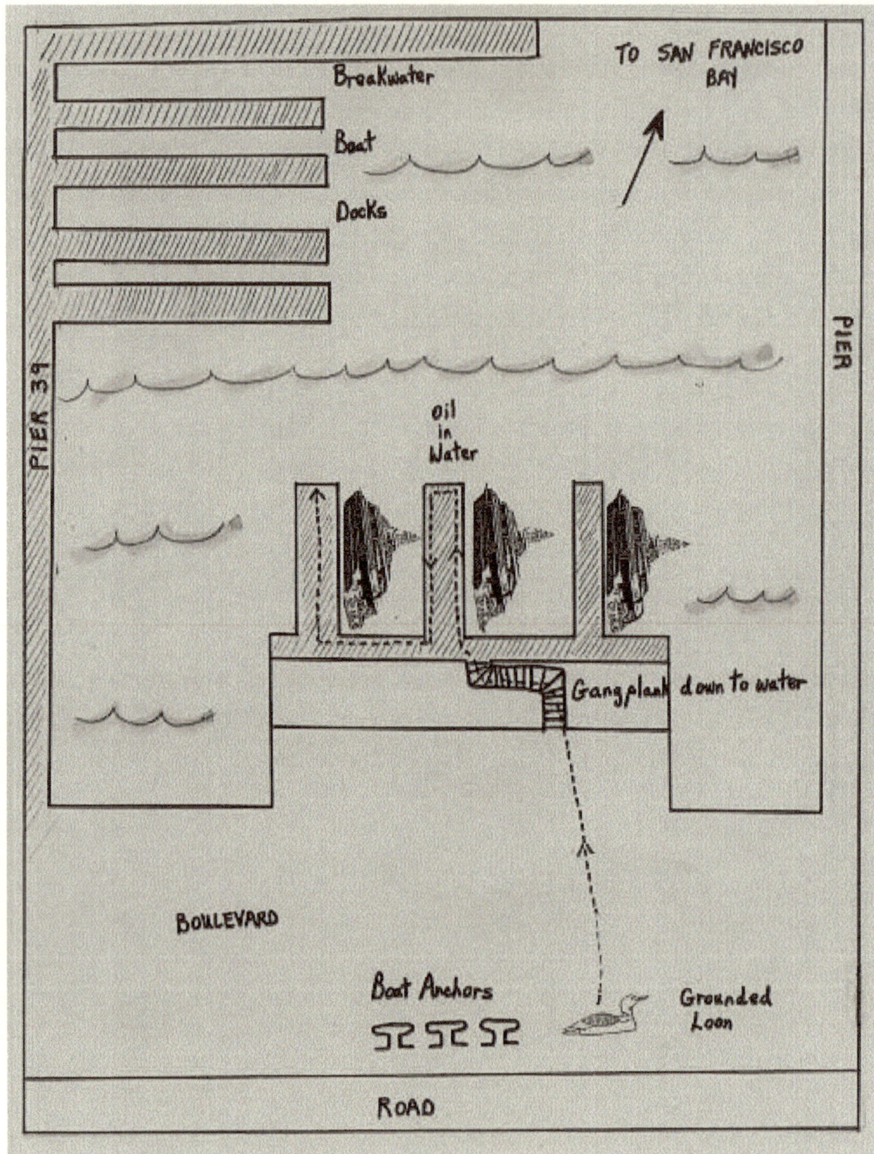

Fig 11-2 - Map showing the route taken to carry the grounded loon to the water and safety.

Later that afternoon, I walked by the area where I had set the loon in the water. It was gone. I felt very satisfied to think I had had a chance to help this noble, wondrous creature find its way again.

Loons have long held a special place in the hearts of many North Americans due to their beauty, habits, and voice. They are a symbol of wilderness and solitude. A. C. Bent describes this affection well: "Among the picturesque lakes of the wilder, wooded portions of the Northern States and Canada – where dark firs and spruces mingled with graceful white birches, cast their reflections in the still, clear waters – sportsmen and appreciative nature lovers have found attractive summer resorts. Here, far from the cares of the busy world, one finds true recreation in his pursuit of speckled trout, real rest in his camp among the fragrant balsams, and genuine joy in his communion with nature in her wildest solitudes. The woodland lakes would be solitudes, indeed, did they lack the finishing touch to make the picture complete, the tinge of wildness which adds color to the scene, the weird and mournful cry of the loon, as he calls to his mate or greets some new arrival. Whoever paddled a canoe, or cast a fly, or pitched a tent in the north woods and has not stopped to listen to this wail of the wilderness? And what would the wilderness be without it?" (Ref 11-2)

All five species of North American Loons – Red-throated, Pacific, Yellow-billed, Arctic, and Common – migrate to warmer areas around the Gulf of Mexico and on the east and west coasts of North America to winter, returning to breed on northern lakes when the ice melts in the spring. Loons in their summer plumage are striking with a black and white checkered back, glossy black head, and white collar. All loons have grayish feathers in the winter, while immature birds resemble adult birds in their winter plumage.

The voice of the Loon is unique. Loon calls have been identified into four classifications: wail, tremolo, yodel and hoot. The wail is perhaps the call most frequently heard. A loon will wail when it becomes separated from its chick, or if its mate fails to return. The tremolo is an aggressive response given when disturbed by a boater or predator. The yodel is also an expression of aggression and is given by the male during a confrontation. The hoot symbolizes a call of curiosity and/

or happiness. The sounds are apparently a learned communication between the birds. To hear the richness of their harmonics is a thrilling experience.

The skeletal and muscular structures of loons have evolved to favor swimming and diving. Their legs are placed far back on their bodies, allowing for excellent movement in the water. The legs have powerful muscles for swimming. The fact that many bones in the loon's body are solid, rather than hollow like other birds', helps them to dive. However, these same adaptations for efficient diving work against the loons' ability to take flight. In taking off from a lake, loons run along the surface into the wind. The distance needed to take flight depends on the wind speed. Once in the air, the loon can migrate at average speeds of 60 miles per hour.

Loons can live for 15 to 30 years. They typically mate for life. They show a strong attachment to their old home and return year after year to their chosen lake site to nest. They tend not to desert a locality unless one or both of the pair are killed.

An incubating loon is not as conspicuous as its striking colors would indicate. While incubating, the loon sits very low and is spread out quite flat. The distinctive designs on their bodies may actually serve to conceal them. The patches of white and black on their back may serve as visual disruptions because the patterns are positioned "out-of-line" with the body's contours. That is, the pattern seems to be a separate design superimposed on top of the animal. This makes it hard for a predator to get a clear sense of where the animal begins and ends as the pattern on the body seems to run off in every direction.

Once young loons can fly well, their mother coaxes them to leave the pond or lake on which they were bred, and leads them on the wing to the nearest part of the sea. Once there, she leaves them to fend for themselves. This usually happens around the end of August or beginning of September. The young soon afterwards travel southwards, usually alone. Their migration precedes that of the adults by about three weeks and they go much farther south. The principal flight is along the coast. They usually fly high in the air, singly, or in small widely-scattered groups.

During the winter, loons may stay on inland lakes and streams within their wintering range, which extends as far north to where they can find plenty of open water. As they require a large open space in which to rise from the water, they may be caught by the freezing of ponds and may subsequently starve. However, the great majority of them spend the winter on the seacoast, where they are usually seen singly, but sometimes form large gatherings far out at sea.

A. C. Bent comments: "I believe they usually sleep on the water, but when it is safe to do so they often come ashore to sleep. I have several times surprised one well up on a sandy beach, where it had been spending the night or had gone ashore to dry and sand its plumage. Its attempts to regain the water were more precipitous than graceful, as it scrambled or stumbled down the beach, falling on its breast at every few yards, darting its head and neck about, humping its back and straining every muscle to make speed." (Ref 11-3)

Observers have noticed that under certain circumstances, loons show both playfulness and curiosity. Dr. P. L. Hatch (1892) relates the following earliest dawn performance: "The night is spent in proximity to each other on the water, somewhat removed from the land. And in the earliest morning, notes of the parent male soon call out a response from the other members of the family, when they all draw near, and after cavorting around each other after the manner of graceful skaters for a brief time, they fall into line, side by side, and lifting their wings simultaneously, they start off in a foot race on the water like a line of school children, running with incredible speed a full quarter of a mile without lowering their wings or pausing an instant, wheel around in a short circle (in which some of them get a little behind) and retrace their course to the place of starting. This race, after but a moment's pause, is repeated over and over again, with unabated zest, until by some undiscoverable signal it ceases as suddenly as it began. Its termination is characterized by a subsequent general congratulation manifested by the medley of loon notes. This walking, or rather running, upon the face of the quiet lake waters is a marvel of pedal performance, so swiftly do the thin, sharp, legs move in the race, the wings being continuously held at about half extent. Soon after this is over, the male parent takes to wing to seek his food in some distant part of the same or some other lake, which is soon followed by the departure of the female in another direction, while the young swim away in various directions to seek their supplies nearer the place of nightly rendezvous." (Ref 11-4)

Fig 11-3 - Loons swimming in San Francisco Bay.

Fig 11-4 – Loon with its eyes below the water searching for food.

Fig 11-5 – Loon in San Francisco Bay with Alcatraz in the background.

CONCLUSION

WHEN I AM IN PLACES like Crissy Field Marsh or the Coastal Trail, a sense of comfort comes over me and I feel the world is as it should be. I am at peace. I have a lot of patience to stop and watch something happening in nature for a long time. I am all alone in a special place, but I am not lonely.

These natural places are close to extremely busy automobile and pedestrian traffic. They are literally surrounded by urban concrete. For example, the Coastal Trail goes underneath the south approach to the Golden Gate Bridge. Hundreds of cars and people are pouring across the bridge overhead, but a short distance from all this human-made activity, there is another world, a world a thousand miles away in terms of its natural habitat as contrasted with man-made habitat.

Similarly, Crissy Field Marsh is beside the Golden Gate Promenade which is heavily-traveled by people and dogs, yet within a few yards, there is an area that is wild and inhabited by totally different creatures with incredibly different lives. The importance of these natural, wild areas to the many creatures who use them during the year is paramount.

To have these types of habitat within walking distance of urban high rises and areas of intense human activity means a great deal to me, whom I consider a bird lover and a naturalist. The value of these places to people like me who love and appreciate nature, and who feel a sense of peace when immersed in them, is priceless.

The importance of these natural, wild areas to the many creatures who use them during the year is paramount. When I look into the eyes of birds and other animals, and they look back at me, I see a universality of all creatures and all living things. As I see them watching me as I watch them, I feel a strong bond with them. I see they are curious about me, just as I am curious about them.

REFERENCES

CHAPTER 1 – CRISSY Field Marsh

1-1 San Francisco Bay Joint Venture. *Restoring the Estuary: An Implementation Strategy for the San Francisco Bay Joint Venture – A Strategic Vision for the Restoration of Wetlands and Wildlife in the San Francisco Bay Area*, Chapter 2, "Biological Foundations of the San Francisco Bay Joint Venture", January, 2001. http://www.sfbayjv.org/pdfs/strategy/007-022-Chap2.pdf.

Chapter 2 - Mrs. Long-billed Curlew and the Willet

2-1 O'Brien, Michael, Richard Crossley, and Kevin Karlson. *The Shorebird Guide.* (Boston, New York: Houghton Mifflin Company, 2006),384.

2-2 Brown, Stephen, Catherine Hickey, Brian Harrington, and Robert Gill, editors. *United States Shorebird Conservation Plan, Second Edition*, (Mamomet, Massachusetts: Mamomet Center for Conservation Sciences, May 2001), 52. https://www.shorebirdplan.org/wp-content/uploads/2013/01/USShorebirdPlan2Ed.pdf

2-3 Haig, Susan M., Lewis W. Oring, Peter M. Sanzenbacher, and Oriane W. Taft. "Space Use, Migratory Connectivity, and Population Segregation Among Willets Breeding in the Western Great Basin". *The Condor,* Volume 104, Issue 3, 1 August 2002, pages 620-630. https://academic.oup.com/condor/article-abstract/104/3/620/5151823.

Chapter 3 –Aquatic Park to Golden Gate Bridge

3-1 Higman, Harry and Earl Larrison. *Union Bay, the Life of a City Marsh*. Seattle: University of Washington Press, 1951.

3-2 Clowater, James S. "Distribution and Foraging Behaviour of Wintering Western Grebes", thesis submitted in partial fulfillment of the requirements for the degree of Master of Science in the Department of Biological Sciences, Simon Fraser University, November, 1998.

3-3 Kaufman, Kenn. *Lives of North American Birds*. (Boston, New York: Houghton Mifflin Company, 1996), 209.

3-4 Macwhirter, R. Bruce, Peter Austin-Smith Jr. and Donald E. Kroodsma. (2002). Sanderling (*Calidris alba*), *The Birds of North America* (P. G. Rodewald, Ed.). Ithaca: Cornell Lab of Ornithology; Retrieved from the *Birds of North America*: *https://birdsna.org/Species-Account/bna/species/sander*.

3-5 "Surf Scoter." *Audubon*, Pacific Flyway, California. http://ca.audubon.org/birds-0/surf-scoter (accessed September 2, 2019).

3-6 Takekawa, John. "Finding the Needle in a Big Haystack – Locating Surf Scoter Nests in the Northern Boreal Forest". *Sound Waves*, Coastal Science and Research News from Across the USGS, Volume FY 2005, Issue No. 75, August 2005.

3-7 Takekawa, J. Y.et al. "Breeding distribution and ecology of Pacific coast Surf Scoters. Boreal birds of North America: a hemispheric view of their conservation links and significance. *Studies in Avian Biology* (2011) 41: 41-64.

3-8 De La Cruz, S. E. W.et al. "Spring migration routes and chronology of surf scoters (*Melanitta perspicillata*): a synthesis of Pacific coast studies". *Canadian Journal of Zoology* (2009) 87(11): 1069-1086.

3-9 McClain, Joe. "Winnie the Whimbrel: RIP". William and Mary News & Media, September 9, 2008, https://www.wm.edu/news/stories/2008/winnie-is-down-3006.php (accessed July 23, 2020).

3-10 Watts, Bryan. "Mackenzie Whimbrels Complete Loop Migration". The Center for Conservation Biology, William & Mary and Virginia Commonwealth University, July 15, 2013 https://ccbbirds.org/2013/07/15/mackenzie-whimbrels-complete-loop-migration/ (accessed July 23, 2020).

3-11 Semeniuk, Ivan. "In New Brunswick's blueberry country, a 'nuisance' bird earns respect and allies". The Globe and Mail, August 27,2018, updated August 29, 2018 https://www.theglobeandmail.com/canada/article-in-new-brunswicks-blueberry-country-a-nuisance-bird-earns-respect/ (accessed July 23, 2020).

3-12 Kaufman, Kenn. *Lives of North American Birds*. (Boston, New York: Houghton Mifflin Company, 1996), 273.

3-13 Lebbin, Daniel J., Michael J. Parr, and George H. Fenwick. *The American Bird Conservancy Guide to Bird Conservation*. (Lynx Edicions, Barcelona, and The University of Chicago Press, Chicago and London, 2010), 338.

3-14 Leslie, Scott. *Sea & Coastal Birds of North America: A Guide to Observation, Understanding and Conservation*. (Toronto, Canada: Key Porter Books Limited, 2008), 198.

3-15 Bent, Arthur Cleveland. *Life Histories of North American Shore Birds, Order Limicolae (Part 1)*. Smithsonian Institution, United States National Museum, Bulletin No. 142. (Washington, D.C.: United States Government Printing Office, 1927), 277.

3-16 Ibid, 280.

3-17 Ibid, 286.

3-18 Barrow, Mark V. Jr. *A Passion For Birds – American Ornithology After Audubon.* (Princeton, New Jersey: Princeton University Press, 1998), 174.

3-19 Ibid, 175.

3-20 Bent, A. C., *Life Histories of North American Marsh Birds.* Smithsonian Institution, United States National Museum Bulletin 135. (Washington, D.C.: United States Government Printing Office, March 11, 1927), 101-114.

<u>Chapter 4 - Coastal Trail West of the Golden Gate Bridge</u>

4-1 Bent, A. C., and Collaborators, compiled and edited by Oliver L. Austin, Jr. *Life Histories of North American Cardinals, Grosbeaks, Buntings, Towhees, Finches, Sparrows, and Allies.* Smithsonian Institution, United States National Museum Bulletin 237 (Part 3). (Washington, D.C.: United States Government Printing Office, 1968), 1273 – 1291.

4-2 Ibid

4-3 Graustein, Jeannette E. "Audubon and Nuttall." *The Scientific Monthly* 74, no. 2 (1952), 84-90.

4-4 Graustein, Jeannette E. *Thom, Naturalist: Explorations in America, 1805-1841* (Cambridge: Harvard University Press, 1967), 51.

4-5 Ibid

4-6 Dana, Richard Henry. *Two Years Before the Mast* (London: T Nelson and Sons Ltd., 1912), chapter 30.

4-7 Cook, Kevin. "The American Goldfinch." *Bird Watcher's Digest.* July/August 1994.

4-8 Audubon, John James. *The Birds of America, from Drawings Made in the United States and Their Territories, Volume III.* (New York: J.J. Audubon, Philadelphia: J.B. Chevalier, 1841), 130.

4-9 Bent, A. C., *Life Histories of North American Cuckoos, Goatsuckers, Hummingbirds, and Their Allies.* Smithsonian Institution, United States National Museum Bulletin 176. (Washington, D.C.: United States Government Printing Office, July 20, 1940), 332-352.

4-10 Bonta, Marcia Myers. *Women in the Field – America's Pioneering Women Naturalists.* (Texas A&M University Press, 1991), 203.

4-11 Kaufman, Kenn. *Lives of North American Birds.* (Boston, New York: Houghton Mifflin Company, 1996), 460.

4-12. *Field Guide to the Birds of North America, Third Edition.* (Washington, D.C.: National Geographic Society, 1999), 452.

Chapter 5 – Marshall's Beach

Chapter 6 – Mercer Slough

6-1 Kaufman, Kenn. *Lives of North American Birds.* (Boston, New York: Houghton Mifflin Company, 1996), 365.

6-2 Bent, A.C., *Life Histories of North American Woodpeckers.* Smithsonian Institution, United States National Museum Bulletin 174. (Washington, D.C.: United States Government Printing Office, May 23, 1939), 52-68.

6-3 Bent, A.C., *Life Histories of North American Thrushes, Kinglets, and Their Allies*. Smithsonian Institution, United States National Museum Bulletin 196. (Washington, D.C.: United States Government Printing Office, June 28, 1949), 142-162.

6-4 Bent, A.C., *Life Histories of North American Wild Fowl*. Smithsonian Institution, United States National Museum Bulletin 126 (Part 1). (Washington, D.C.: United States Government Printing Office, May 25, 1923), 155-171.

6-5 Bent, A.C. and Collaborators, compiled and edited by Oliver L. Austin Jr., *Life Histories of North American Cardinals, Grosbeaks, Buntings, Towhees, Finches, Sparrows, and Allies*. Smithsonian Institution, United States National Museum Bulletin 237 (Part 3). (Washington, D.C.: United States Government Printing Office,1968), 1491-1512.

6-6 Ibid

6-7 Bonta, Marcia Myers, *Women in the Field – America's Pioneering Women Naturalists*. (Texas A&M University Press, 1991), 222.

6-8 Ibid, 222.

6-9 Ibid, 228

6-10 Ibid, 228

6-11 Ibid, 230

6-12 Ibid, 23

6-13 Glase, J. C., "Ecology of social organization in the Black-capped Chickadee". *Living Bird*, 1973, 12:235-267.

6-14 Bent, A.C., *Life Histories of North American Woodpeckers*. Smithsonian Institution, United States National Museum Bulletin 174. (Washington, D.C.: United States Government Printing Office, May 23, 1939), 265-287.

6-15 Ibid

6-16 Dugger, B.D., K.M.Dugger, and L.H. Fredrickson, 1994, Hooded Merganser (*Lophodytes cucullatus*), in *The Birds of North America*, No. 98, (A. Poole and F. Gill, Eds.), Philadelphia: The Academy of Natural Sciences; Washington, D.C.: The American Ornithologists' Union.

6-17 Ibid

6-18 Bent, A.C., *Life Histories of North American Nuthatches, Wrens, Thrashers, and Their Allies*. Smithsonian Institution, United States National Museum Bulletin 195. (Washington, D.C.: United States Government Printing Office, July 7, 1948), 245-259.

6-19 Kroodsma, D.E. and J. Verner, 1997, Marsh Wren (*Cistothorus palustris*), in The Birds of North America, No. 308, 1997, The Academy of Natural Sciences and the American Ornithologists Union, Philadelphia, PA and Washington, D.C.

6-20 Kaufman, Kenn. *Lives of North American Birds*. (Boston, New York: Houghton Mifflin Company, 1996), 566.

6-21 Bent, A.C. and Collaborators, compiled and edited by Oliver L. Austin Jr., *Life Histories of North American Cardinals, Grosbeaks, Buntings, Towhees, Finches, Sparrows, and Allies*. Smithsonian Institution, United States National Museum Bulletin 237 (Part 3). (Washington, D.C.: United States Government Printing Office,1968), 1491-1512.

6-22 Ibid

6-23 Ibid

6-24 Ibid

Chapter 7 – Burnaby Lake and Still Creek

7-1 Burnaby Lake Regional Park, https://en.wikipedia.org/wiki/Burnaby_Lake_Regional_Park (accessed August 22, 2020).

7-2 Kaufman, Kenn. *Lives of North American Birds*. (Boston, New York: Houghton Mifflin Company, 1996), 223.

7-3 Clulow, George, "Sad End for First Breeding Record of Sandhill Cranes in Burnaby", July 6, 2015, https://burnabybirdguy.wordpress.com/category/breedingnesting-birds/ (accessed August 22, 2020).

7-4 Moreau, Jennifer, "First-ever sandhill crane chick in Burnaby now feared dead:, in Burnaby Now, July 6, 2015. http://www.burnabynow.com/community/first-ever-sandhill-crane-chick-in-burnaby-now-feared-dead-1.1991007/ (accessed August 22, 2020).

7-5 Clulow, George, "Sad End for First Breeding Record of Sandhill Cranes in Burnaby", July 6, 2015, https://burnabybirdguy.wordpress.com/category/breedingnesting-birds/ (accessed August 22, 2020).

7-6 Wakelin, Kimberley, "The Sandhill Crane in British Columbia", October 30, 2009, http://ladywoodpecker.blogspot.ca/2009/10/sandhill-crane-in-british-columbia.html (accessed November 21, 2016).

7-7 Kaufman, Kenn. *Lives of North American Birds*. (Boston, New York: Houghton Mifflin Company, 1996), 409.

7-8 "Swainson's Thrush", on The Cornell Lab of Ornithology's *All About Birds.* https://www.allaboutbirds.org/guide/Swainsons_Thrush/lifehistory (accessed August 22, 2020).

7-9 Starzomski, B. 2015. Swainson's Thrush in Davidson, P.J.A., R.J. Cannings, A.R. Couturier, D. Lepage, and C.M. DiCorrado (eds). 2015. *The Atlas of the Breeding Birds of British Columbia, 2008-2012.* Bird Studies Canada. Delta, B.C.

7-10 Delmore, Kira E., James W. Fox, and Darren E. Irwin, :Dramatic intraspecific differences in migratory routes, stopover sites and wintering areas, revealed using light-level geolocators", in *Proceedings of the Royal Society B*, doi: 10.1098/rspb.2012.1229.

7-11 The University of British Columbia, Media release July 22, 2014 "Mixed genes mix up the migrations of hybrid birds".

7-12 Kaufman, Kenn and Kimberly Kaufman, "Field Guide to Nature of New England". (New York: Houghton Mifflin Company, 2012), 174.

7-13 Smith, Dr. Chris, "Why don't ducks get hypothermia". *The Naked Scientists 2000-2016*, University of Cambridge.

Chapter 8 - Volunteering at WildCare

8-1 *National Geographic Complete Birds of North America, 2nd Edition.* Edited by Jonathan Alderfer. (Washington, D.C.: National Geographic Society, 2014), 475.

8-2 Kaufman, Kenn. *Lives of North American Birds.* (Boston, New York: Houghton Mifflin Company, 1996), 227.

8-3 *Field Guide to the Birds of North America, Third Edition.* (Washington, D.C.: National Geographic Society, 1999), 350.

8-4 *WildCare News Spring/Summer, 2007.* San Rafael, California: WildCare.

8-5 Bonta, Marcia Myers. *Women in the Field – America's Pioneering Women Naturalists.* (College Station, Texas: Texas A & M University Press, 1991), 232-233.

8-6 Ibid, 238.

8-7 Ibid, 239.

8-8 Ibid, 234.

8-9 Ibid, 218.

8-10 Ibid, 216.

8-11 Bent, Arthur Cleveland. *Life Histories of North American Thrushes, Kinglets, and Their Allies: Order Passeriformes.* Smithsonian Institution, United States National Museum Bulletin 196. (Washington, D.C.: United States Government Printing Office, 1949), 151.

8-12 Bonta, Marcia Myers. *Women in the Field – America's Pioneering Women Naturalists.* (College Station, Texas: Texas A & M University Press, 1991), 220.

Chapter 9 - Oil Spill in San Francisco Bay

9-1 "Our Process for Helping Oiled Birds." *International Bird Rescue Every Bird Matters.* The work we do every day keeps International Bird Rescue prepared to meet the challenges of an oiled wildlife emergency, https://www.bird-rescue.org/our-work/aquatic-bird-rehabilitation/our-process-for-helping-oiled-birds.aspx (accessed 26 July 2020).

9-2 Kay, Jane. "Around S.F. Bay, oiled birds still found nearly 3 weeks after spill." *SFGate.* November 27, 2007. https://www.sfgate.com/news/article/Around-S-F-Bay-oiled-birds-still-found-nearly-3-3235702.php (accessed 26 July 2020).

9-3 Sullivan, Ron and Joe Eaton. "In wake of oil spill, bird rescuers work against the clock, the odds." *SF Gate, Special to The Chronicle.* November 17, 2007. https://www.sfgate.com/bayarea/article/In-wake-of-oil-spill-bird-rescuers-work-against-3234791.php (accessed 26 July 2020).

9-4 Kay, Jane. "Birds' savior: For over 30 years, wildlife lover has come to the rescue." *SFGate.* January 22, 2003. https://www.sfgate.com/green/article/Birds-savior-For-over-30-years-wildlife-lover-2638690.php (accessed 26 July 2020).

9-5 Ibid.

9-6 Ibid.

9-7 Jones, Carolyn. "Jay Holcomb, leader of International Bird Rescue, dies." *SFGate,* June 13, 2014. https://www.sfgate.com/bayarea/article/Jay-Holcomb-beloved-bird-rescuer-dead-at-63-5548497.php (accessed 26 July 2020).

9-8 Jones, Carolyn. "International Bird Rescue celebrates 40th year." SFGate, April 24, 2012, updated August 6, 2012. https://www.sfgate.com/science/article/International-Bird-Rescue-celebrates-40th-years-3504432.php (accessed 26 July 2020).

9-9 Holcomb, Jay. "Jay Holcomb's 25 years of IBRRC leadership." *Every Bird Matters, News and Views from International Bird Rescue.* January 25, 2011. http://blog.bird-rescue.org/index.php/tag/jay-holcomb/ (accessed 26 July 2020).

9-10 "Why Rehabilitate Wild Birds?" *International Bird Rescue Every Bird Matters*. Perhaps you have heard this wonderful story before, it is especially pertinent to International Bird Rescue's work. https://www.bird-rescue.org/our-work/aquatic-bird-rehabilitation/why-rehabilitate-oiled-birds/ (accessed 26 July 2020).

Chapter 10 - Ode to an American Goldfinch

Chapter 11 - A Stranded Loon

11-1 Berger, Cynthia. "Applied Science." *Bird Watcher's Digest*. May/June 1994, 76.

11-2 Bent, Arthur Cleveland. *Life Histories of North American Diving Birds: Order Pygopodes*. Smithsonian Institution, United States National Museum Bulletin 107. (Washington, D.C.: United States Government Printing Office, 1919), 47-48.

11-3 Ibid, 58.

11-4 Ibid, 56.

APPENDIX I - Migration Maps for Some of the Birds Seen

<u>NOTE ON BIRD MIGRATION</u>

Bird migration may appear to be communal, especially as large numbers of birds are often seen congregated at specific staging and stopover sites. However, migration is in reality a very individual bird phenomenon. Both breeding and non-breeding areas may be large territories. Birds often stay for variable lengths of time at a given site. Often no simple single migratory route connects breeding with non-breeding regions. It is therefore difficult to draw general conclusions about the migrations of any single bird.

Individuals often do not migrate together, with males, females and young all departing at different times. Sometimes the same two individuals may meet again on the breeding grounds year after year, but their paths getting there are not necessarily the same. Other pairs may form on the wintering grounds and travel together to their breeding ground, but make the return journey to their wintering ground separately.

Some individuals of the same species may not migrate at all; others may migrate short distances; while still others have long migrations. Individuals may migrate singly, in small groups, or in large flocks consisting of either all birds of the same species or a mixture of species.

The conclusion concerning bird migration is that one cannot apply generalizations to an individual of a species. Migration is really about the travels of individual birds, no two of whom are the same.

<u>List of Migration Maps</u>

(typical wintering area is shown by a box and typical breeding area is shown by a circle in below maps)

Migration Map 1 - Typical Migration Routes – Pacific Flyway

Migration Map 2 - A Typical Migration Route –Surf Scoter

Migration Map 3 – A Typical Migration Route – Sanderling

Migration Map 4 – A Typical Migration Route – Greater Scaup

Migration Map 5 – A Typical Migration Route – Marbled Godwit

Migration Map 6 – A Typical Migration Route – Western Willet

Migration Map 7 – A Typical Migration Route – Black-bellied Plover

Migration Map 8 – A Typical Migration Route – Long-billed Curlew

Migration Map 9a– A Typical Migration Route –Red-throated Loon

Migration Map 9b– A Typical Migration Route –Common Loon

Migration Map 10 – A Typical Migration Route – Least Sandpiper

Migration Map 11 – A Typical Migration Route – Townsend's Warbler

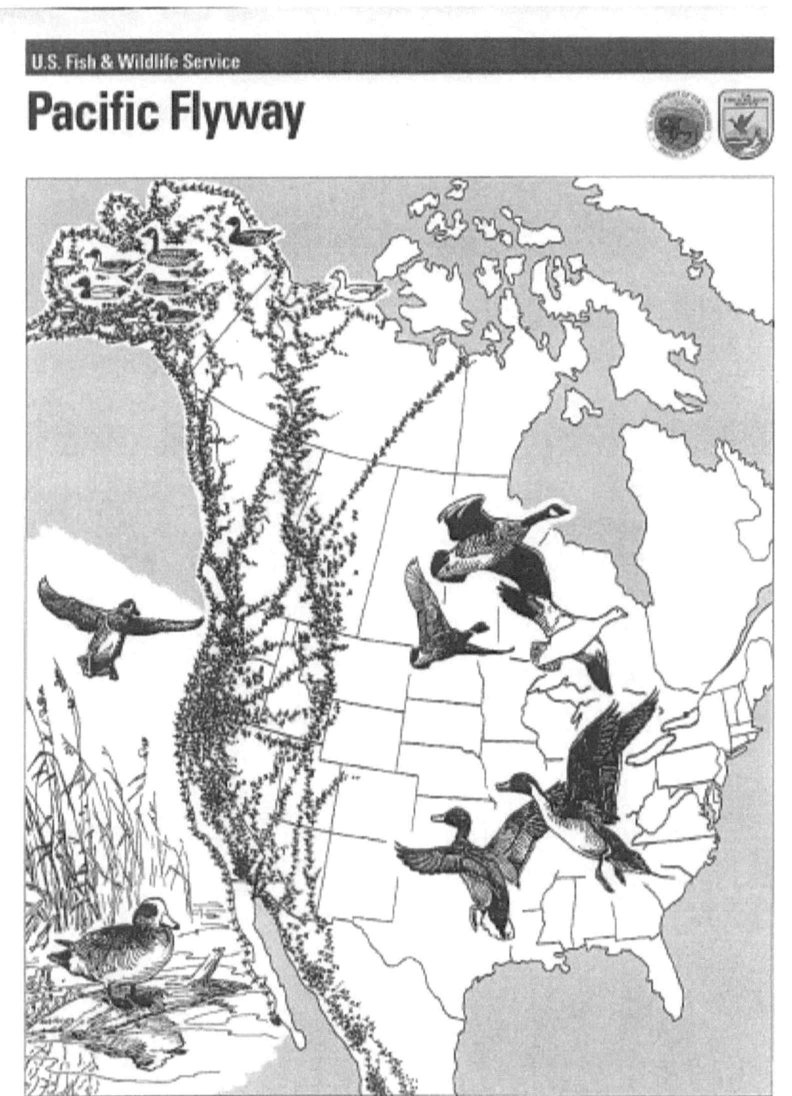

Migration Map 1 – The San Francisco Bay is a key wintering and stopover area along the Pacific Flyway. Courtesy of US Fish and Wildlife Service. sonic.net/~sfbayjv.pdfs.strategy/007-022-Chapw.pdf. (accessed on October 13, 2019).

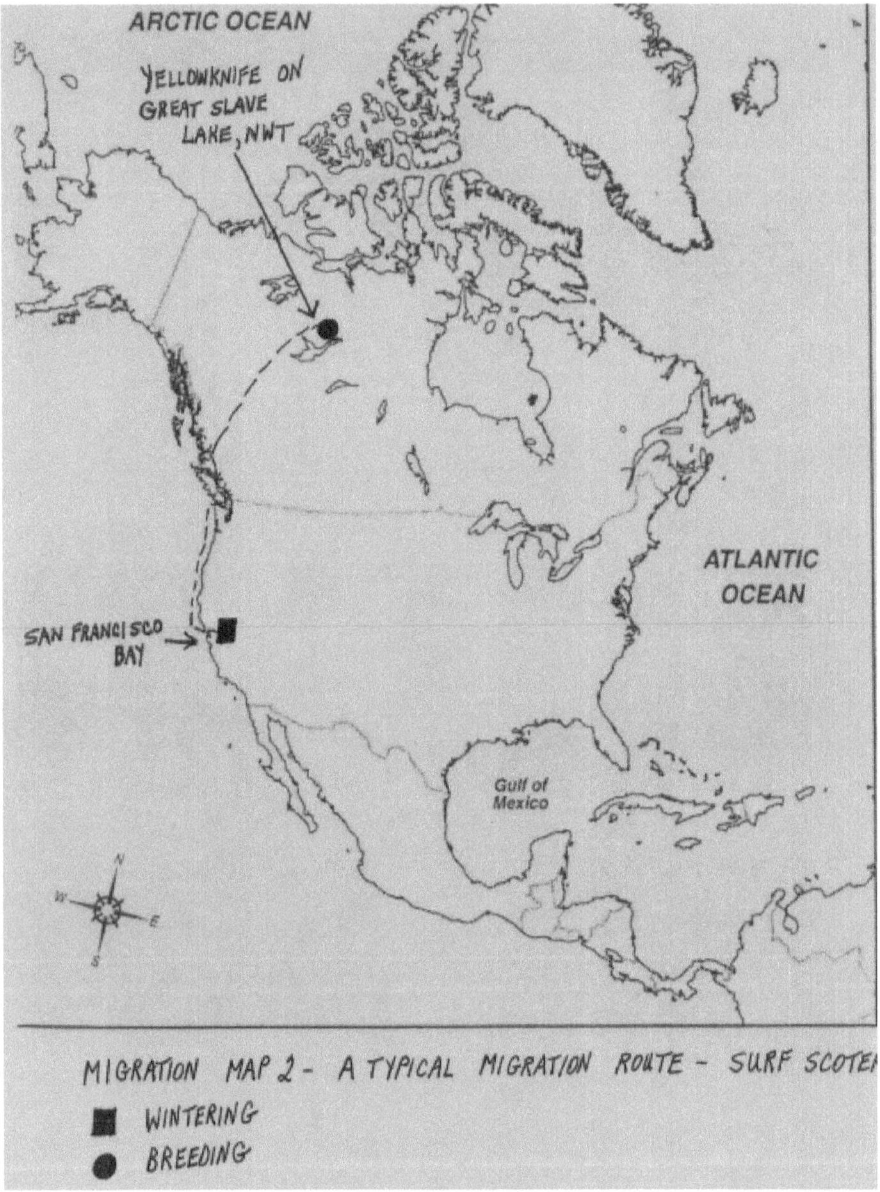

ARCTIC OCEAN
YELLOWKNIFE ON GREAT SLAVE LAKE, NWT
ATLANTIC OCEAN
SAN FRANCISCO BAY
Gulf of Mexico
N
W
E
S
MIGRATION MAP 2 - A TYPICAL MIGRATION ROUTE - SURF SCOTER
WINTERING
BREEDING

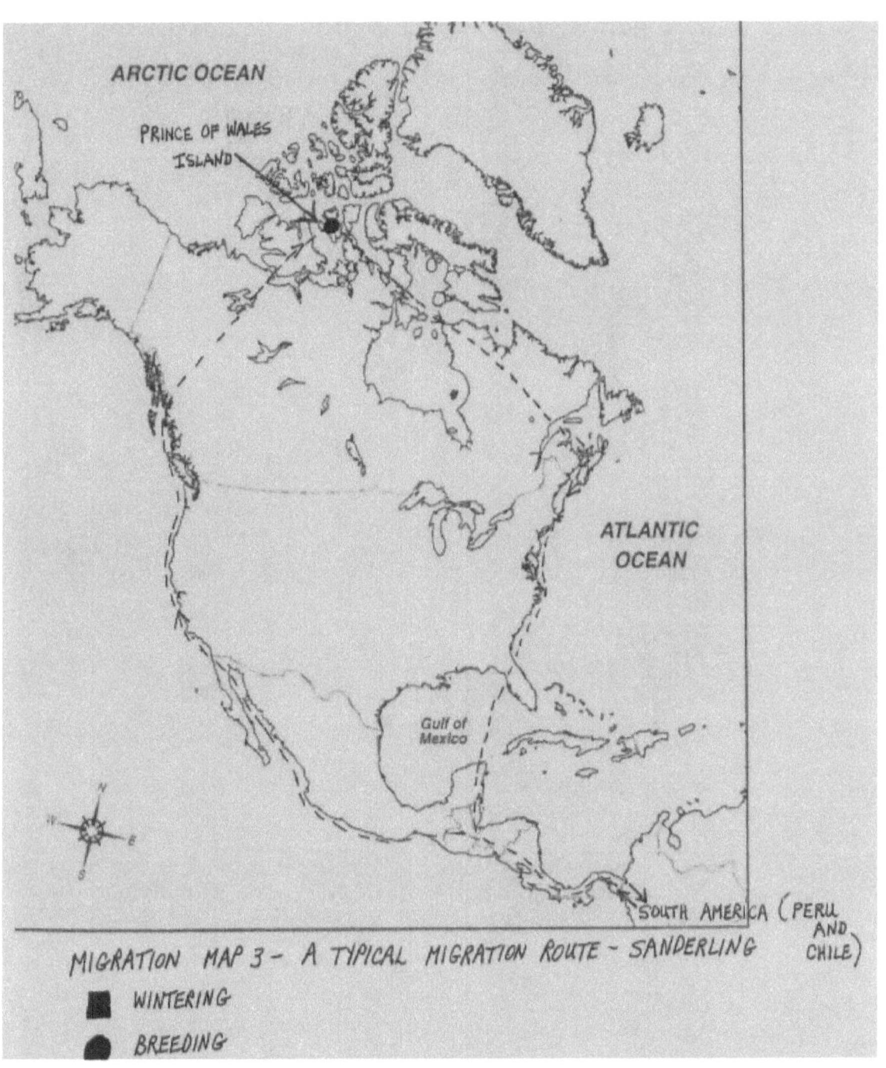
ARCTIC OCEAN
PRINCE OF WALES ISLAND
ATLANTIC OCEAN
Gulf of Mexico
N
W E
S
SOUTH AMERICA (PERU AND CHILE)
MIGRATION MAP 3 - A TYPICAL MIGRATION ROUTE - SANDERLING
WINTERING
BREEDING

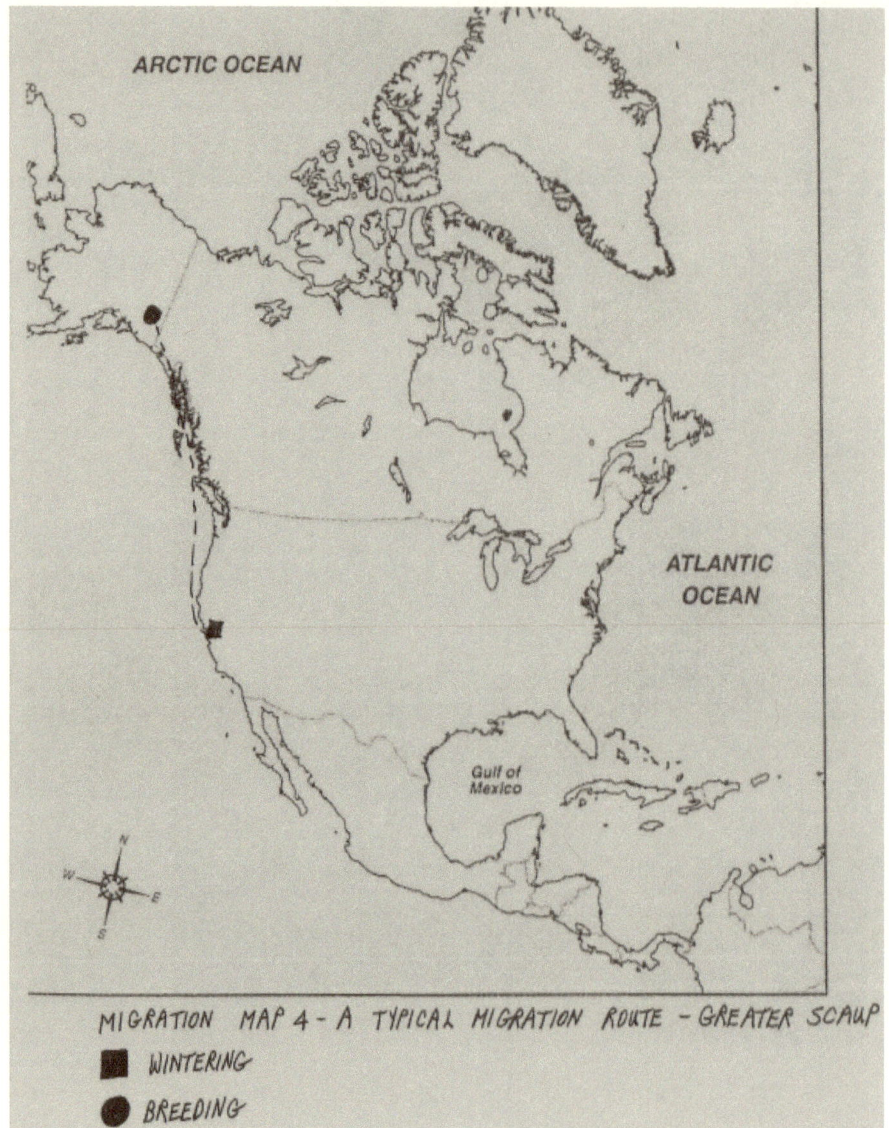

ARCTIC OCEAN
ATLANTIC OCEAN
Gulf of Mexico
N
W
E
S
MIGRATION MAP 4 - A TYPICAL MIGRATION ROUTE - GREATER SCAUP
WINTERING
BREEDING

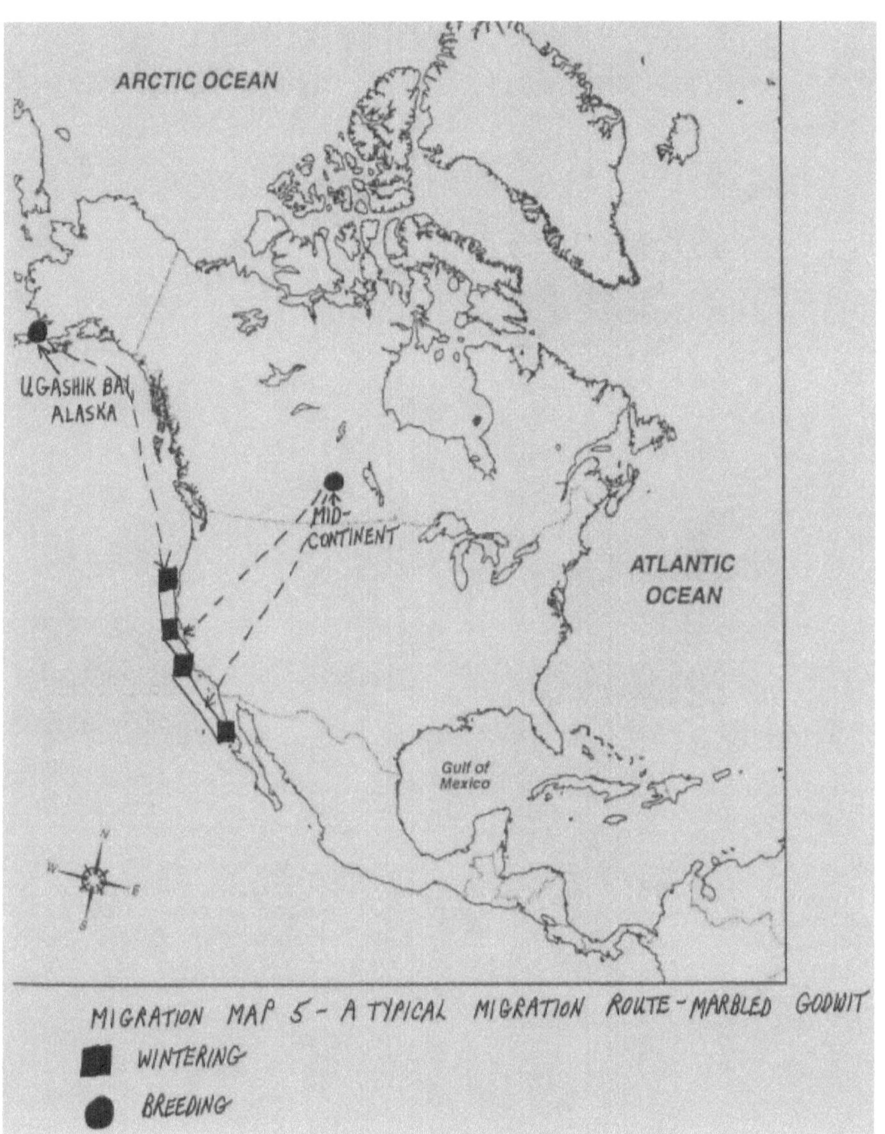
ARCTIC OCEAN
UGASHIK BAY ALASKA
MID-CONTINENT
ATLANTIC OCEAN
Gulf of Mexico
N
W   E
S
MIGRATION MAP 5 - A TYPICAL MIGRATION ROUTE - MARBLED GODWIT
WINTERING
BREEDING

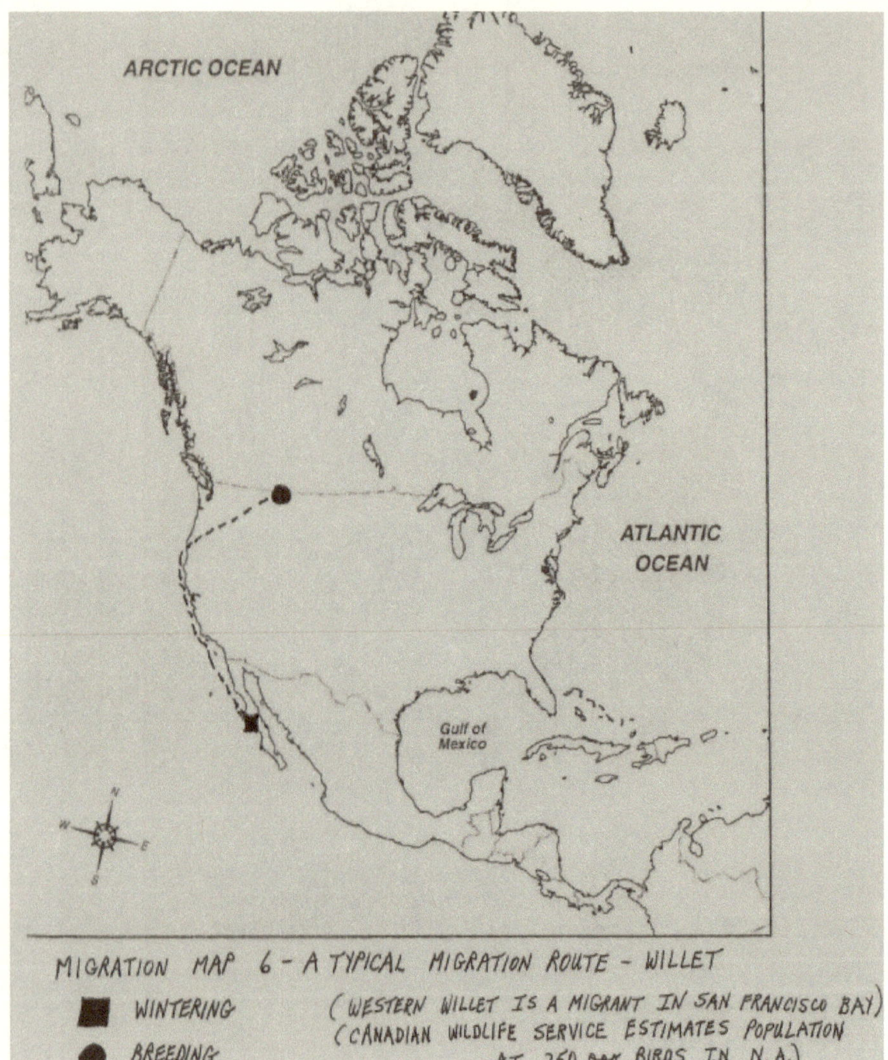

MIGRATION MAP 6 - A TYPICAL MIGRATION ROUTE - WILLET

WINTERING

BREEDING

(WESTERN WILLET IS A MIGRANT IN SAN FRANCISCO BAY)
(CANADIAN WILDLIFE SERVICE ESTIMATES POPULATION
AT 250,000 BIRDS IN N.A.)

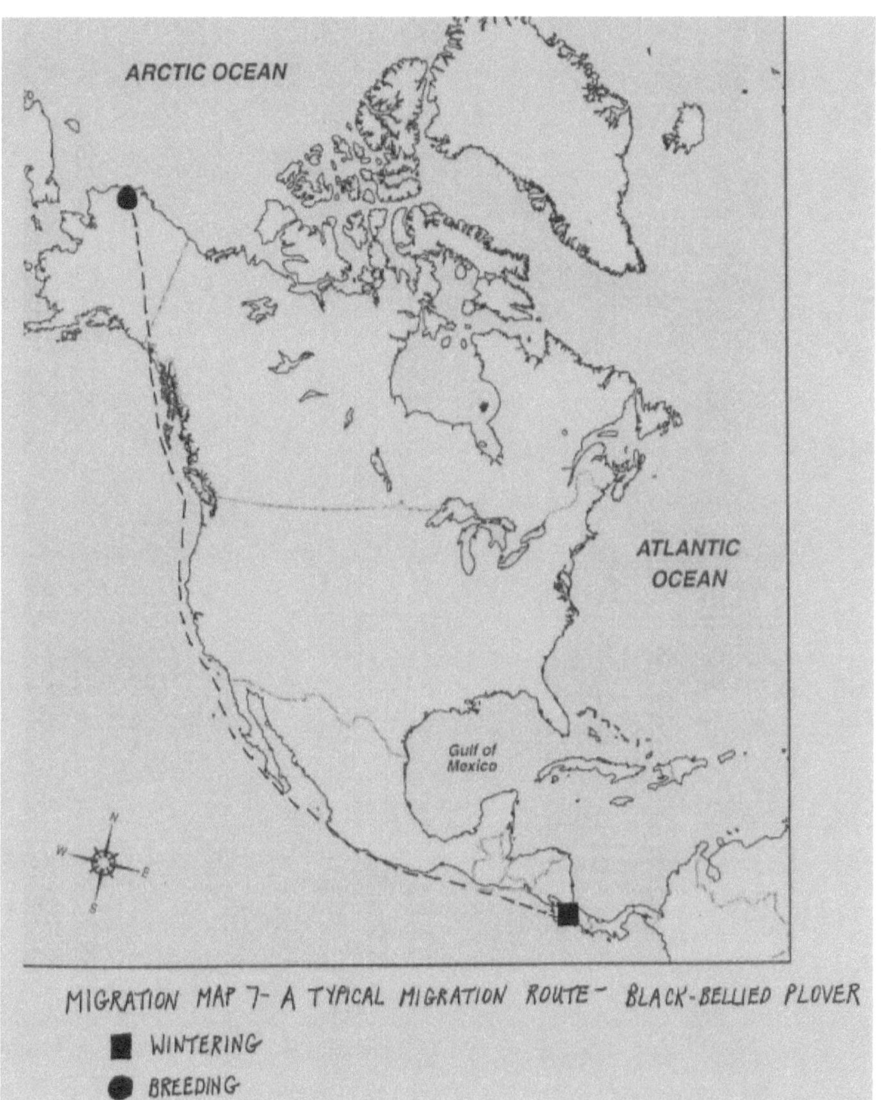
ARCTIC OCEAN
ATLANTIC OCEAN
Gulf of Mexico
N
W E
S
MIGRATION MAP 7 - A TYPICAL MIGRATION ROUTE - BLACK-BELLIED PLOVER
WINTERING
BREEDING

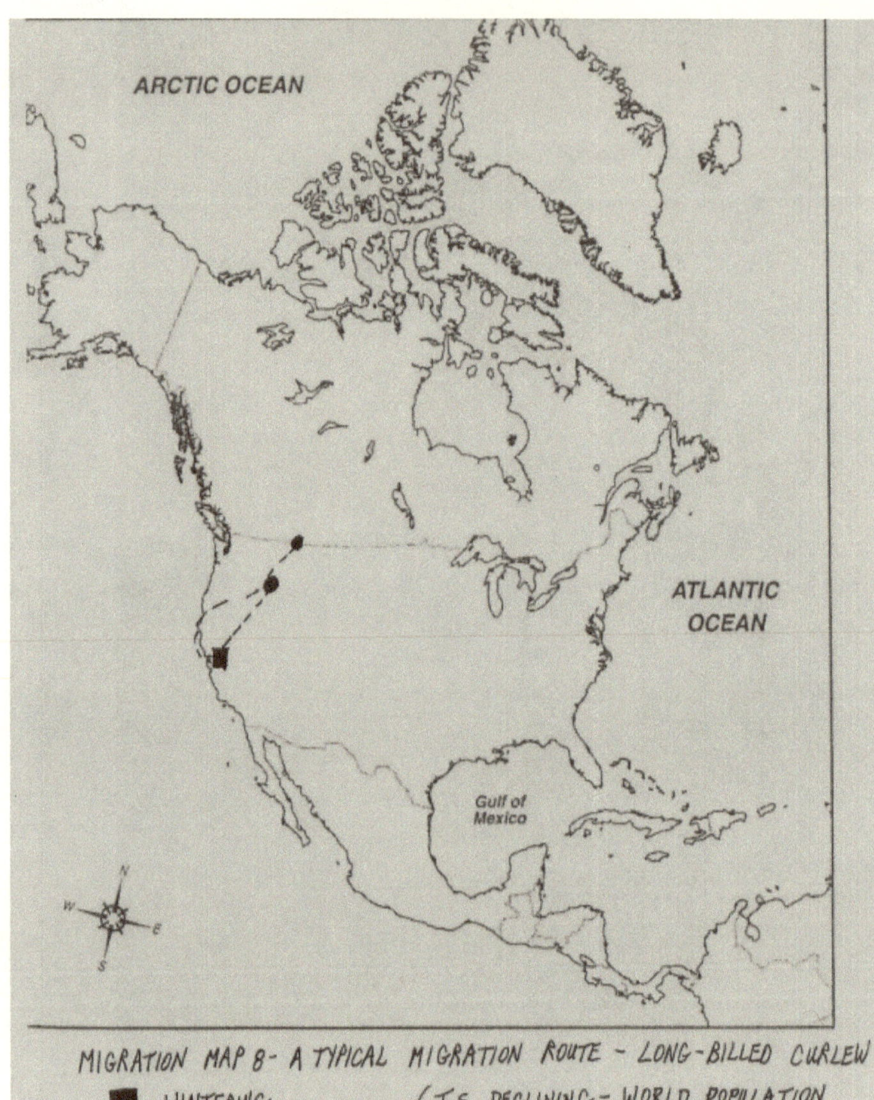

MIGRATION MAP 8 - A TYPICAL MIGRATION ROUTE - LONG-BILLED CURLEW

■ WINTERING

● BREEDING

(IS DECLINING - WORLD POPULATION IS 20,000!)

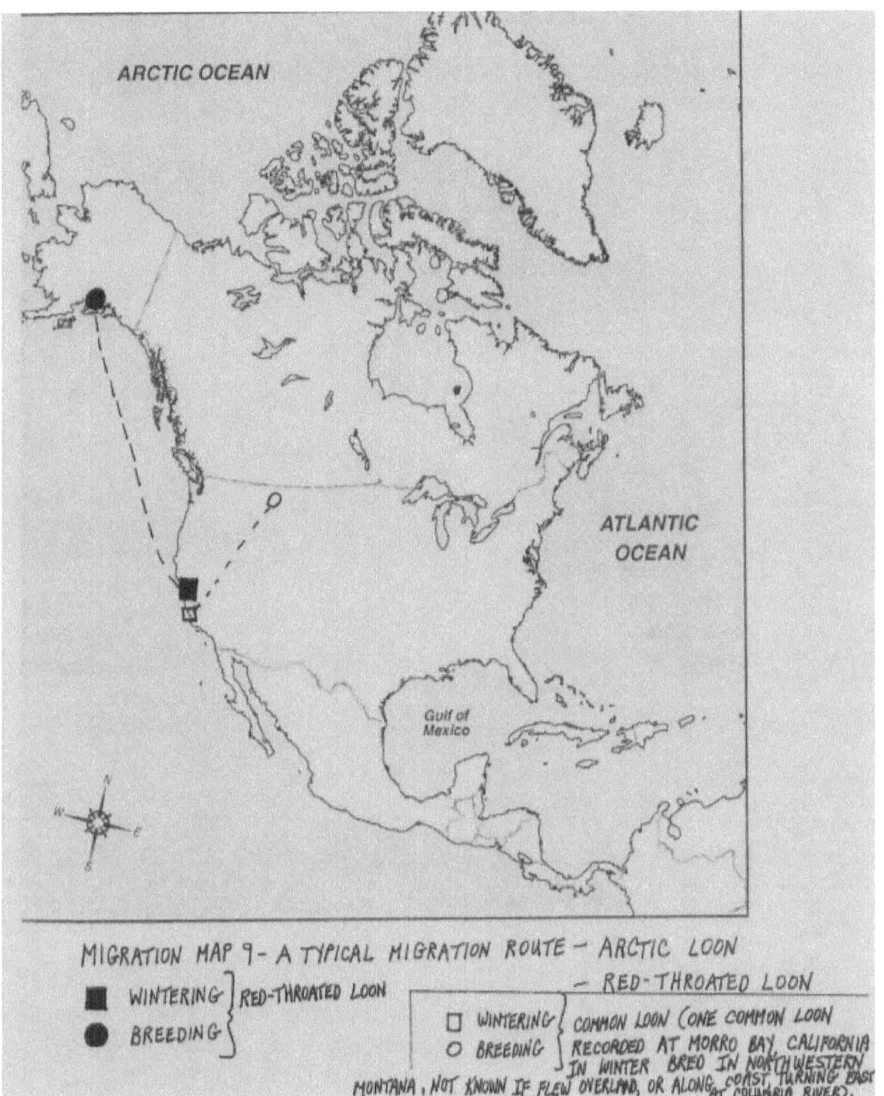
ARCTIC OCEAN
ATLANTIC OCEAN
Gulf of Mexico
N
W   E
S
MIGRATION MAP 9 - A TYPICAL MIGRATION ROUTE - ARCTIC LOON
WINTERING } RED-THROATED LOON
BREEDING }
- RED-THROATED LOON
WINTERING } COMMON LOON (ONE COMMON LOON
BREEDING } RECORDED AT MORRO BAY CALIFORNIA
IN WINTER BRED IN NORTHWESTERN
MONTANA. NOT KNOWN IF FLEW OVERLAND, OR ALONG COAST, TURNING EAST AT COLUMBIA RIVER).

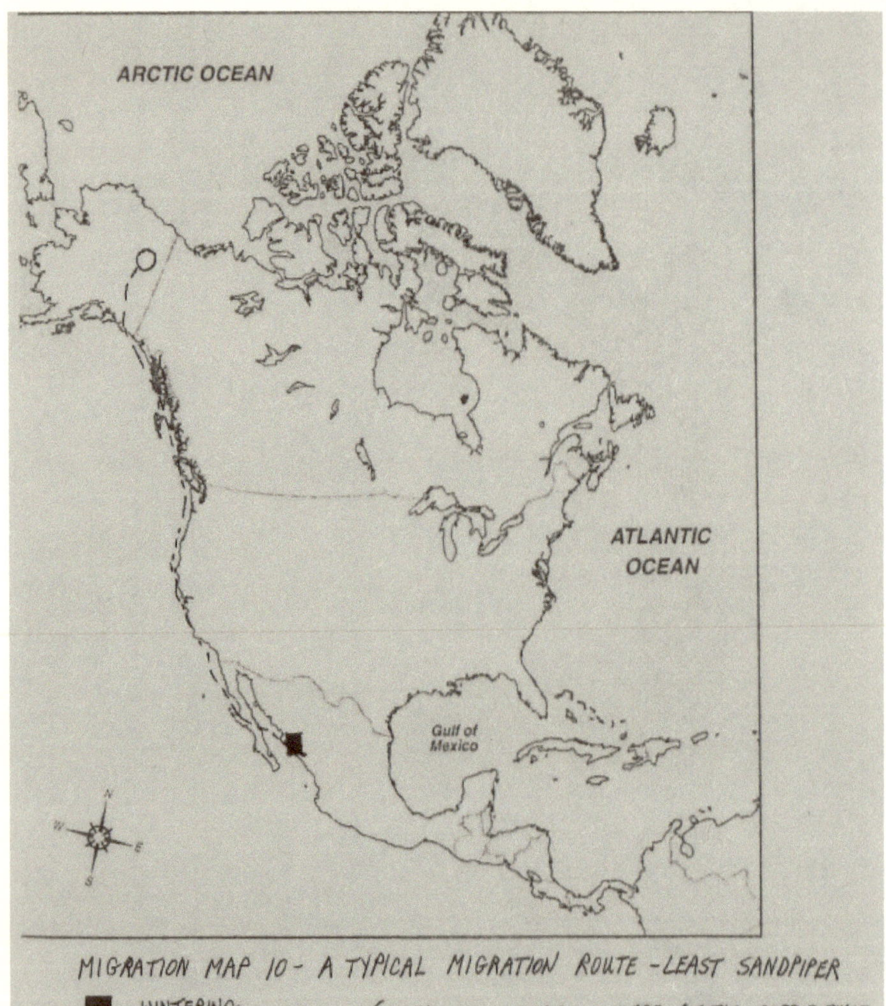

MIGRATION MAP 10 - A TYPICAL MIGRATION ROUTE - LEAST SANDPIPER

■ WINTERING
● BREEDING

(MANY LEAST SANDPIPERS STAGE AT THE COPPER RIVER DELTA IN SOUTHWESTERN ALASKA IN SPRING BEFORE HEADING TO WINTERING AREAS).

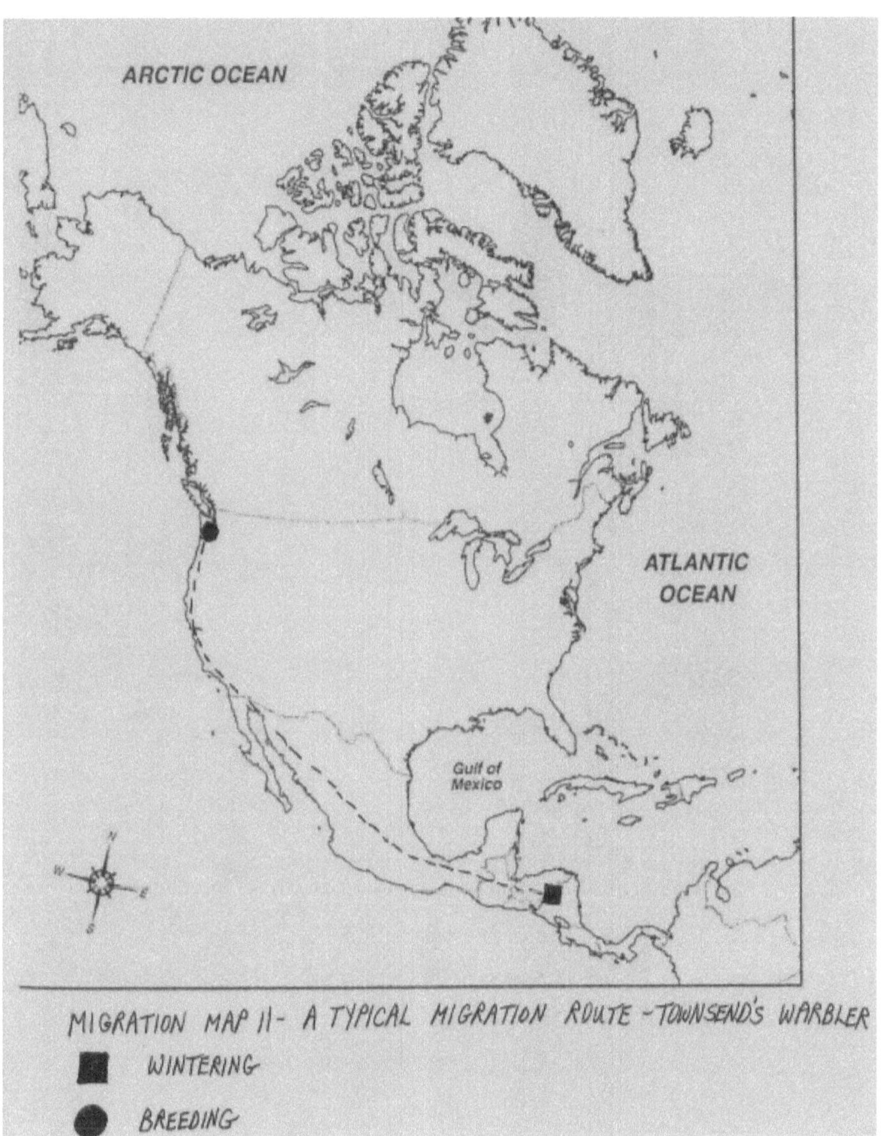

ARCTIC OCEAN
ATLANTIC OCEAN
Gulf of Mexico
N
W E
S
MIGRATION MAP II - A TYPICAL MIGRATION ROUTE - TOWNSEND'S WARBLER
WINTERING
BREEDING

ABOUT THE AUTHOR

RESEARCH AND WRITING have long been Val's personal interest, particularly in the world of nature and birds. She likes to take compact binoculars and observe birds on "slow jogs" in natural areas. She keeps journals of the birds she observes.

Val's interest in birds led her to volunteer in the baby bird room at Wildcare, a wildlife rehabilitation center located near San Francisco. She received training from the Oiled Wildlife Care Network, and when there was the devastating Cosco Busan oil spill in San Francisco Bay in 2007—which affected thousands of migrating and overwintering birds—she was able to use her acquired skills and knowledge to help in efforts to save oiled birds at the worldwide-known International Bird Rescue center in Cordelia, California.

Val received a Bachelor of Arts degree, majoring in history and anthropology. She has an MBA from the University of Toronto and is a Chartered Financial Analyst (CFA).

PUBLISHED BOOKS

1. ___The Real Winnie - A One-of-a-Kind Bear___, Toronto: Natural Heritage Books, 2003; second printing 2005. There are Japanese and Czechoslovakian editions of this book.

The Real Winnie: A One-of-a-Kind Bear is the story of the special real black bear who was the inspiration for the Winnie The Pooh stories. While visiting Assiniboine Park Zoo with her parents in Winnipeg, Manitoba, Canada, Val was captivated by the statue of a soldier and a small bear cub. The soldier was Harry Colebourn, a veterinarian with the Fort Garry Horse cavalry regiment and part of the Canadian Expeditionary Force of World War One. He rescued the orphaned black bear cub and named the bear Winnipeg, or Winnie for short. Winnie accompanied the regiment to training grounds in England and then was taken to the London Zoo when Harry was ordered to the front lines in France. Winnie was an extraordinary bear who became a star attraction at the London Zoo. A. A. Milne's son, Christopher, loved to visit her, and Winnie became immortalized in the Winnie the Pooh stories.

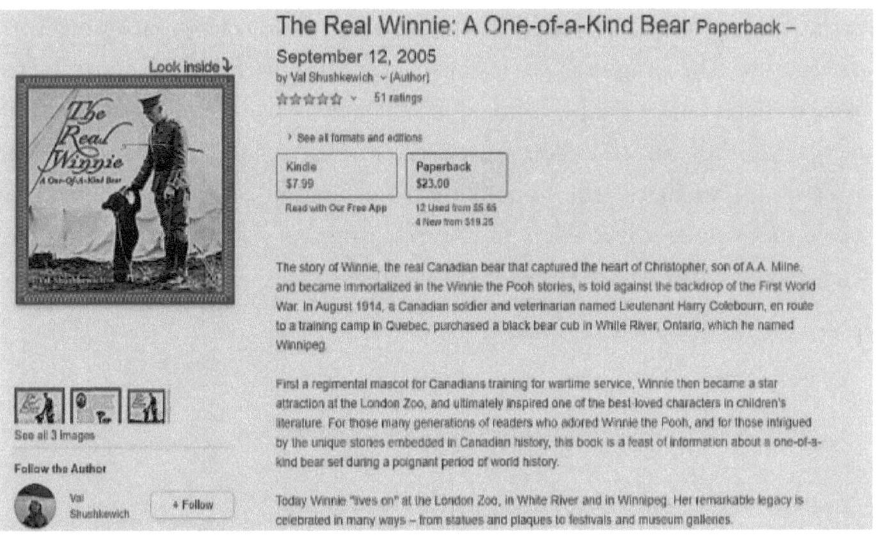

The Real Winnie: A One-of-a-Kind Bear Paperback –
September 12, 2005
by Val Shushkewich ~ (Author)
☆☆☆☆☆ ~ 51 ratings

› See all formats and editions

Kindle $7.99	Paperback $23.00
Read with Our Free App	12 Used from $5.65
	4 New from $19.25

The story of Winnie, the real Canadian bear that captured the heart of Christopher, son of A.A. Milne, and became immortalized in the Winnie the Pooh stories, is told against the backdrop of the First World War. In August 1914, a Canadian soldier and veterinarian named Lieutenant Harry Colebourn, en route to a training camp in Quebec, purchased a black bear cub in White River, Ontario, which he named Winnipeg.

First a regimental mascot for Canadians training for wartime service, Winnie then became a star attraction at the London Zoo, and ultimately inspired one of the best-loved characters in children's literature. For those many generations of readers who adored Winnie the Pooh, and for those intrigued by the unique stories embedded in Canadian history, this book is a feast of information about a one-of-a-kind bear set during a poignant period of world history.

Today Winnie "lives on" at the London Zoo, in White River and in Winnipeg. Her remarkable legacy is celebrated in many ways – from statues and plaques to festivals and museum galleries.

Look inside ↓

See all 3 images

Follow the Author

Val Shushkewich   + Follow

2. ___More Than Birds - Adventurous Lives of North American Naturalists___,
Toronto: Dundurn Press, 2012.

After researching the interesting lives of 22 naturalists who have contributed
to people's understanding about birds, Val wrote *More Than Birds -
Adventurous Lives of North American Naturalists*.

A reviewer in GoodReads said this about *More Than Birds – Adventurous
Lives of North American Naturalists*: "I picked up this book because I was
interested in only a couple of the mini biographies of well-known naturalists,
but I ended up reading almost the entire book. Shushkewich has a writing
style that is clear, easy to read, and she manages to delve into details of lives
and research while managing to stay succinct. As a result, the biographies
kept my interest, and I was thoroughly engaged."

The 1800s saw early North American naturalists describing and illustrating
the spectacular flora and fauna they found in the New World. Then
collectors and scientists of the Smithsonian Institution and the Canadian
Museum of Nature worked feverishly to describe and catalogue the species
that exist on the continent. After that came the naturalists who were
interested in describing the birds and how they lead their lives.

Early conservationists were instrumental in the creation of great bird
sanctuaries. The emphasis of today's naturalists, including Robert Nero,
Robert Bateman, Kenn Kaufman, and David Allen Sibley, is on doing
everything they can to encourage people to experience nature and wildlife
directly in their lives. The hope is that once people encounter the natural
world more and became aware of its beauty, intricacy, and fragility, they will
want to protect and preserve it.

More Than Birds: Adventurous Lives of North American Naturalists Kindle Edition

by Val Shushkewich ∨ (Author) | Format: Kindle Edition

☆☆☆☆☆ ∨ 2 ratings

› See all formats and editions

Kindle	Paperback
$9.99	$27.92
Read with Our Free App	11 Used from $12.74 17 New from $18.93

Once people encounter the natural world and become aware of its intricacy, fragility, beauty, and significance, they will recognize the need for conservation.

The fascinating development of natural history studies in North America is portrayed through the life stories of 22 naturalists. The 19th century saw early North American naturalists such as Alexander Wilson, the "Father of American Ornithology," John James Audubon, and Thomas Nuttall describing and illustrating the spectacular flora and fauna they found in the New World.

Scientists of the Smithsonian Institution and the Canadian Museum of Nature worked feverishly to describe and catalogue the species that exist on the continent. Great nature writers such as Florence Merriam Bailey, Cordelia Stanwood, Margaret Morse Nice, Louise de Kiriline Lawrence, and Roger Tory Peterson wrote in depth about the lives and behaviours of birds. Early conservationists such as Jack Miner, the "Father of Conservation," created nature preserves.

Today, noted naturalists such as Robert Nero, Robert Bateman, Kenn Kaufman, and David Allen Sibley do everything they can to encourage people to experience nature directly in their lives and to care about